Las Hermanas

Lara Medina is Associate Professor, Department of Chicano and Chicana Studies at California State University, Northridge.

Las Hermanas

Chicana/Latina Religious-Political Activism in the U.S. Catholic Church

Lara Medina

 Temple University Press

Philadelphia

To "those valiant women whose ideals, dreams, and
personal sacrifice made *Las Hermanas* a reality."
—Carmelita Espinoza, SGS,
and María de Jesús Ybarra, OP, 1974

Temple University Press, Philadelphia 19122
Copyright © 2004 by Temple University,
except "About the Cover" copyright © 2004 Yreina D. Cervántez
All rights reserved
Cloth edition published 2004
Paper edition published 2005
Printed in the United States of America

⊗The paper used in this publication meets the requirements of the
American National Standard for Information Sciences—Permanence
of Paper for Printed Library Materials, ANSI Z39.48-1984

Library of Congress Cataloging-in-Publication Data

Medina, Lara, 1953–
Las Hermanas : Chicana/Latina religious-political activism in the U.S. Catholic Church /
Lara Medina.
p.   cm.
Includes bibliographical references (p.) and index.
ISBN 1-59213-483-1 (pbk : alk. paper)
ISBN 1-59213-250-2 (cloth : alk. paper)
1. Hermanas (Organization)—History.   2. Hispanic American Catholics—Political
activity.   3. Catholic women—Political activity.   I. Title.
BX810.H57M43   2004
267'.44273—dc22   2003064591

ISBN 13: 978-1-59213-483-0 (paper : alk. paper)

120507P

Contents

Photograph gallery follows page 82

Acknowledgments

THIS BOOK could not have been written without the permission of Las Hermanas. I am indebted to the numerous women who graciously shared with me their memories and experiences of challenging and transforming the Roman Catholic Church. I am particularly grateful to Gregoria Ortega, Yolanda Tarango, Teresita Basso, Ada María Isasi-Díaz, María Iglesias, Margarita Castañeda, Rosa Martha Zárate, Tess Browne, Alicia Salcido, Sylvia Sedillo, and Dolores Florez, who agreed to more than one interview and always pointed me in the right direction of who else I should talk with. From PADRES, I thank Juan Romero, Patricio Guillen, and Virgilio Elizondo, clergy who honestly shared the challenges of collaborating with very strong and vocal women. Acknowledgment is also due to Dr. María Carolina Flores, archivist of the Las Hermanas papers, who saw to it that the primary documents would be preserved at Our Lady of the Lake University in San Antonio. Without this collection of papers, newsletters, and reports, this history of Las Hermanas would have been lacking in its reconstruction. The voices, however, of the women involved in Las Hermanas over the past three decades provided the central interpretive lens.

Prior to this book, I reconstructed the history of Las Hermanas for my dissertation under the astute guidance of Dr. Vicki L. Ruiz. As one of the few Chicana historians, Dr. Ruiz understood immediately the significance of Las Hermanas and the vacuum in Chicana/o historiography that this work fills. (The use of the term Chicana/o is a gender inclusive term. It can be used interchangeably with Chicano/a and at times depends on the emphasis of the context.) I thank Dr. Ruiz immensely for her steadfast encouragement and insightful comments. Through her mentoring I learned the method of oral history and its importance in recovering the histories of marginalized peoples. I also want to thank Dr. David Yoo and Dr. Lourdes Arguelles who also served on my dissertation committee and whose own works on race, religion, and gender helped guide my theoretical perspective. Gratitude also goes to Dr. Timothy Matovina, a colleague who first suggested Las Hermanas for my dissertation topic. His own previous work on Las Hermanas and PADRES gave him the insight that there was a fuller story to tell. His critical reading of dissertation chapters helped tremendously. For the reading of this publication, I am grateful to Dr. Marta Lopez-Garza, an astute scholar of women's studies and Chicano/a studies. Her expertise in feminist theory, social movements, and Chicano/a studies helped to strengthen the narrative as a whole.

Institutional support made the completion of the dissertation as well as manuscript revisions possible. The Hispanic Theological Initiative (HIT) offered me predissertation, dissertation year, and postdissertation year support. I am grateful to HTI not only for monetary support, but also for the invaluable networking among other Latina/o scholars of religion and theology. The Louisville Institute granted dissertation year support, as did the Claremont Graduate University. The National Endowment for the Humanities (NEH) Extending the Reach Award supplied a two-year grant so I could conduct further research and complete revisions for the manuscript. I would like to acknowledge Dr. Eduardo Pagán of the NEH for his helpful recommendations on my proposal. California State University at Northridge provided release time from the classroom through its Faculty Support Programs promoting research, scholarship, and creativity. I especially thank Dr. Jorge García, who served as dean of the College of Humanities for many years, including my first four tenure-track years at California State University at Northridge, for his support and interest in this endeavor.

These acknowledgments would not be complete without respect and gratitude given to my family: my father, Florial Medina Lara; my husband, Gilbert R. Cadena; my son, Armando Lara Millán; and my daughter, Marisol Ixchel Medina y Cadena. My father ensured my entry into college, my husband encouraged me to pursue a doctorate, and my children never complained about the hours I spent researching and writing. Their own commitment to studying shows that they, too, value education. My love also goes to my sister, who passed into the spirit world on 8 March 1999, and to my mother and ancestors with whom she now resides. To them and to my extended family and friends who offered emotional support and unconditional love, I am grateful.

About the Cover

THE BOOK'S cover image is by Yreina D. Cervántez, a third-generation Chicana whose work combines pre-Columbian concepts with autobiographical elements and political commentary. The images and symbols used speak to the legacy of Chicana/Mexicana and Latina subversive religious agency and political action.

"Mujer De Mucha Enagua," PA'TI XICANA by Yreina D. Cervántez

In Mexico when one speaks of a "mujer de mucha enagua," you are talking about a woman of strength, courage, and integrity. To quote Ellen Calmus from her article "We Are All Ramona: Artists, Revolutionaries and Zapatistas With Petticoat":

> They told me that when a woman is very *activista* they call her *mujer de mucha enagua*: "woman with a lot of petticoat." (A revealing image and key to understanding the women Zapatistas: unlike the European tradition of women who may assume political and military prowess, but whose doing so is assumed to involve a loss of femininity, these women consider a woman's activism to mean she has "a lot of petticoat": she is a real woman).

In my serigraph I am adopting this "Mujer De Mucha Enagua" metaphor to represent all women united in the struggle for a better life. The second half of the title, PA'TI XICANA, is a dedication to my sister Xicana/Latinas in the United States who have their own unique brand of activism.

"Mujer De Mucha Enagua," PA'TI XICANA is an affirmation of the feminine spirit, or more precisely the subversive feminine spirit, and her/our ongoing commitment to and search for "another way to be, another way to be human and free" (Rosario Castellanos). This search is portrayed and embodied in the essence of three women, a powerful trinity, who all address the tenacious struggle of the indigenous peoples of Mexico and the Americas.

This trinity includes, on the left, la mujer Zapatista (woman Zapatista), who declares "todos somos Ramona," we *are all Ramona* (Comandante Ramona, a leader in the Zapatista movement) and wears inscribed on her apron a message from the Popul Vuh reminding us to "conjure up the faces and words" of our ancestors. At right, Sor Juana Ines de la Cruz, "ella nacida en Nepantla" (she who was born in Nepantla) speaks in Nahuatl, Mexico's principal indigenous language, to invoke the assistance of Tonantzin, the Mother Goddess (also known as Toci). Doing so is perhaps a subversive act, considering the prejudices of colonial New Spain against the Mother Tongue and the religious traditions associated with it. The voice of Rosario Castellanos resonates with the feminist conviction and inspiration of Sor Juana, whose bosom holds a portrait of this daughter of Chiapas. Castellanos declares in her poem Madre India: "pan, luz y justicia" (bread, light and justice).

Also included in "Mujer De Much Enagua," PA'TI XICANA are the colors of the earth, the stylized spots/pattern of the pelt of the jaguar, and, between the two central figures, the hand of the "Goddess," inspired by the frescos at Teotihuacan. Tattooed on the hand is the spiral symbol representing the eternal as well as the Native American concept of timelessness, reinforced by the Mayan words "mixik balamil" (the navel of the universe). At the feet of the two women are Mayan glyphs combined with Nahua (Aztec) glyphs and words, all meaning *Tlalliyolo*, the heart of the earth, representing both the jaguar and Tonantzin. The double heart, the symbol for Toci/Tonantzin, overlaps the Nahua symbol for the "mountain of Cihuacoatl (Snake Woman)," yet another aspect of the mother goddess.

At the far right are six Mayan hand mudras, done in the compositional style of Mayan stelae reliefs. They are ancient symbolic representations related to woman, the goddess, death, and maize/corn (sustenance). At the bottom of this panel of mudras is an image of "la mujer que simboliza fecundidad" (woman symbolizing fecundity). In this instance, fecundity represents creativity/creation, the engendering of fertile ideas, and the actualization of dreams.

Introduction

En la frente de liberación del pueblo Mexico-Americano existen mujeres,
lindas y valientes,
existen mujeres que saben luchar.

[*In the forefront of the liberation of the Mexican American community*
are beautiful and courageous women,
women who know how to fight.]
—*Canción de Las Hermanas*

THIS VERSE from *Canción de Las Hermanas* declares
passionately the self-understanding of the women forming the first
national religious-political organization of Chicana and Latina
Roman Catholics in the United States. Envisioning its participants as beautiful and valiant warrior women in the front lines of
the Chicano movement, Las Hermanas proclaimed a self-identity
transcending the traditional boundaries for women religious in
the early 1970s.[1] As agents of change, they transformed religious
life to be intimately connected to the struggles of their ethnic and
gendered communities. Through direct involvement in the Chicano movement, Las Hermanas expanded the ministerial role of
the U.S. Roman Catholic Church as it bridged the civil rights
struggles of Chicanos and Chicanas and their religious needs.[2] As
feminists they joined the ranks of Chicanas who battled the gender oppression rampant in the Chicano cultural nationalist movement and brought Chicana feminism into the Catholic Church.
Chicana sociologist Mary Pardo indicates that although an organi-

zation might not identify itself as feminist, it is the outcomes of the organization that signifies it as feminist or not. Feminist outcomes would include female agency, women's empowerment, and social change.[3] Thus, I identify Las Hermanas as a feminist organization, as they are primarily concerned with the empowerment of Latinas within the context of social change. Their distinct arena, the sanctified patriarchy of the Catholic Church, made them keenly aware of the forces of male domination. The women of Las Hermanas defy long-standing stereotypes of Latina Catholics as apolitical and asexual passive bearers of their faith.

Within Las Hermanas laywomen interacted closely with women religious, as well as Chicanas with other Latinas, primarily Puerto Ricans and Cubans. Their collective identity as sisters, as *hermanas*, transcended the distinction between clergy and laity imposed by a hierarchical Church. Their eagerness to collaborate across Latina cultural specifics also contrasted with the strong nationalist tendencies of some sectors of the Chicano movement during the 1970s. Las Hermanas created a model of church based on mutuality and solidarity among Chicanas and Latinas and one that superseded the boundaries and limitations of the institutional Church and nationalist ideologies. Thus, when I refer to a member of Las Hermanas, I will indicate her association with religious life in the first reference only. This is meant to deemphasize whether a member is a woman religious or laywoman, as both are considered of equal status within Las Hermanas. I also will not always identify the specific ethnicity of each woman, as the pan ethnic identifier *Latina* encompasses the self-perception of the members. The term *Chicana/Latina* further emphasizes the *comadrazgo* (female bonding) between Chicanas and Latinas in the organization.[4] I do want to emphasize, however, that the initial cohort of members were primarily Chicana and the majority of the members today are of Mexican origin. Contrary to the broader feminist movement, the concept of sisterhood within Las Hermanas allowed for differences among Latinas and created solidarity among its members. The spiritual foundation of Las Hermanas, combined with its call for justice, sustained the bonds of sisterhood over the years.[5]

Las Hermanas organized in 1971 during a time of intense social upheaval for the Roman Catholic Church and for the world. Civil rights movements, feminism, antiwar protests, gay and lesbian activism, Latin American liberation movements, and Vatican II contributed to a milieu of social unrest and radical transformation. Influenced by the politics of mass protest, primarily Chicana women religious mobilized to challenge the overt discrimination toward Chicanos and Latinos in the Catholic Church and in society at large. Their own experiences with racism and sexism in the Church amplified their desire to push for change. Their early concerns included institutional representation and accountability for a rapidly growing Latino Catholic population, culturally sensitive ministry and educational programs, church and secular labor practices, women's empowerment, and ecclesial support for the Chicano movement. By its third year of organizing, Puerto Rican and Cuban women joined the organization. After their first decade of activism, attention turned specifically to empowerment for grassroots[6] Latinas, including issues of leadership development, moral agency, reproductive rights, sexuality, and domestic abuse. National biennial conferences, regional retreats, meetings, and newsletters created the spaces to analyze issues integral to the daily lives of Latinas, issues silenced by the institutional Church.

Between 1971 and 1985, Las Hermanas influenced the policy decisions of major ecclesial bodies such as the National Conference of Catholic Bishops/United States Catholic Conference (NCCB/USCC), the Leadership Conference of Women Religious (LCWR), and the Secretariat for Hispanic Affairs of the United States Catholic Conference. By 1974, Las Hermanas had conducted two national surveys, one on the absence of Latino ministry programs in parishes across the nation, and one on the exploitation of Mexican sisters as domestics in U.S. rectories and seminaries. Early on members joined forces with Padres Asociados para Derechos Religiosos, Educativos y Sociales (PADRES), an organization of Chicano priests, for numerous projects. Together they lobbied successfully for the appointment of Chicano bishops; developed the Mexican American Cultural Center (MACC), the first national Chicano pastoral institute; co-planned and facilitated the first national *encuentros* of Latino Catholics; and contributed to the first formulations of raza theology.[7] During the 1970s Las Hermanas and PADRES, along with numerous individual laity, represented the emerging Latina/o religious leadership of the U.S. Catholic Church. Many remain in leadership positions. A new generation of Latina/o leaders in the Church today inherits a path forged by the courageous women of Las Hermanas, the men of PADRES, and their supporters.

Collaborative work between Las Hermanas and PADRES did not occur without tension. A long-term association never materialized. Ultimately, an attitude of male clerical superiority within PADRES hampered its ability to relate to the Hermanas as equals and endorse fully the equal status of women in the Church. Recognizing the powerful role of the Church in justifying patriarchy and shaping Chicano/Latino cultures, accompanied by a sense of entitlement to their own religious tradition, compelled Las Hermanas to continue the fight against sexism inherent in the Church's structure. As one Hermana stated, "If the boys want me to go, they are going to have to carry me out because it is not their Church!"[8]

In addition to influencing ecclesial matters in their first decade of organizing, Las Hermanas's members participated in Chicano student protests for educational rights, the farmworker struggle for labor rights, and widespread community organizing. Their activism represents the first time that Chicana and Latina religious leaders collectively challenged public and private institutions to address ethnic, gender, and class discrimination. Their presence brought the Chicano movement into the Church and the Church into the Chicano movement.

From its inception, Las Hermanas espoused feminist ideas, yet a specifically feminist agenda did not shape the organization until its second decade. According to Catalina Fresquez, "From the beginning we had a very strong message that women count, that women can be agents of change."[9] A "community-centered consciousness"[10] with women as central actors describes their activism. Shared leadership, reflecting "one of the basic themes of Chicana feminism,"[11] continues to shape their organizational structure. By 1980, Las Hermanas actively pushed for women's ordination, tirelessly bringing the subjectivity of Latinas to the national agenda of the predominantly Euroamerican Women-church movement. Although no longer focused on ordination for women, Las Hermanas has consistently provided Latinas with the opportunity to experience their own sacred authority in rituals and prayers conducted at conferences and retreats.

I identify the activism of Las Hermanas as political activism and I seek to make a clear connection between their religious work and its political significance. Contrary to male-centered political science theory, political work extends far beyond the arenas of electoral politics and public policy. As feminist social scientists have helped us to understand, political action occurs whenever and wherever persons attempt to shape their personal and/or communal lives in opposition to social orders sustained by inequality. As sociologist Mary Pardo states, "The significance of politics occurring outside political institutions, and women's community activism particularly, continue to be largely excluded from conventional notions of political activity."[12] Although operating in relation to an established institution, Las Hermanas emerged as a purely organic effort to transform the Catholic Church and has chosen autonomy over institutional dependency. It remains an organic grassroots effort and its work continues to hold political significance for empowering Latinas.

By the beginning of its third decade, theologians within Las Hermanas recorded and analyzed the spirituality and theology of its members. The first book on U.S. Latina religious praxis titled *Hispanic Women: Prophetic Voice in the Church*, was published in 1988 with the assistance of Las Hermanas and several other social justice and women religious organizations.[13] Spirituality based on transformative struggle would later give shape to *mujerista* theology, a unique blending of feminist concerns, Latina cultures, and liberation theology. Clearly unrecognized is Las Hermanas's contribution to this now internationally recognized Latina feminist theology.

Representing diverse regions, the women drawn to Las Hermanas shared certain experiences: working-class origins, Catholic education, and varying degrees of cultural alienation either in religious life or as lay members of the Roman Catholic Church. When Las Hermanas first mobilized, some of the members were ministering in Spanish-speaking communities, while the majority had been denied the opportunity.[14] Collectively they understood their power to claim their right to minister to Latinos/as. The idea for an organization immediately attracted women such as Teresita Basso (California), Ramona Jean Corrales (Arizona), Yolanda Tarango (Texas), María de Jesús Ybarra (Washington), Linda Chávez (New Mexico), Sylvia Sedillo (New Mexico), Mario (Lucie) Barron (California), María Iglesias (New York), Olga Villa Parra (Indiana), Margarita Castañeda (New York), María Carolina Flores (Texas), Carmelita Espinoza (Colorado), Clarita Trujillo (New Mexico), Consuelo Covarrubias (Wisconsin), and Irene and Molly Muñoz (Iowa). The majority of these women would rise to leadership positions in the organization. Other women, including Rosamaría Elías (New York), Rosa Martha Zárate (California), Elisa Rodríguez (Texas), Sara Murrieta (California), Catalina Fresquez (Texas), María Carolina López (Colorado), Carmen Villegas (New York), Ada María Isasi-Díaz (New York), Clara Herrera (Colorado), María Luisa Gastón (New York), Dolores Florez (Colorado), and Lucie Ortiz (Florida), joined at different times and contributed immensely to the leadership of Las Hermanas. Each woman brought to the organization a determination to create a new way of being church in a conflicted society, "*la Nueva Iglesia Latina.*"[15] They have been joined by numerous other women over the years, some very active on a regional basis and others participating on the sidelines.

This book broadens the scope of three disciplines: Chicano/a studies, women's studies, and religious studies. As the first in-depth study of Chicanas and Latinas as religious leaders and agents of transformation, it offers an interdisciplinary examination of religion, ethnicity, gender, and politics. Previous scholarship on the Chicano movement has virtually ignored the presence of religious leaders among its participants, particularly women religious. My focus on women activists within the social context of the 1970s, 1980s, and 1990s offers a necessary corrective to this absence and to the male-centered historical treatment of the Chicano movement. I argue that Las Hermanas and PADRES brought the Chicano movement into the religious arena, and the Catholic Church into the Chicano movement.

Contrary to popular and scholarly belief, Chicana/o and Latina/o religious leaders, sisters, priests, and laity fought valiantly in the struggle for civil rights and self-determination. They have been overlooked in large part because of the estrangement of many Chicano/a activists and scholars from institutionalized religion, specifically Roman Catholicism. As Chicanos/as critiqued their history shaped by colonizing powers intertwined with Christian missionaries, many saw rejecting Catholicism as an essential element for self-determination. Furthermore, for Chicana feminists the Catholic faith had for too long determined their subjugation in a patriarchal culture. For many activists, a fervent Mesoamerican indigenous spirituality replaced the European religion of their parents. Marxist influence on some sectors of the movement stressed "religion as an opiate of the masses," and further alienated many

Chicanos from religion in any form. [16] Some Marxist Chicanos/as, however, understood the power of religion and religious leaders to influence social change due to their exposure to Latin American liberation theology. These interrelated factors combined with the absence, or at times negative presence, of the Catholic Church in Chicano struggles convinced the majority of a generation of activists that the Catholic Church and its representatives had little to offer. In complete antithesis, Las Hermanas chose to confront the Church from within.

In religious studies the Catholic story is traditionally marginal to and eclipsed by the extensive attention scholars devote to Protestant Christianity. And within the field of American Catholicism, the narrative centers on Euroamerican devotees. Chicano/Latino Catholics are for the most part absent from historical treatments of U.S. Catholic history. This study brings to the discipline the contributions of Latina Catholics in the "religious landscape" of the Americas.

Women's studies will also benefit from this book with its focus on the agency of Latinas, an ongoing neglected area within the discipline. Its close look into how one group of Latinas organize and strategize to combat the interrelated forces of racism, sexism, and classism offers a model of praxis to all feminist scholars. My integration of oral history and archival research brings to life a story yet untold.

In many ways my personal background prepared me well to write this book. I am Chicana, raised in a Catholic family, and have been a participant in the Chicano movement since the early 1970s. During my college years at the University of California at Santa Barbara, my consciousness-raising process also led me to reject the Catholic faith as part of my struggle for self-determination. Little did I realize that years later I would return to the Church in need of spiritual direction. My deep questioning about life and faith eventually led me to graduate work in theology at the Graduate Theological Union in Berkeley. It was there that I first met Las Hermanas. The book *Hispanic Women: Prophetic Voice in the Church* by Ada María Isasi-Díaz and Yolanda Tarango had just been published. How affirming to finally hear my experiences as a Chicana reflected in theological discourse! Soon after, another member of Las Hermanas, Teresita Basso, gave a guest lecture in a class on Latino religiosity taught by Allan Figueroa Deck. I still recall her confidence and ease in speaking about Las Hermanas and its history of challenging the institutional Church. In the midst of learning about Latin American liberation theology, feminist theology, and the history of Chicana/o Catholic activism, I began to see the need for a Chicana/o theology, the subject of my master's thesis.

After graduating, I relocated to Los Angeles, where I worked as a lay minister in the Catholic student center at University of California at Los Angeles. Through my contacts in the Chicano community, I met another Las Hermanas member, Rosa Martha Zárate. She quickly showed me how to apply liberation theology in southern California. I visited the self-help economic cooperative, CALPULLI, and the small base communities organized by Zárate and Fr. Patricio Guillen, where I was encouraged in my pastoral work among Chicano/Latino students. I saw little distinction in the roles of this priest and this sister. They both functioned as religious leaders, sharing power and responsibility, regardless of gender. Father Guillen had been a longtime member of PADRES and Sister Zárate, a *veterana* of Las Hermanas. Together they represented a microcosm of the numerous Chicano and Chicana priests and sisters who understood themselves as part of the Chicano movement and continued to carry on the struggle. I knew then that their stories must be told. When a colleague, Timothy Matovina, suggested that I write the history of Las Hermanas for my doctoral dissertation, I welcomed the opportunity to interpret its significance as the first and only national religious-political organization of Chicana and Latina Roman Catholics.[17]

This study draws on the voices and collective memories of many of the women who helped shape the organization. A total of forty-five oral interviews, including several with members of PADRES, provided me with insight into their stories of protest, strategic planning, and prophetic witness. I supplemented the oral interviews with the primary documents of Las Hermanas archived in Special Collections at Our Lady of the Lake University in San Antonio, Texas, and with secondary sources. The papers and newsletters of PADRES also provided primary documentation on the events of the 1970s. Las Hermanas members María de Jesús Ybarra, Silvia Sedillo, Rosa Martha Zárate, Teresita Basso, and Clarita Trujillo supplied materials from their private collections. Juan Romero of PADRES also gave me some of his own writings on the historical events. Newspapers, including the *Abilene Reporter-News, Dallas Morning News, Los Angeles Times,* and the *National Catholic Reporter,* added context. The stories told to me, however, yielded the deepest insight into the events recorded. Although I have gained much information through numerous interviews and secondary sources, I realize that many more members of Las Hermanas and PADRES were not interviewed, and that my interpretations may be contested. I welcome the dialogue generated by my interpretation and preservation of this history.

Chapter 1 sets the social context in which Las Hermanas emerged. Vatican Council II opened the Catholic Church to "the modern world" and created new opportunities for women in religious life to choose their own ministries. Institutionalized patterns of discrimination against Chicano Catholics offered an immediate agenda for Chicana sisters. As the North American church underwent dramatic change so did the Church in Latin America. Liberation theology inspired a generation of religious leaders to live out their faith by choosing "a preferential option for the poor." The civil rights and ethnic nationalist movements in the United States coincided with these global changes. Chicana women religious enthusiastically joined the Chicano movement and bridged religion and politics.

Chapter 2 looks at specific events in West Texas that spurred the founders of Las Hermanas to mobilize other Chicana sisters nationwide. An immediate membership set in motion a long-lasting commitment of sisterhood "united in action and prayer." Early organizational goals specified "effective service to *el pueblo.*" The consciousness-raising process experienced by those attending Las Hermanas soon gave the organization a reputation of radicalizing previously "obedient" sisters.

Chapter 3 examines the early activism of Las Hermanas, including Proyecto Mexico, a project designed to rectify the exploitation of Mexican sisters employed as domestics in church-related institutions. Collaborative work with PADRES for institutional accountability and culturally specific ministry programs exemplified their efforts to make visible Chicana/o/Latina leadership within the U.S. Catholic Church. Their work with the United Farm Workers of America receives attention in order to fill the gap in scholarship regarding Chicano/a religious leaders involved in the labor movement. Political activism shaped theological insights and

Las Hermanas contributed to an emerging Chicano/Latino theology. Las Hermanas's participation in Theology of the Americas, a multiracial project intended to explore the significance of Latin American liberation theology for North Americans, enhanced the preparation for their own theological discourse rooted in the experiences of grassroots women.

Chapter 4 considers the challenges faced by Chicana/Latina Catholic feminists, a complex identity that manages the intersection of gender, ethnicity, class, and religion. A keen awareness of the influence of Catholicism on gender expectations within Latino cultures compelled Las Hermanas to engage clerical male counterparts in the praxis of gender equality. Their commitment to women as full participants in the life of the Church and society met the same kind of exclusion encountered by Chicana feminists in the secular arena. This chapter examines the experiences of Rosa Martha Zárate, Sara Murrieta, and Yolanda Tarango, experiences that exemplify the obstacles placed in the paths of strong and vocal women. Besides battling "intragroup sexism,"[18] Las Hermanas challenged the discrimination operating within the predominantly Euroamerican Women-church movement, a struggle that ultimately led to their renewed commitment to their own autonomous feminist organization.

The final chapter discusses the spirituality and theology of Las Hermanas based on transformative struggle, or the process of embracing struggle for the goal of making justice a reality. Articulated through mujerista theology, this spirituality finds expression not only in social activism, but also in women's creativity, women-centered rituals, and nurturing relationships. Through ritual, song, poetry, and activism, Las Hermanas continues its legacy of living in the intersection of politics and religion.

This examination of feminist praxis and Latina sisterhood provides insights for the future of an expanding U.S. Latina/o Catholic population. Latinos currently comprise at least 40 percent of the U.S. Catholic Church and are the majority in more than a dozen archdioceses. Over twenty-seven archdioceses are between 25 and 50 percent Latino.[19] Yet underrepresentation of Latinos and Latinas in decision-making positions of the ecclesial structure, a lack of culturally sensitive services, the closing of viable Latino ministry programs, and increased centralization of male authority continue to plague the Church in the twenty-first century.[20]

According to the United States Catholic Conference of Bishops (USCCB), about 3.8 percent of Catholic priests are Latino, or about 1,818 out of 47,582 Catholic clergy in the United States. Of these about 500 are U.S.-born Latino. There is one Latino priest for every 9,925 Latino Catholics, compared to one Euroamerican priest for every 1,230 Catholics. Of the 75,000 sisters, less than 750 are Latina. Of the nearly 280 Catholic bishops, about 9 percent, or 25, are Latino. Of these, less than a quarter are Chicano. The ratio of Latino bishops to Latino Catholics is 1,000,000 to one, compared to the general Catholic population, where the ratio of bishops to parishioners is 231,000 to one. If we look at the pipeline of future Chicano priests and sisters and the pool of potential bishops, the numbers are not promising. While half of the dioceses claim to offer special programs in "Hispanic" ministry, Latinos make up only 11 percent of seminarians.[21]

The Church today faces a significant loss of its clergy. From 1965 to 2005, the Church will lose 40 percent of ordained ministers, and the average age for ministers will be fifty-five years old.[22] At the same time, the U.S. Catholic Church will increase about one percent a year, due primarily to Latina fertility rates and immigration. Euroamerican Catholics will decrease in numbers, due to low fertility rates and an aging population. Whether the Church is prepared or not, the numbers of Latino/a Catholics will continue to grow.

Las Hermanas, an autonomous feminist Catholic organization, continues to offer a critical response to the marginalization of Latino/a leadership and women within the Roman Catholic Church. Las Hermanas expands our understanding of the role that women and religion have played and continue to play in the struggle for self-determination.

1

The Emergence of Las Hermanas

The Social Context

*Times are changing rapidly and by necessity . . . the Church must also "change". . . .
The "church" . . . is seeking ways and means of identifying more closely with the people
of God. This "identity role" must also be ours.*
—*Gloria Gallardo, co-founder of Las Hermanas, 1971*

*The religious are to embody themselves into the real world with greater daring to-
day than ever before: they cannot consider themselves removed from social problems,
from democratic awareness, or from the pluralistic mentality of the society in which
they live.*
—*Second General Council of Latin American Bishops, 1979*

FOR THREE days in early April 1971, fifty primarily
Chicana women religious met in Houston, Texas, to discuss and
pray about the implications of the Chicano movement for the
Catholic Church. The seeds planted during those three spring days
became the roots of Las Hermanas, a national religious-political
organization of Chicana/Latina feminist Catholics. During the
past three decades, Las Hermanas has offered a counter-discourse
to the patriarchy and Eurocentrism of the U.S. Roman Catholic
Church by creating an alternative space for Latinas to express a
feminist spirituality and theology.

Las Hermanas emerged in the context of the Church's renewal
through Vatican Council II, Latin American liberation struggles,
the civil rights movements, Vietnam War protests, and feminism.
The ferment of change combined with a legacy of discrimination

in the U.S. Catholic Church toward Chicanos and other Spanish-speaking persons convinced Chicana sisters to mobilize in 1971.

Encouraged by the organizing efforts of Chicano clergy in 1969 known as PADRES, Gregoria Ortega, a Victoryknoll sister from El Paso, and Gloria Graciela Gallardo, a Holy Ghost sister from San Antonio, contacted Mexican American sisters nationwide. A letter dated 20 October 1970 expressed their reasons for uniting as Chicana sisters:

> We, as religious exert much influence among our Spanish-speaking people because of their deep-seated religious principles. Many of us feel that we are not doing this to our fullest capacity. On the other hand, there are some of us who have tried to become more relevant to our people and because of this, find themselves in "trouble" with either our own congregation or other members of the hierarchy. Then there are some of us who would like to be able to do more among our people but cannot, either because they are not yet quite sure of themselves or because they are being constrained by the lack of understanding or communication in their congregation.[1]

Six months later fifty women religious from twenty congregations gathered in Houston. The decision to form Las Hermanas quickly took root, and a motto, "*Unidas en Acción y Oración*" [United in Action and Prayer], was chosen. The participants unanimously supported four goals in order to effectively serve "the Spanish-speaking people of God using our unique resources as Spanish-speaking religious women"[2]: (1) activate leadership among themselves and the laity; (2) affect social change; (3) contribute to the cultural renaissance of *La Raza;* and (4) educate their Anglo-dominant congregations concerning the needs of Spanish-speaking communities.[3]

The second meeting eight months later (25–27 November 1971, in Santa Fe, New Mexico), drew four times as many participants. The first issue of *Informes,* the organizational newsletter, dated September of that year, stated, "Our current 'membership' is over 900, giving HERMANAS members in twenty-five [U.S.] states, Mexico, Guatemala, Bolivia, Ecuador, and Peru."[4] Fourteen states elected state coordinators, and Colorado, Texas, and California held regional conferences.[5]

This remarkable response to the invitation to unite as Mexican American sisters was also a response to a long history of overt discrimination within the Church toward Chicano and Latino Catholics as well as the current·climate of activism and reform. Chicano and Latino communities were seeing the demands of Chicano activists for Church support, transformations of the Church after Vatican Council II, the growing influence of Latin American liberation theology, and feminism, which merged and set in motion the ethnic and political consciousness of Chicana women religious.

Ecclesiastic Discrimination

A pattern of second-class status in the Roman Catholic Church for Mexican Americans and extreme cultural alienation and discrimination experienced by many Chicanas in religious life compelled Las Hermanas to organize for change. Yolanda Tarango of the Sisters of Charity of the Incarnate Word recalls the racism she and other Chicanas experienced:

> At that time you were supposed to leave behind your past as it was not desirable to work with one's people. I experienced much racism. Nothing cultural was valued. We were forbidden to speak Spanish even in hospitals, schools, not even to the janitors. This is the climate we walked into. For everyone it was a culture shock; anything Hispanic was devalued. It was a violent tearing away from our pasts.[6]

In some situations Chicana sisters were encouraged to draw on their cultural capital. Exceptions to a pattern of discrimination in religious life did exist; for example, the Victoryknoll sisters were established principally to work in Mexican American communities and thus had a percentage of Chicana sisters. Leadership, however, remained dominated by Euroamerican sisters.[7] Other orders such as the Congregation of Divine Providence welcomed Mexican American women, but before the 1960s did not encourage them to pursue higher education. Euroamerican sisters consistently received greater educational opportunities.[8] The Sisters of Loretto established a novitiate in Santa Fe in 1852 with primarily Mexican American women. According to Sylvia Sedillo, SL, "I always felt like I belonged."[9] Teresita Basso also always felt supported by her congregation, the Presentation of the Blessed Virgin Mary.[10]

The treatment of most Chicana sisters did not differ much from the discrimination that Spanish-speaking Catholics encountered historically in the Church. An overview of Chicano-Catholic history beginning in 1848 is helpful to assess the legacy of institutionalized racism. Following the signing of the Treaty of Guadalupe Hidalgo in 1848, Mexican Catholics in the annexed territories became members of the U.S. Roman Catholic Church overnight. These now Mexican Americans soon experienced discriminatory practices under the authority of European-born pastors and bishops. With Spanish, French, Irish, and German clergy, recruited to minister to the Spanish-speaking, a lack of cultural understanding reigned.[11] The actions of the first bishop of the New Mexico territory, including present-day Arizona and southern Colorado, Fr. Jean Batiste Lamy of France, exemplify the religious struggles of the era. Arriving in 1851, Lamy expelled the sixteen native Mexican clergy ministering in New Mexico. In 1854 in a pastoral letter, Lamy instituted tithing and threatened to excommunicate any pastor who did not comply. Uncooperative parishioners would be denied the sacraments. Mexican-born Fr. José Martínez refused and was subsequently banished from his ministry among native New Mexicans. Lamy proceeded to insult further the native Catholics by recruiting additional priests from France and replacing indigenous religious art with European statues.[12]

Further examples of institutional efforts to strip Mexican Americans of their cultural and religious identity abound. With no understanding of the communal and family-centered religious customs of Mexican Catholics, Bishop Taddues Amat of the Monterey–Los Angeles diocese attempted to regulate religious orthodoxy. Between 1862 and 1876, Amat published three decrees prohibiting any popular devotions that "offended clerical sensitivities."[13] Mexican public celebrations such as *Los Pastores*, a Christmas play, *Los Judeaos*, a Holy Week drama, and funeral customs were among the first traditions declared scandalous. Concern for Protestant nativism convinced the Spanish bishop to refashion Mexican Catholicism according to the rubrics of Roman ritual.[14] By the late 1800s, Mexican Catholics in southern California retained a distant relationship with the Church.[15] Ironically, the insensitivity of Amat and others encouraged the "unofficial" rituals of a community and family-centered faith to take on even greater significance for the people.[16]

By the turn of the century, many Catholic parishes with a substantial number of Mexican American members forced these parishioners into the church basement for separate Masses.[17] In the early 1900s, in Phoenix, Arizona, a German cleric, Fr. Novatus Benzing, expected Mexicans to sit on the church floor while Anglos occupied the pews. He denied Mexican Americans the sacraments unless they enrolled their children in the parochial school.[18] Southwest Mexican communities often responded to such blatant discrimination by building their own churches.[19]

Whereas the majority of Mexican Americans remained faithful to their Catholic roots, some did convert to Protestantism.[20] Presbyterian, Methodist, and Baptist ministers made the first inroads into Mexican communities throughout the Southwest in the 1820s. By the turn of the century, "a significant number of Hispanic churches had been planted. They were ministered mostly by Hispanics, though under the 'tutelage' of Anglo missionaries."[21] The Pentecostal Azusa Street revival in Los Angeles in the early 1900s marked a significant expansion of Latino Protestants and attracted even "devout [Mexican] Catholics."[22] Issues of paternalistic control, however, shaped the patterns and structures of Mexican American Protestantism in the Southwest well into the late twentieth century.[23]

By the second decade of the twentieth century, the Catholic Church increased its efforts to respond positively to its Mexican members. Fear of Protestant conversions rather than cultural acceptance, however, characterized its motivations.[24] As examples, Bishop Cantwell of Los Angeles appointed Fr. Robert E. Lucey as director of the Bureau of Catholic Charities. By 1929 Lucey had established five diocesan community centers serving Mexican American neighborhoods. In addition, a medical clinic and a recreation center including an employment bureau tried to meet the needs of the growing Mexican Catholic population.[25] These efforts, however, focused extensively on Americanizing the Mexicans with little analysis of the root cause of poverty.[26] With the onset of the Depression, charity programs decreased and the Church turned to religious education as a means of continuing Americanization efforts. Raising good Catholics meant forming good Americans.[27]

A few Catholic settlement houses in the Midwest serviced Mexican immigrants; however, none ever matched those established by Protestants such as Hull House and the University of Chicago Settlement.[28] In fact, the Catholic-sponsored Gary-Alerding House in Gary, Indiana, opened in 1923, yet blatant anti-Mexican sentiments expressed by its director, Fr. John deVille, discouraged Mexicans from utilizing settlement services.[29]

The efforts of Mexican sisters at times offered a different experience. In the 1930s, a Mexican order, the Company of Mary, fled the anti-Catholic Mexican government under Plutarco Calles, and established their convent in Douglas, Arizona. Finding themselves in a heavily populated Mexican town dominated by an Anglo Protestant society, these women offered their teaching services to Mexican women and children. According to historian Raquel Rubio Goldsmith,

> For Mexicanas in Douglas, the convent symbolized a Mexican world . . . no other building housed Mexican culture so grandly . . . [it] stood proudly for that which was pushed into corners in the rest of the town. There, Mexican culture found a home, and Mexicanas . . . reveled in its existence, feeling pride along with comfort.[30]

Such unusual circumstances, however, did not have a broader impact beyond the fortunate women and children who encountered these Mexican sisters in Arizona.

The post–World War II Church hierarchy succeeded in building a massive parochial school system that aimed to further Americanize and strengthen Catholic ties among Mexican Americans.[31] Despite these efforts, discrimination on the pastoral level persisted. In 1945 in Riverside, California, the Zuniga family suffered public chastisement for entering the church during the Mass designated for Euroamerican Catholics. Numerous other stories describe Mexicans being forced to occupy the pews in the back of the church and having to wait to receive the Eucharist until after their fellow white Christians had.[32]

Councils for the Spanish-speaking began to appear in the early 1950s as an outgrowth of the Bishops' Committee for the Spanish Speaking first organized in 1945. Under the leadership of Robert E. Lucey, then archbishop of the San Antonio archdiocese, the bishops' committee agreed to construct medical clinics, settlement houses, and community and catechetical centers in Los Angeles, Santa Fe, Denver, and San Antonio.[33]

By the mid-1960s, diocesan councils, and in some areas regional offices for urbanized Chicano/Latino Catholics, began to appear, at times under the leadership of Latino laity. Moíses

Sandoval states that by 1965, representatives of seventy dioceses worked in liaison with the bishops' committee. The archdioceses of New York, Chicago, and Denver had offices, committees, or projects dedicated to Latino ministries. The dioceses of Cleveland, Miami, Madison, Wisconsin, and Baker, Oregon, also had offices devoted to Latino ministry and migrant needs.[34]

Not until 1970, however, did the institutionalization of Latino leadership on a national basis occur when the Office for the Spanish Speaking (OSS), established in 1945, relocated to Washington, D.C., under the direction of Pablo Sedillo, a layman from New Mexico. Housed within the building of the NCCB, the OSS proved ineffective as Sedillo lacked both staff and a budget. Initially Sedillo led OSS as a division in the Department of Social Development and World Peace, but the new director lacked access to the policy-making committees of the NCCB. After four years of lobbying with the help of PADRES, Las Hermanas, and Latino laity, Sedillo's office was elevated to the Secretariat for the Spanish Speaking in 1974.[35]

Accompanying this success was the gradual development of regional offices for Latino ministry in the Midwest (1968), the West (1973), and the Northeast and the Southwest (1974). Small budgets and understaffing, however, characterized the operational limits of these programs.

Regional Latino/a directors, including Las Hermanas members Olga Villa, director of the Midwest office, and Lupe Anguiano, director of the Southwest office, lobbied tirelessly for more Latinos at the decision-making level, from chanceries to parish councils. Culturally relevant services, liturgies in Spanish, and social justice concerns held top priority as Villa and Anguiano sought to minister to immigrants, farmworkers, and the urban poor. Leadership development and the preparation of Latino lay ministers also received primary attention.[36]

Overall, however, institutionalized patterns of discrimination continued to characterize Chicano–Catholic Church relations. As sociologist Gilbert Cadena states, "From 1848 to 1970, Mexicans/Chicanos had virtually no voice in the national decision-making process of the church . . . nor did they plan pastoral or social policy."[37] Not until 1970 did the Catholic hierarchy appoint its first Mexican American, Fr. Patricio Flores, as an auxiliary bishop even though Latinos comprised approximately 27 percent of the U.S. Catholic population. In comparison, Irish Americans comprised 17 percent of the U.S. Catholic population yet had a representation of 56 percent among American Catholic bishops. Chicanos represented only 200 members of the 54,000 priests and Latinas less than 5 percent, or 1,000 of 104,000, women religious in the United States.[38] In many regions Spanish-speaking Catholics still had to worship in substandard conditions. In the 1970s ecclesiastical employment practices relegated sisters from Mexico to domestic tasks in rectories and seminaries; their meager earnings were sent to their communities in Mexico.[39] Inheriting this legacy of discrimination compelled Chicana sisters in 1971 to challenge the racism in the Catholic Church and immerse themselves in national and international secular/political struggles for justice. They courageously brought the Chicano movement into the Catholic Church.

The collaboration between Chicana and Latina sisters and Chicano priests in the early 1970s reflects an era of intense action and optimism. In the words of Las Hermanas member Carmelita Espinoza, RGS, "It was a real decade of conversion and change!"[40] Latina/o Catholics became very visible as these women and men struggled to empower themselves as leaders for the sake of Latino communities. María Iglesias, SC, remembers the energy and excitement: "All of us were calling for dialogue with the hierarchy. It was the first time we had a voice."[41]

Vatican Council II

The Second Vatican Council (1962–65) convened by Pope John XXIII called upon the Church to modernize in response to the "signs of the times." The cries for self-determination among colonized peoples, protests for workers' economic rights, and the struggle for women's equality in public and private arenas were singled out as significant pressures requiring the attention of religious leaders.[42] The papal mandate for the Church to engage in the concerns of the world encouraged an unprecedented involvement of religious leaders, both men and women, in social and political affairs.

The Council's "recognition that God speaks through cultures"[43] broadened the Church's identity in the world. By bringing together bishops from numerous countries and cultures, approving vernacular languages for liturgical use, affirming historical consciousness, and pronouncing the validity of other religions, Vatican Council II opened the door to culturally specific ministries. [44] For Teresita Basso, a member of Las Hermanas from its inception, the Church's validation of culture as an expression of the sacred pointed her to ministry in Chicano communities. "I realized I knew the language and the culture: The Church had been absent for so long among our people." [45]

The Council produced sixteen documents providing direction to religious leaders and laity, endorsing principals such as a ministry of collegiality among clerics and laity, ecumenism, correction of the Church's errors, regional and local diversity, scriptural reflection by the laity, and a recommitment to the social mission of the Church. [46] The longest document, *Gaudium et spes: The Church in the Modern World*, declared social justice activity as a primary way of fulfilling the mission of the Church. As a synthesis of Catholic social teaching, the document declared that the Church could no longer remain indifferent to the world and its changes. According to historian John O'Malley,

> never before in the history of Catholicism have so many and such sudden changes been legislated and implemented which immediately touched the lives of the faithful, and never before had such a radical adjustment of viewpoint been required of them. [47]

Such sudden changes affected Church leaders and laity in diverse ways.

Divisions among the 2,700 bishops present at the Council reflected the heterogeneity of the Church. Conservatives maintained that the weakening of ecclesial authority stemmed from "a growing secularization in the world, a decrease in faith, and a lessening of respect for authority." [48] The progressive sector believed that "the institutional church needed restructuring and reform because it was too hierarchical, too impersonal, and too detached from modernity. Service to all humankind should be the church's first priority." [49] These distinctly different positions resulted in final documents marked by inconsistencies and evident compromises. For example, article nine of *Gaudium et spes* emphasizes the mission of the Church to accompany humanity as it seeks "to establish a political, social, and economic order which will to an ever better extent serve man [*sic*] and help individuals as well as groups to affirm and develop the dignity proper to them."[50] In contrast, article forty-two clearly states that the Church has "no proper mission in the political, economic, or social order. The purpose which Christ set before her is a religious one."[51] Such inconsistencies later supported politically divergent interpretations.

Perfectae caritatis: Decree on the Appropriate Renewal of Religious Life urged religious orders of priests and sisters to critical self-examination and renewal of religious life; it advocated a return to the community's original inspiration and its adjustment to the conditions of the times.[52] According to Basso, who entered the convent at the start of Vatican Council II in 1962, "We were allowed to interpret our vows differently. It was no longer merely answering to hierarchical power but rather a striving to listen to the spirit within each of us . . . what the spirit was calling us to do with our particular gifts."[53] Yolanda Tarango, who joined religious life at the end of Vatican Council II, recalls:

> It was an exciting time as it was the beginning of designing what religious life was to be. We were considered the new school. We were able to appreciate what was, but grateful that we didn't have to adhere to it. There was much social and religious upheaval.[54]

Vatican II uprooted the earlier understanding of religious life as following specific mandates to a state of perfection by opening communication between religious life and the modern world.[55]

Many sisters eagerly accepted new ministerial and professional challenges that required advanced education and focused on eliminating the causes of poverty.[56] Basso reflects on this redirection:

> We questioned our vows, what did obedience, poverty, and chastity mean? Poverty was not just a style of living, but what were we doing to critically look around us at the middle class we lived. We were challenged to look at the real poverty in the world. We were attempting something different.[57]

María Iglesias emphasizes the shift in the level of freedom and responsibility that Vatican Council II demanded of women religious:

> We became more responsible for our own lives. When I first entered, the order was responsible for every move we made. Before we never questioned where we were sent to work. That was up to the

institution. Then the institution turned around and said, "Now think!"[58]

As a result of this new freedom, many women changed from teaching professions to social work. In Iglesias's community, many of the Euroamerican sisters chose to work in housing projects or with the homeless, while others learned Spanish for ministries in Latin America.

But for Chicana sisters who had joined religious life prior to Vatican Council II, the challenge to address social ills required far more than redirecting their ministry. Accepting the challenge meant coming to terms with their own ethnic identities previously denied by many of their religious communities. Remember that life in the convent had demanded that these women leave their cultural backgrounds, families, traditions, and languages behind. The forced cultural alienation led many sisters to extreme levels of self-denial. Carmelita Espinoza speaks symbolically of her own ethnic identity in the late 1960s: "At that time I was an Anglo sister. If you were a bright and nice Hispanic woman, they sent you to college. You became the cream of the crop but you were not allowed to work among Latinos."[59] Yolanda Tarango echoes this alienation along with the impact Las Hermanas made on their lives:

> Most of us had been pretty brainwashed or repressed. Coming together at the first [Las Hermanas] conference was a call to action and a personal call to our own identity and that of the struggling Hispanic community . . . We realized we needed to all go back to our orders and demand to work with the Hispanic community.[60]

By the time of the farmworkers' struggle under the leadership of César Chávez and Dolores Huerta in the mid-1960s, it became increasingly difficult for Chicana and Latina sisters to remain distant from their own ethnic communities.

In addition to opportunities for individual choice after Vatican Council II, the privilege of being educated broadened occupational horizons for women religious. Within Las Hermanas, Catalina Fresquez, CCVI, earned a doctorate in biology; María Carolina Flores, CDP, achieved a degree in library science and later earned a doctoral degree in history; Lydia Peña, SL, earned a doctorate in art history and now holds an administrative position at Regis University in Denver, Colorado. Although only a few sisters in Las Hermanas hold doctorates, several have earned master's degrees.

For many Chicana and Latina sisters, the privilege of being educated led to a self-awareness of "being the voice of our people."[61] Carmelita Espinoza elaborates: "We realized we could speak out because we were educated. We had the clout of being educated within the system."[62]

Understanding the relative degree of power they held within the Church to advocate for the rights of Chicano Catholics spurred these women to intense levels of activism. Knowing "how the [Church] system worked"[63] encouraged these women to hold the institution accountable to its Spanish-speaking members. María Iglesias explains: "I saw that I was to be a bridge between my people and the Church."[64]

Differing opinions, however, among religious congregations prevailed regarding efforts for renewal. Although some religious embraced the social gospel, others did not.[65] Confusion within religious orders often reflected a general reluctance to adopt the new mission of the Church.[66] For example, defining "the poor" could not be resolved easily for the Sisters of Charity in New York. Iglesias explains:

> When our order first started in the early 1800s we were working with very poor Irish immigrants. As the families became more settled our institutions benefited from their wealth. By the time of Vatican Council II we found ourselves teaching the children of those who had resources, yet our founding mission was to work with the very poor. We had to ask ourselves, "Who are we serving?" Many sisters did not want to deal with that, they were afraid . . . the new poor immigrants were not of their same ethnic group.[67]

Iglesias asked for permission to work exclusively with the Puerto Rican children of a parish in the South Bronx who could not afford to attend the parochial school. Some members of her community felt she was setting up a dichotomy between teaching and pastoral work. The parish priest fired Iglesias after she had dedicated two years to the work. Through the support of a "few valiant women" in her congregation and her introduction to Las Hermanas, Iglesias found the courage to remain in religious life.

Mario (Lucie) Barron, a member of St. Joseph's of Carondelet, also experienced the confusion that Vatican Council II caused for some religious communities. Reading the social encyclicals supporting the rights of laborers inspired Barron to contact César Chávez and Dolores Huerta. "She began making the connections between the social teachings of Vatican Council II and the plight of farmworkers, yet she had no one in her order to participate in the conversation. They weren't making the same connections."[68] Barron became determined to change her teaching assignment in a Catholic school among the children of farm growers in Oxnard, California, to teaching the children of the farmworkers. Although her religious community did not fully understand her, it supported her as long as she continued to teach.

Overall, renewal within congregations cooperated with papal authority throughout the years of Vatican Council II. By the end of the decade, however, relations began to weaken. Little had changed in the line of authority between the Vatican and women religious. Considered as laity, sisters retained the lowest position in the ecclesial hierarchy. The Vatican refused to enter into dialogue with congregational leaders even when conducting commissions on the lives of sisters. North American sisters, motivated by their own renewal efforts and the growing influence of feminist and liberation movements, charted their own course for effective ministry.[69] Las Hermanas exemplified the growing autonomy of women in religious orders.[70]

Clear divisions among women's religious communities appeared in 1971, when the Congregation of Major Superiors of Women changed its name to the LCWR to reflect a broader understanding of leadership, authority, and independence from the Vatican and the American hierarchy. Revised bylaws eliminated any reference to the LCWR being under the authority of the papacy.[71] While 90 percent of women religious remained with the LCWR, fifty congregational superiors formed their own group, Consortium Perfectae Caritatis; others formed the Institute for Religious Life. Both were very conservative responses to the LCWR.[72] In outlining "seven essentials for religious life," which included wearing a religious habit, Consortium pledged their support of a strong hierarchical relationship between women religious and the Vatican.[73]

The LCWR wasted no time in clarifying their independence from ecclesial authority. In 1972 they rejected papal orders that religious communities "may not abolish [the religious habit] altogether or leave it to the judgment of individual sisters."[74] Five years later, the American bishops criticized the LCWR publication, *Choose Life,* for taking a "weak position" against abortion. By implying that abortion is the result of other social problems, the LCWR crossed the sensitive boundaries of Church authority. According to church historian George Kelley, Rome informed religious superiors in 1979 that the LCWR was not an official organization for American nuns.[75] Ironically, the Vatican has continued to deal publicly and officially with the LCWR. Despite Vatican disapproval, the LCWR has continued its mission as an autonomous group of women religious. In 1971, the LCWR assisted in identifying Chicana sisters for membership in Las Hermanas, and one year later the LCWR publicly supported the United Farm Workers by endorsing the lettuce boycott. The LCWR has consistently provided limited financial support to Las Hermanas.

Latin American Liberation Theology

As North American sisters and priests responded to the challenges of Vatican Council II, religious leaders in Latin America responded similarly given their particular social context. While the Vatican Council envisioned a new role for the Church in the world, it did so from a Western European and North American worldview. This perspective claimed that the benefits of modernity, namely capitalist development, could solve much of the economic injustices in "underdeveloped" countries. Vatican Council II supported social activism as a way to assist the poor and acknowledged personal sin in the world as the human inclination to do evil. It failed to discuss social sin or institutionalized systems of oppression that keep the majority of the world's population living in extreme poverty.[76]

As Latin American religious leaders applied the spirit of Council documents to their context, they confronted the reality of poverty and misery that developmental reforms caused and could not change. Clearly exploitation and foreign aid created persistent poverty for the majority of Latin Americans.[77] As an example, in the 1960s, the United States intervened in a broad economic plan for the five countries of Central America. The Central American Common Market (CACM) tried to balance the industrialization process and ensure that new industries would be in the hands of Central Americans. Fearing that the plan ran counter to the free market, the United States offered $100 million to "aid economic integration" and reshape the plan. Ultimately, the U.S.

intervention forced the CACM to serve foreign investors such as Kellogg, Ritz, and Firestone, rather than aid the growth of autonomous Central American industries.[78]

Only three years after the close of Vatican Council II, Latin American bishops convened in Medellín, Colombia, to discern the role of the Church in the midst of extreme poverty and growing military repression. The United Nations Economic Commission for Latin America had reported that 1.2 percent of landowners owned 71.6 percent of the total farm areas (excluding Cuba and Bolivia, where huge land holdings have been outlawed).[79] With the majority of land and investment devoted to one-crop export items, the dietary needs of the masses remained unmet. In the late 1960s, 42.2 percent of Latin America's population was farmworkers; the majority were paid in "chits," negotiable only at the landowner's store, a tactic further exacerbating the poverty and dependency of workers. Small plots of land for personal use held substantial surcharge fees payable to the landlord. Eighty-six million Latin Americans in rural areas had substandard water supplies, leaving more than one-half of the total population subject to epidemic diseases such as typhoid.[80] Economic insecurity and social and family instability characterized rural life.[81]

The urban masses did not fare any better. Displaced farmers migrated to cities for low-wage work in factories, industries, and domestic services. In Nicaragua alone, between 1960 and 1977 the rural population declined from 60 percent to 48 percent, with a large portion being single women with children.[82] Families headed solely by females comprised one-half of the impoverished class. Poor women had a life expectancy of fifty years; three out of ten never attended school; one of every two remained illiterate.[83] With no job security, benefits, unions, or even regulated work schedules, the majority of women and their children faced insurmountable poverty.[84] This brutal reality accompanied by growing military-backed dictatorships convinced Latin American bishops to apply Vatican Council II's spirit of radical change to their context.[85]

The documents produced by the Congreso Episcopal Latioamericano (CELAM—Latin American Conference of Bishops) in 1968 at Medellín pronounced a radically new role for the Church in society. The bishops argued that the Church must assist the poor in their struggle for liberation. In analyzing the external and internal colonialism of Latin America, the bishops moved beyond a concern for personal sin and identified the reality of structural sin or institutionalized systems of oppression. The bishops called for structural change of oppressive social institutions *and* a new consciousness of liberation. Liberation meant the poor acting as agents of social transformation or subjects of their own history. Justice would prevail only as a result of the liberation struggle of the people themselves. Solidarity with the poor in seeking justice must comprise an essential element of the faithful Christian life.[86]

Identifying "social struggle as a form of Christian discipleship" marked a significant challenge for the Church in Latin America because of its legacy of extreme conservatism. Close alliances with political and economic powers, defensive positions toward change, and adherence to a paternalistic treatment of the "ever-present poor" had shaped the ministry of the Church since European Christian colonization in the sixteenth century.[87]

Church reform, however, actually began a decade prior to Vatican Council II. In Brazil, for example, under the leadership of Archbishop Dom Helder Cámara, the National Conference of Brazilian Bishops (Conferencia Nacional Episcopal Brazileño, CNBB) formed in 1952, during a time when bishops' conferences were rare. The CNBB became the principal activist vehicle for social change in Brazil and throughout Latin America. Early on it persuaded the hierarchy to support the Movement for Grassroots Education (Movimiento para Educación de Base, MEB), a national and regional organization of laity concerned with social justice. The MEB developed literacy circles that brought the poor together to analyze the region's poverty, malnutrition, and illiteracy. Literacy tools included both the Bible and Paulo Freire's consciousness-raising techniques, the process by which people become aware of their rights and responsibilities.[88] According to Freire, they "achieve a deepening awareness of the socio-cultural reality that shapes their lives and of their capacity to transform that reality."[89]

In parts of Latin America where a scarcity of priests existed, individual clergy and sisters promoted *comunidades eclesiales de base*, or small base church communities led by the laity. These small groups became the seeds of the base community movement that fostered a radical Christian faith critical of systems of oppression.[90] By the late 1950s, the strengthening of lay movements among workers, farmers, and students, educational programs like the MEB, the mobilization of bishops in the CNBB, and revolutionary unrest in many parts of Central and South America created "the presence of a broad disposition to change in Latin American Catholicism that was legitimated and enhanced, but not created de novo, by the encyclicals of Pope John XXIII and the Council."[91] In 1968, the CNBB played a leadership role in the historic meeting of CELAM at Medellín.

The bishops' emphasis on activism, justice, and liberation would become the hallmark tenets of liberation theology. The insights of the Latin American bishops and the theologians among them culminated in the first major book on liberation theology in 1971, authored by Gustavo Gutiérrez, a Peruvian bishop who attended Vatican Council II.[92] Numerous works followed elaborating further a theology of liberation that influenced colonized peoples worldwide.[93] Liberation themes even found their way into papal documents as early as 1971. In *Justitia in mundo*, the Synod of Bishops declared the Church to be in solidarity with those struggling to liberate themselves from oppression, domination, and abuse.[94] CELAM convened again in 1979 at Puebla, Mexico, to champion further the ideas and language used at Medellín and to "affirm the need for conversion on the part of the whole church to a preferential option for the poor, an option aimed at their integral liberation."[95]

Liberation theology transformed the ministries of religious leaders and pastoral workers throughout Latin America as they participated in political education and supported popular movements to fight military dictatorships, national security states, and U.S. military intervention.[96] By 1970 military-dominated regimes ruled in Brazil, Chile, and Argentina, followed by reactionary governments in Central America. The 1970 democratic election of the first socialist president in the Americas, Salvador Allende in Chile, and a successful socialist revolution in Nicaragua in 1979, marked a promising change of direction for Latin America. However, a U.S.-backed military coup in Chile only three years after Allende's election and civil war in El Salvador beginning in 1980 shattered hopes for self-determining populations.

As the crises deepened, many religious leaders became "major public protagonists" and openly criticized the oppression.[97] Between 1968 and 1978, more than 1,500 active religious and lay leaders became victims of threats, arrests, tortures, and murders.

Thousands of others disappeared or were forced into exile. The assassination of El Salvador's Archbishop Oscar Romero in March 1980, followed by the rape and brutal killing of three North American sisters and one lay missionary in December 1980, exemplify "the savagery of the repression."[98] In 1982, five Guatemalan lay catechists of Santa Cruz El Quiché met their death in retaliation for using the Bible to teach their peers how to read and write. The townspeople were forced by the military to kill the "subversive" catechists themselves, or the army would raze Santa Cruz and neighboring villages. Such indictments claimed that "The Bible was, of all books, the most subversive because it taught that everyone was equal in the sight of God—hence the ferocious persecution of catechists."[99] In 1989, six Jesuit priests, their housekeeper, and her daughter were massacred by the Salvadoran military at the Jesuit-run University of Central America. The priests had been leading spokespersons for a nonviolent, negotiated settlement to El Salvador's ten-year civil war.[100]

The experiences of the Church in Latin America had a tremendous impact on Christian theology and praxis worldwide. The challenge to all Christians to "make a preferential option for the poor" influenced the commitments of North American priests, sisters, and laity. Many made serving the poor a top priority. According to historian Mary Jo Weaver, the 1960s witnessed 20,000 American sisters training and working in Latin America.[101] Ministering in Latin America also shaped the consciousness of Chicana and Latina sisters, many of whom traveled south to study with liberation theologians and minister among the poor. According to Carmelita Espinoza,

> We chose Quito, Ecuador, because they were training ministers at the Pastoral Institute of Latin America. We had been in white institutions for so long that we really wanted a different exposure. It was clear that the laity had to be empowered and that Western theology was so limiting.[102]

For Dominga Zapata, SH, the training in Latin America attracted "Hermanas who believe that *La Raza* Church depends upon what Church we introduce our people to and how their faith is kept alive and growing."[103] Most of these women ultimately worked among Latino communities in the United States, yet their exposure to Latin America had long-lasting effects. As María de Jesús

Ybarra, OP, shares, "One of the things I learned [in Latin America] was that the Church is not the end but the means to help our people."[104]

Learning firsthand the tenets of liberation theology dramatically affected Chicana and Latina sisters. Many underwent radical transformations in their own identities and commitments. According to Ada María Isasi-Díaz, a member of a religious community in the mid-1960s who had ministered in Peru,

> Though I was not to articulate it until years later, it was then that I began to realize that the lived experience of the poor and oppressed was to be the source of my theology . . . Since those days in Peru in the mid-1960s I have understood myself as a justice-activist.[105]

Understanding the role of the Church in the systems of oppression in Latin America led members of Las Hermanas to confront poverty in the United States among their own ethnic communities. Chicana sisters previously isolated from the secular world now openly defied racism and poverty. The Chicano movement for civil rights coincided with the emergence of liberation theology, placing the struggle for justice close to home.

The Chicano Movement

The 1960s and 1970s witnessed a continuation of but also a transformation in political activism within Mexican American communities. Since the signing of the Treaty of Guadalupe Hidalgo in 1848, when the United States annexed one-half of Mexico's territory, Mexican Americans were disenfranchised from their land and from economic, social, and political power. Each generation responded with distinct strategies of resistance that enabled cultural survival.[106] For Mexican American youth coming of age during the 1960s, the legacy of resistance forged by previous generations would be carried on through the politics of mass protest.

Chicano and *Chicana* emerged as the terms of identity in the quest for self-determination, cultural pride, political and economic power, and social change. Despite being rejected by Mexican Americans of middle-class status and conservative politics, masses of youth intent on reclaiming their long-denied place in society were unified by these terms. By appropriating "a pejorative barrio term 'Chicano' into a symbol of pride,"[107] young men and women created an identity that challenged the assumptions, policies, and principles of mainstream white America.

Economic and educational disparity plagued a rapidly growing Chicano/Latino population. The 1970 census reported a total population of "persons of Spanish origin" at 9,073,237. Persons of Mexican origin comprised the majority at approximately four and one-half million and resided primarily in urban areas within the five southwestern states of California, Texas, Arizona, Colorado, and New Mexico.[108] Approximately 20 percent of Latino families headed by two parents survived below the poverty level in comparison to 8.6 percent of Euroamerican families. The median income for these families totaled $7,534 versus $9,961 respectively. For "Spanish heritage" single female heads of households the mean income totaled $4,565 in comparison to $6,871 for white women.[109]

Educational achievement levels fared worse for "persons of Spanish heritage" than for the rest of the population, with an average of 9.6 years of school completed versus 12.1 for the rest of the nation. Only 2.3 percent held a bachelor's degree or higher, versus 6.7 percent for whites.[110] According to *U.S. News and World Report*, a 1964 study disclosed that 18 percent of Chicanos and 22 percent of Chicanas in Los Angeles alone were "functionally illiterate" and their school "dropout" rate was the worst of any group in California. Eurocentric curriculum and a lack of bilingual, bicultural teachers effectively pushed Chicano students out of the educational system. The study found that Chicano youth faced the same de facto segregation in schools as that faced by African Americans. "About 80 percent of the Mexican Americans and 93 percent of the Negroes are concentrated in three of the city's six school districts."[111] De facto segregation inevitably led to separate and inferior institutions. In 1970, educator and sociologist Thomas P. Carter published a major study on the complex reasons contributing to low educational levels among Mexican American youth. According to Carter, "the failure of the school[s] to provide them with the skills, knowledge, and credentials essential for entrance into the higher levels of society" played a major factor in the inequities and injustices faced by Chicanos.[112]

The rapid demographic increase and economic and educational inequalities caught the attention of politicians. Lyndon B. Johnson's War on Poverty of the mid-1960s directed funding to Mexican American communities "to an extent unimaginable under previous presidents."[113] Federal programs focused on health care, job training, adult education, food stamps, and housing. Governmental appointments provided unprecedented opportunities for community organizing and leadership development.[114]

Federal educational programs made possible by the struggles of black Americans directly benefited Chicano youth by opening doors to colleges and universities. The increasing number of Chicano students enrolled in institutions of higher education did little to rectify the educational and economic disparity among the majority of Chicanos, however.[115]

A critical awareness of the inequalities fueled the Chicano communities' outrage at U.S. intervention in the Vietnam War. The disproportionate number of Chicano and African American casualties in the war fueled the rage among Chicanos and Chicanas. As one Chicano stated, "How can they tell us we are fighting for freedom and democracy 8,000 miles away, when we don't have freedom and democracy here at home?"[116]

The Spanish-speaking population as a whole sorely lacked political representation. In California, no Mexican American sat in either house of the California legislature despite the state's three million Spanish-speaking persons. In Los Angeles County, where one million Chicanos resided, neither the city council nor the board of education had any Mexican American representation.[117] On the federal level, the U.S. Senate claimed one Spanish surnamed member, and the House of Representatives had only five congressional representatives with Spanish surnames.[118] A lack of political representation, socioeconomic injustices, cultural denigration in schools, and overrepresentation among Vietnam War casualties propelled Chicano and Chicana activists into a social movement demanding change.

The Chicano movement, or *el movimiento,* was not a homogeneous struggle. According to historian Ernesto Chávez,

> It was not a unified entity but rather a series of separate actions waged by organizations that used a common anti-American language to press their demands. Although sharing the common goal of self-determination for the Mexican community, how to achieve this aim varied from one group to another.[119]

The striving for self-determination took place in multiple arenas with young, middle-aged, and elderly participants, both male and female. Numerous organizations emerged out of their specific social, political, and regional contexts. The Brown Berets, the Chicano Moratorium Committee, La Raza Unida Party (LRUP), Centro de Acción Social Autónomo (CASA), El Movimiento Estudantil Chicano de Aztlán (MEChA), Comisión Femenil Mexicana, and the United Farm Workers of America (UFWA) were among many that organized to address the inequalities facing Chicanos. Las Hermanas and PADRES mobilized to address specifically inequalities within the Catholic Church and to bridge political and religious concerns. Activism among these distinct organizations took many forms, from boycotts to protests, from house meetings to conventions, from sit-ins to voter registration drives. I limit my discussion to the arenas where members of Las Hermanas were most present—the farm labor movement, the Chicano student movement, the Chicano moratorium, the Roman Catholic Church, and Chicana feminism.

The Farm Labor Movement

The struggle of Mexican American farmworkers under the leadership of César Chávez and Dolores Huerta beginning in 1962 had a great impact on the emerging Chicano movement. Though Chávez and Huerta led a labor movement, they and the National Farm Workers Association (NFWA) helped to inaugurate an era of Chicano/a political activism.[120] "As the first Mexican American leader to receive national recognition and support for his cause," Chávez helped to validate the "quest for identity and power" among Chicana/o youth.[121] By the time of the NFWA's march from Delano to Sacramento in 1965 to garner public support for a joint strike with the Agricultural Workers Organizing Committee (AWOC) against grape growers in San Joaquin Valley, "thousands of Mexican American students and youth . . . flocked to Sacramento to join the marchers and received a hearty dose of inspiration."[122] The 300-mile march resulted in the signing of contracts with several major California grape growers. The following year, Chávez requested a hearing before the U.S. Senate Migratory Subcommittee, which included Senator Robert Kennedy, to further publicize the farm workers' grievances. By August 1966, the NFWA joined with AWOC to form the United Farm Workers Organizing Committee (UFWOC); soon UFWOC organized the largest boycott against table grapes in the history of U.S. labor. Between 1966 and 1970, the UFWOC had union representatives in every metropolitan area, and "many Americans forgot what a grape tasted like."[123]

Halfway through the boycott the strain of decreasing resources and the growing presence of strikebreakers influenced some union members to use violent tactics such as burning farm buildings and harming "scabs." In opposition to the violence, Chávez held a twenty-five-day fast to increase national attention and revitalize the boycott.[124] In 1969 Chávez requested official support for the boycott from the Roman Catholic hierarchy. Although denying his request, California bishops appointed a mediating committee to negotiate a labor contract. In 1970, Lionel Steinberg, the largest table grape grower of Coachella Valley, along with three-quarters of the state's grape growers signed a three-year contract with the UFWOC.[125]

Throughout the national boycotts and labor strikes Chávez often directly challenged Catholic religious leaders. In a 1968 address at the Second Annual Mexican American Conference in Sacramento, California, he chastised the church for failing to support UFWOC in their early years of organizing. Chávez stated:

> It was not until some of us moved to Delano . . . that we really saw how far removed from the people the parish Church was. In fact, we could not get any help at all from the priests of Delano. When the strike began, they told us we could not even use the Church's auditorium for the meetings. The farmworkers' money helped build that auditorium![126]

Chávez's words conveyed the alienation and anger toward the Roman Catholic Church that many Chicana/o activists felt. As students strove for self-determination they openly rebelled against the Church's lack of financial and political support and discriminatory practices toward Mexican Americans. The following statement, written in 1971, emphasizes the growing antagonism among Chicano youth toward the Catholic Church: "the Catholic Church hierarchy has continuously insulted its Chicano membership by its racist practices and refusal to use its immense resources to support the Chicano movement."[127]

Despite the estranged relationship, Chávez, a devout Catholic, understood the power of the Church and he challenged Chicano activists not to ignore it:

THERE IS TREMENDOUS SPIRITUAL AND ECONOMIC POWER IN THE CHURCH. [It] has millions of dollars earmarked for the poor. But often the money is spent for food baskets for the needy instead of for effective action to eradicate the causes of poverty . . . I am calling for Mexican American groups to stop ignoring this source of power. It is not just our right to appeal to the Church to use its power effectively for the poor, it is our duty to do so. It should be as natural as appealing to government.[128]

Chávez's plea challenged the hierarchy of the Church as well as inspired new directions of ministry taking shape among women religious and priests. His message held a particular significance for Chicana sisters and Chicano priests previously denied the opportunity to work within their ethnic communities. As for many Chicano youth of the 1960s and 1970s, the farmworkers' struggle for labor rights provided the impetus "for their first experiences of militancy."[129]

Gaining support for boycotts within religious communities was not always an easy task for Chicana sisters. According to Teresita Basso, "boycotting grapes often created a point of polarity in religious orders as not everyone was supportive . . . we wanted to do it as a community."[130] Irene Muñoz described her experience with the Sisters of the Humility of Mary in the Midwest:

At one of our meetings, the sisters were discussing whether we should smoke or not. We said, "Wait! We have farmworkers out here and they are being treated this way . . . we have to fight for them." When it came time to boycott lettuce, the sisters said to us, "Why are you creating so much ruckus, who do you think you are?" It was painful. We were part of the community but not really part of it.[131]

Harassment did not stop Muñoz or her sister Molly, who belonged to the same religious community. They and many other sisters volunteered in the farm labor movement and continued to raise the consciousness of their peers. In reflecting on the impact they had, Muñoz stated, "Our community has come a long way."[132]

Student Activism

By 1967 Chicano and Chicana students on college campuses across the Southwest began to express their own struggle for educational and civil rights. Various student organizations emerged. As examples, the Mexican American Student Organization (MASO) mobilized at the University of Texas at Austin and the United Mexican American Students (UMAS) organized at Loyola University, the University of California at Los Angeles, and the University of Southern California. Agendas included support for the farmworkers, community involvement, and increased recruitment of Chicano students with financial and academic support. By 1968, student pressure resulted in the first Chicano Studies program at California State University at Los Angeles. [133]

Chicano high school students did not remain immune from the rising activism. In 1968, over 10,000 Chicano students representing five high schools in East Los Angeles walked out of classes during a one-week period. Student leaders, both male and female, orchestrated the massive resistance effort, called the "blow-outs." [134] Collectively they took a stand against inadequate and biased curriculum, a lack of Mexican American teachers, the tracking of Chicano students into vocational programs, and overall racist treatment. [135] The "blow-outs" took a violent turn when Los Angeles police overreacted and clubbed and arrested numerous students. Despite varying opinions among parents regarding the walkouts, many adults joined with college students to form the Educational Issues Coordinating Committee (EICC). The EICC drafted demands for reform, picketed the police department, and conducted a sit-in at the school board to protest the firing of a Chicano teacher, Sal Castro, who had supported the protests. [136]

Student activism had a long-range impact on the broader Chicano community. Teresita Basso, a sister at the time and elementary school teacher in East Los Angeles, recalls her participation in the school board sit-ins and the effect it had on her life: "I saw what was happening to the Chicano community. I decided that for my further studies I wanted something that would take me back into the Chicano community. I ended up pursuing a master's in Mexican American Studies at San Jose State College." [137] Basso went on to teach some of the first courses on Chicanas at community colleges in the San Francisco Bay Area.[138] As for many Chicanos and Chicanas, public protests of the 1960s provided the impetus for a lifelong commitment to the advancement of Chicano communities.

The Crusade for Social Justice, under the leadership of Corky Gonzales, sought to provide further direction to the increasingly militant urban Chicano and Chicana youth. Bringing together college students, community activists, gang members, and ex-convicts, the Crusade hosted the National Chicano Youth Liberation Conference in March 1969 in Denver, Colorado. Espousing a strong cultural nationalist agenda, Chicano youth emerged from the week-long conference with a mission to maintain a revolutionary stance whereby the rejection of Anglo culture and a reclamation of Mexican culture would provide a national unifying force. *El Plan Espiritual de Aztlán* compiled the resolutions of the conference. The need to replace capitalism with communal values and the call for a separate political party were among the resolutions; however, *El Plan* did not clearly articulate a process for such radical social change. Rather, it emphasized the reclamation of a mythical Aztec homeland, Aztlán, and pride in Mexican and Mexica or Aztec culture as the effective means of transformation.[139] The Crusade made an impact on the local adult community as well. Carmelita Espinoza recalls "being very green to the movement. The Crusade politicized me and made me proud of my background."[140]

The Chicano Moratorium

Opposition to the Vietnam War increased among Chicano communities, as their young men represented almost 20 percent of the casualties between 1961 and 1969—a glaring disparity for a total population of 10 to 12 percent.[141] On 29 August 1970, 30,000 demonstrators, including families with children and elderly, attended a peaceful march and protest ending in Laguna Park in East Los Angeles. Police, ready for riot control, "decided to end the rally and started to force the participants to leave."[142] By the end of the day, sixty people had been wounded, and three Chicanos, including a journalist for the *Los Angeles Times*, Rubén Salazar, had been killed.[143] Clarita Trujillo, OLVN, remembers the event with great emotion:

The sisters present had on modified habits and we walked on the edges of the march as a sign of peace. There were priests, sisters, people with their children, old women, it was a community affair. At the rally I remember sitting on the grass. I heard a yell and saw the police coming from behind. A tear gas canister fell at my feet. A boy helped me jump a fence and we walked all the way home. I knew it was a terrible betrayal by the police.[144]

The Chicano priests and sisters present convened a meeting shortly after, joined by the first and newly appointed Chicano bishop, Patricio Flores, who was in Los Angeles for other business. According to Trujillo, "We organized to hold together and we agreed to keep on marching and protesting."[145]

The U.S. Roman Catholic Church

Las Hermanas organized within the context of a tremendous awakening among Chicano clergy and laity throughout the United States. In 1969 a small group of Chicano priests in San Antonio, Texas, began to have weekly discussions about their own priestly formation programs and the overall treatment of Chicanos in the Church. Fr. Juan Romero shared memories of restrictions on his ministry:

In my first parish in Los Angeles, I was not permitted to celebrate Mass or preach in Spanish, although 80 percent of my Confessions and about 90 percent of parlor calls were in Spanish. My experience was similar in subsequent parishes during the first five years after ordination.[146]

Similar experiences convinced a group of twenty-five priests (along with a few Protestant Chicano ministers) from Texas, New Mexico, Arizona, and Colorado to gather in San Antonio in response to an invitation by Fr. Ralph Ruiz, then director of the Inner City Apostolate for the San Antonio diocese. The enthusiastic response of the participants to "unite their efforts on behalf of their people"[147] and a grant of $7,000 from the Protestant agency, Interreligious Foundation for Community Organization, convinced the group to organize as PADRES. PADRES convened its first national congress on 2–6 February 1970, in the Pioneer Hotel in Tucson, Arizona. Ironically, the more than one hundred participants included a majority of Euroamerican priests, sisters, and laity. Chicano clergy comprised less than one-quarter of the assembly.[148]

Restricting their membership to clergy raised significant conflict among the participants, but the majority were convinced of the need to solidify their identity as a priests' group before extending membership to laity.[149] Concern for Chicano Catholics focused the agenda on issues including support for the farm labor struggle, bilingual education, immigration, welfare reform, equitable distribution of Church resources, the promotion of Spanish-speaking priests, the appointment of Chicano bishops, and mobile team ministries.[150]

Soon after its first meeting, PADRES was awarded a $50,000 grant from the National Catholic Conference of Bishops and an additional $100,000 from the Campaign for Human Development for the implementation of mobile team ministries. On 5 May 1970, PADRES member Patricio Flores became the first Chicano bishop in the history of the U.S. Roman Catholic Church. PADRES's early success coincided with the growing criticism of the Catholic Church by Chicano and Chicana student activists and most certainly encouraged the vision of Sisters Gregoria Ortega and Gloria Gallardo for an organization of Chicana nuns.

In 1969, a group of Chicano Catholics, Católicos Por La Raza (CPLR), challenged the San Diego and Los Angeles archdioceses on the Church's absence in their struggle for social, political, and economic justice. "They were beginning to ask, 'Is the institutional Church Christian, or is it just another paternalistic White racist institution?'"[151] Organized protests, including confrontation tactics, transpired in San Diego and Los Angeles to demand that the Church redistribute its resources for the benefit of the Chicano community.

On 30 November 1969, CPLR took over Camp Oliver, a youth camp owned and operated by the Sisters of Social Service, in Descanso, California, near San Diego. They had been meeting for the weekend with representatives from the diocesan Office of Ethnic Affairs to discuss how the Catholic Church could be more responsive to the Chicano community. As the conference was underway, participants decided to coalesce as Católicos Por La Raza and to "liberate the camp."[152] Six students seized the main building and renamed the site Campo Cultural de La Raza. Demands sent to San Diego's Bishop Leo T. Maher included the appointment of

Chicano clergy to positions of authority within the Catholic hierarchy; an active campaign to support César Chávez; and free Catholic schooling and hospital services for Chicanos. The following day, six CPLR activists were arrested but released after several hours. A subsequent meeting with Bishop Maher produced no immediate results. Not until three years later did the diocese establish El Centro Padre Hidalgo to serve the Chicano Catholic community.[153] According to sociologist Albert Pulido, the end result "did not worsen the relationship between the Mexican American community and the Church—it actually started one."[154]

Weeks later, on Christmas Eve, CPLR once again challenged the hierarchy of the Church, this time in Los Angeles. The closing of a Catholic high school in East Los Angeles due to "lack of funds" angered the activists, who simultaneously witnessed the building of a $3 million cathedral near downtown Los Angeles. On 31 December 1969, members of CPLR marched to St. Basil's Cathedral on Wilshire Boulevard to hold vigil at the midnight Mass. Upon entering the church, they met the force of off-duty sheriff deputies posing as ushers. The "ushers" used clubs to expel the demonstrators and arrested twenty-one of them once they were outside the church.[155] Although Las Hermanas did not organize until two years later, the actions of these young Chicano Catholics and the early success of PADRES were powerful reminders that more needed to be done.

As criticism of the Church received national attention, many Mexican American sisters experienced the transformation to a "Chicana" identity. Teresita Basso explains:

> As a result of my convictions, my experiences, in religious life, and especially my Mexican-American background, I have come to realize my responsibility to . . . the Mexican-American people. The impact of this realization has led me to reevaluate my identity as a "Chicana" religious woman.[156]

Responsibility to her people signaled Basso's awakening of a radical ethnic political identity that would soon include a feminist identity as well.

Chicana Feminism

Chicana participation at the Crusade for Justice's National Chicano Youth Liberation Conference in 1969 reflected the emerging feminist consciousness among many female activists. During a workshop on women, Chicanas debated traditional gender roles in the movement that kept women in the home raising children while quietly sacrificing their needs for the family, community, and el movimiento. Chicanas active in the movement were usually relegated by the men to being cooks, secretaries, and janitors or were merely recognized as companions of male activists.[157] The majority of the conference participants, however, did not wish to criticize intraethnic sexism, and the workshop facilitator reported to the entire conference, "It was the consensus of the group that the Chicana woman does not want to be liberated."[158] Although this was a significant blow to the women who felt differently, their voices rose above those willing to accommodate their male peers.

Chicanas began forming student organizations and editing feminist newspapers specifically to analyze and propose solutions to the gender politics they encountered.[159] As historian Ramón Gutiérrez points out, "Although the movement persistently had advocated the self-actualization of all Chicanos, Chicanos still actually meant only males."[160] It would be up to Chicanas to broaden the discourse.

While Chicana feminists confronted the struggle to end sexism within a nationalist struggle to end racism, they continued to address broader issues of inequality facing Chicano communities. As historian Vicki Ruiz points out, "Chicanas have articulated a community centered-consciousness."[161] The early 1970s marked the emergence of a Chicana feminist movement within the broader Chicano movement.[162]

Chicanas soon developed their own political agendas, organizations, and alternative presses.[163] Chicanas articulated the emerging Chicana feminism in speeches, essays, and articles published in Chicano, and specifically Chicana, journals and newspapers beginning in the early 1970s. The earliest feminist newspapers included *Regeneración, El Popo Femenil, Hijas de Cuauhtémoc, La Razón Mestiza,* and *Comadre.*[164] *El Grito Del Norte* and *El Chicano* were among the newspapers founded and edited by women.[165]

In spite of being ostracized by their male-identified peers, feminists in the Chicano movement designed various strategies to develop their leadership abilities. Simply by "taking leadership" in male-dominated organizations, or by forming separate organizations, women's caucuses, and conferences, Chicana feminists focused their energies on being "consistent fighters against their own oppression as Chicanas, around their own specific demands."[166] Comisíon Femenil Mexicana, an independent organization founded by young Chicana professionals, emerged from a women's workshop at the Mexican American National Issues Conference meeting in Sacramento, California, in 1970. Women in the Mexican American Political Association formed a caucus and all three Chicano Youth Liberation Conferences in 1969, 1970, and 1971 had a workshop on women.[167] More than 600 Chicanas attended the First National Chicana Conference held in Houston, Texas. Women in El Centro de Acción Autonoma-Hermandad General de Trabajadores (CASA), a labor and immigrant rights organization, involved themselves as "organizers, writers and service providers," even amid organizational pressure to remain traditional.[168] Cross-pollination among groups and among women enhanced the growing consciousness. Teresita Basso remembers her own involvement: "We all affected one another. No one was in isolation."[169]

As strong and vocal women, Las Hermanas was not immune from institutional and intraethnic attempts to marginalize their voices. Members refused to be the traditional helpmates or subordinate members of a movement for change. Their collective struggle with PADRES faced similar obstacles and challenges plaguing "secular" Chicanos and Chicanas. Feminist issues met the same kind of resistance found in the broader society. Fr. Virgilio Elizondo, a member of PADRES, spoke frankly of the impact that Las Hermanas had on the transformations taking place: "In honesty, we were not used to women coming into their power. We welcomed it but at the same time we were threatened by it. We did not know how to do it. Also the barrier of the ordained priest is a structural obstacle."[170] Working within an ecclesial institution that carries an aura of sanctification by its very nature made the struggle against patriarchy perhaps even more arduous than for secular women. As Ana María Díaz-Stevens points out, "the power to govern the institution derives from Holy Orders, which is a sacrament reserved to men. Thus, Catholicism can be considered a patriarchy par excellence."[171] A commitment to the empowerment of Latino communities and a reluctance to leave their faith tradition, convinced Las Hermanas to continue the struggle against sexism embedded in the Church.

Las Hermanas did not organize explicitly out of a direct response to sexism, but by 1976 their agenda focused specifically on women. Yolanda Tarango recalls:

When we first started it was more of a dormant feminist consciousness. Through our involvement in the Chicano movement we began to translate that analysis to the Church and name the racism and sexism that we saw there. We wanted to create an organizational basis to challenge the Church. It was not specifically a women's agenda but the women's version of advocating for rights of Latinos in the Church.[172]

Women religious have traditionally enjoyed the autonomous space afforded to them by their chosen lifestyle. As frequently noted by scholars, historically the convent provided greater access to education and independence.[173] Sor Juana Inéz de la Cruz provides one of the earliest models of an educated woman in the Americas.[174] Mario (Lucie) Barron of Las Hermanas recognized this in the late 1950s when she joined the Sisters of St. Joseph of Carondelet to ensure her completion of a college degree.[175]

What sisters do have to confront, however, is their subordinate status to male clergy. By refusing to ordain women to the priesthood, the patriarchal Church perpetuates a system that treats women religious as second-class citizens.[176] Their status as laity as defined by Vatican Council II "represents the end process of a long effort by the hierarchy to demote nuns from their original status as members of the clergy."[177] Prior to Vatican Council II, sisters did enjoy "a quasi-clerical status."[178] Despite the Vatican's insistence, sisters are still perceived by the majority of lay Catholics as officials within the Church. As laywomen, however, they have very little power in the hierarchical structure of the Church, which makes autonomous organizations such as Las Hermanas extremely subversive to patriarchal power.

Las Hermanas surprised many Chicana activists. Olivia Mercado, a reporter for the feminist newsletter, *COMADRE,* wrote in 1978 following her interview with Las Hermanas's national coordinators: "I heard about a 'new' women's organization. Like Columbus, I thought I had 'discovered' a fledgling group of raza women. In actuality, this organization is eight years old and had local subgroups spread throughout the country."[179] For many emerging Chicana feminists, however, religion as transmitted through the Catholic faith epitomized the patriarchal stronghold on Chicano culture. Reporting on the First National Chicana Conference in Houston, Texas, in 1971, Mirta Vidal wrote, "They are questioning 'machismo,' discrimination in education, the double standard, the role of the Catholic Church, and all the backward ideology designed to keep women subjugated."[180] The first conference resolution elaborated the sentiments held by many Chicanas toward Catholicism: "We, as *mujeres de La Raza*, recognize the Catholic Church as an oppressive institution and do hereby resolve to break away and not go to it to bless our unions."[181] Furthermore, in the section titled "Religion," conference participants voted to "take over already existing Church resources for community use, oppose any institutionalized religion, [demand] revolutionary change of [the] Catholic Church or for it to get out of the way."[182] Recognizing the patriarchal interpretations of the Catholic faith, the proposed resolutions on "Sex and the Chicana" stated:

> We should destroy the myth that religion and culture control our sexual lives. We recognize that we have been oppressed by religion and that the religious writing was done by *men* and interpreted by *men*. Therefore, for those who desire religion, they should interpret their Bible, or Catholic rulings according to their own feelings, what they think is right, without any guilt complexes.[183]

Clearly these statements expressed anger and bitterness toward the Church, and reflected a long overdue religious agency among Chicanas. As Chicana feminists sought to free themselves of sexist constraints, they struggled to develop a healthy sense of their sexuality and their own religious beliefs. Not everyone agreed with the radical stance, and in fact one-half of the conference walked out after workshop resolutions demanded free legal abortions, birth control, childcare, educational support for Chicanas, and freedom from institutionalized religion.[184]

The emergence of a Chicana feminist identity most undeniably influenced the consciousness of Chicana women religious. In her article, "The Emerging 'Chicana' Sister," Teresita Basso echoed the resistance to patriarchal oppression voiced by secular Chicana feminists, and stressed the added burden of a sanctified hierarchy in religious life:

The Mexican American woman religious has an even greater struggle in exploring her womanly role in the decade of the '70s, since her strife is threefold. This triple strife consists of society's limited view of woman as housewife, bedpartner, and inferior intellectual; the Church's governing structure's condescending paternalistic view of woman as a helpless submissive creature incapable of self-determination; the Mexican American culturally restrictive view of woman as mother, cooking and caring for the family, incapable of making decisions outside the home, or as a mistress, an object of male enjoyment. If the Mexican American sister is not conscious of those prevailing stereotypes, it may be that she has chosen to close her eyes to the realities of life or rejects the risks that a conscious awareness of such realities might make her face.[185]

In stark contrast to the complete rejection of the Church by many Chicana activists, members of Las Hermanas chose to confront the Church directly from within. Understanding their role as agents of change within the sanctified patriarchy led them to take an aggressive and proactive stance against the Church's exclusionary policies and teachings. Coming together in Houston at the first Las Hermanas meeting in April 1971 set in motion the process of bringing the Chicano movement *and* Chicana feminism into the U.S. Roman Catholic Church.

2

Unidas en acción y oración

Chicana/Latina Religious Leaders

We, as Spanish speaking Sisters, are greatly concerned with the plight of La Raza . . .
We also feel that as religious women . . . we exert great influence among our people
and that we can be a tremendous source of power for them.
—Las Hermanas[1]

MOST OF the fifty women at the first meeting of Las Hermanas were Chicanas, but Puerto Rican, Mexican, and Anglo sisters who had been working in Spanish-speaking communities also participated. Those gathered responded eagerly to Sister Gallardo and Sister Ortega's invitation to "unite closer, not just for strength and support, but to educate ourselves as to who we are, where we are going, why we're going and how."[2] According to Ortega, the desire to form an organization had been present in both their "hearts and minds for some time" as a result of their work in Chicano communities.[3] This chapter highlights the experiences that motivated Ortega and Gallardo to unify Chicana and Latina women religious and discusses the initial goals of Las Hermanas, goals grounded in effective service to *el pueblo,* or struggling Chicano/Latino communities.

Las Hermanas's emergence as visible and vocal Chicana/Latina religious leaders transpired within the broader context of a growing Chicano/Latino influence within the U.S. Roman Catholic Church. Two years earlier, PADRES had mobilized also with a commitment to more effective service. California bishops had successfully mediated a labor contract between the UFW and grape growers in the Central Valley, and the first Chicano bishop was appointed in 1970. The shared vision by PADRES and Las Hermanas of being agents of change reflects what Chicana feminist theorist Chela Sandoval calls "a differential mode of oppositional consciousness." Sandoval explains:

> Differential [oppositional] consciousness is the expression of the new subject position . . . it permits functioning within yet beyond the demands of dominant ideology . . . [it] depends upon the ability to read the current situation of power and of self-consciously choosing and adopting the ideological form best suited to push against its configurations, a survival skill well known to oppressed peoples . . . [it] requires grace, flexibility, and strength.[4]

As members of an institution founded on hierarchical power, and even sanctified patriarchal power, Las Hermanas read the current situation of power as one of domination, but with tremendous potential for transformative change. In Las Hermanas's perspective, the Church could itself become an agent of change by endorsing a movement for social justice. Las Hermanas responded by relocating power, or the ability to act, among its members and identifying with the liberative aspirations of Chicano/Latino communities facing systems of oppression.

Co-Founders

In the heat of late summer 1969, Gregoria Ortega traveled by train from Fresno, California, to Abilene, West Texas. She arrived ready to teach religion to youth from the public schools. Several months before, Ortega had studied Spanish in Guanajuato, Mexico, the birthplace of the Wars for Independence from Spain in 1810. According to Ortega, "In Mexico, I became a revolutionary with the nickname, *la adelita!*"[5] Little did she realize that her stay in Texas would require revolutionary action. The year ahead would challenge Ortega to broaden her religious vocation to include protesting for civil rights.

Growing up in El Paso, Ortega was quite familiar with poverty and discrimination. At eighteen, she entered religious life. Her first memory of nuns in El Paso was that they "looked like penguins in their black-and-white flowing gowns."[6] In response to her wonderment her father replied, "They are women who dedicate their entire lives to the Church and to God."[7] This statement made a lasting impression on young Ortega. When the parish priest began recruiting volunteers for the Junior Legion of Mary, she eagerly joined since she realized that this would be good training for her life as a nun. Along with a cohort of young women, Ortega assisted the sick and elderly in her neighborhood. By the time she was old enough for vowed religious life, she joined Our Lady of Victory Missionary Sisters, commonly known as Victoryknoll. Fifteen years later, at the age of thirty-three, Ortega accepted a teaching assignment among Chicanos in Abilene.

Ortega described Abilene as "bible belt country . . . they had a real hatred for Mexicans and Catholics. Mexicans had been lynched there."[8] Discrimination in Texas stemmed from the historic conflict between Euroamerican settlers and Mexican landowners in the early 1800s. The Texas–Mexico War settled the question of ownership, but tensions remained well into the twentieth century.[9] Historian Arnoldo De Léon describes the ongoing conflict between whites and Mexicans: "In Central, South, and West Texas, Tejanos [Mexicans] coexisted with unneighborly Anglo Texans who judged them to be a people of a lower caste . . . Into the early twentieth century, lynching remained a method of racial control."[10] Discrimination in the rural areas of South and West Texas persisted much longer than in the metropolitan areas of Central Texas. Segregation in farm districts existed "as complete—and as 'de jure'—as any in the Jim Crow South"[11] well into the early 1970s. According to historian David Montejano, in his review of a typical West Texas town, private businesses, such as barber and beauty shops, remained segregated until 1969; cemeteries, bowling alleys, and swimming pools until the early 1970s.[12]

The battle over segregation in schools continued into the 1970s, as administrators refused to integrate according to federal law. In August 1970, the U.S. Justice Department filed suit against twenty-six Texas school districts "for not adequately desegregating their students and faculty."[13] Segregation, however, was not the only problem within the schools. According to De Léon, students complained that

> principals and teachers . . . criticized their heritage, editorialized about politics and the negative role of Mexican Americans in history, enforced a "no Spanish" rule, discouraged them from in-

volvement in certain school functions, neglected their needs whei it came to charting out career plans, and overlooked Mexican-American applicants when hiring teachers and administrators who might have acted as positive role models.[14]

Ortega found herself in the middle of a battle for civil rights as she ministered in the diocese of San Angelo, an area ranking fifth in the Southwest in terms of where Chicanos were most rigidly segregated.[15]

In Abilene, where schools were slowly being integrated, the issue of fair treatment rather than blatant segregation took center stage for Chicano youth. In her religious education classes, Ortega talked about Martin Luther King Jr. and César Chávez with an emphasis on their commitment to nonviolence. She recalls the incident that began her involvement in student protests: "In October the students asked me, 'As Christians can we have a sit-in if there is an injustice done toward us?' I said of course, as long as there is no violence. The kids were sizing me up with penetrating eyes. I knew something was brewing."[16] With a school play scheduled featuring a lead Chicano and a lead Euroamerican girl, ethnic tensions seemed inevitable. When the actress refused to share the stage with her Chicano counterpart, the students' patience ran out. Ortega explains their situation:

> They had many complaints . . . Being hit just for being Mexican; teachers leaving the room with *gavachos* in charge and never choosing a Mexican student; being the only ones suspended for fights that Anglos were also involved in; having only one Chicano teacher in the whole school.[17]

In response 300 students from several schools walked out of classes and gathered at Sears Center, a community hall. They solicited the support of community representatives, including Catholic sisters.[18] Ortega recalls: "I got a call and me [*sic*] and another sister went. I wore my habit to calm the students down. I got up and reminded them of César Chávez and Martin Luther King. That love is stronger than hate. They had so much anger."[19] After hearing from the school superintendent and the chief of police, the students clarified their position. "It was a beautiful historical moment. The leaders, Johnny Sánchez and Gloria Bryand, said, 'We are not going back to school unless all the discrimination

ven us intelligence and we want to use it.'"[20]
resentatives including Ortega, Lucia and George
ocal GI Forum, Maurice Hernández of the League
n American Citizens (LULAC), Carlos Calderón
merican College, and Methodist Reverend Joe Salas
ed the Mexican American Parent Council to support
s.[21]

e days, the students boycotted the Abilene Public School District, demanding that issues of discrimination be addressed, including prohibitions against speaking Spanish on school campuses, the lack of Chicano teachers and administrators, a lack of representation on student councils, and inadequate student counseling.[22] According to Ortega, students took primary leadership in the boycott. "I told them, 'You are the leaders, we are behind you. The day you resort to violence I won't be with you.'"[23] The parent council set up "huelga schools" teaching the youth the Constitution, U.S. history, and how to conduct voter registration drives.[24]

Meeting day and night with very little sleep, council representatives prepared the grievances for the school board assisted by Alan Exelrod from the Mexican American Legal Defense and Educational Fund (MALDEF) in San Antonio.[25] When the board began stalling, students and the parent council planned a march, this time including 200 elementary school children, intentionally affecting the school district's pocketbook.[26] For Ortega the protest proved life-threatening. She remembers, "I received calls at the convent saying 'You better get out of town or . . .' I replied, 'I do not know fear.' I felt like my time was not up. I had no time to fear."[27]

Harassment did not stop Ortega or the others. In December 1969, the students and their parents filed a suit against the Abilene School Board. School officials had denied the students excused absences and makeup privileges regardless of a physician's statement that the "Mexican American students' mental conditions made their attendance at school inadvisable, due to discrimination."[28] Furthermore, the board had responded inadequately to their demands. Claiming their right to free speech and protest, MALDEF counsel including Pete Tijerina, Mario Obledo, Alan Exelrod, and an independent lawyer, Mark Smith, represented the students in court under District Judge Leo Brewster.[29] With a predominantly

Euroamerican jury and a judge who refused to include "plaintiff's expert witnesses and evidence," the students lost their case.[30] Following the jury's decision, Judge Brewster stated: "I'm glad people are out to better their race, but they must . . . realize they cannot get what they want whether they are entitled to it or not."[31] Having been "treated like garbage" and learning that Mexicans had been screened out of the jury process taught the plaintiffs much. According to Ortega, "It was not just the schools we had to fight. We felt like we were holding back the ocean with a finger. It made us more angry and willing to fight."[32]

Publicity of the conflict soon reached surrounding towns. At a fund-raising dinner, the parent council received a visit from a Chicano family living in Rotan, Texas. Their daughter, María Hernández, had been severely beaten by her principal. The family sought their help as the local doctor agreed to testify. According to Ortega, "The doctor told them, 'You don't even whip horses this bad. She is not the only child I have seen like this.' "[33] Ortega and the others accompanied the family back to Rotan where they remained, documenting the incident. Contacting the Community Relations Service of the U.S. Justice Department proved worthwhile as Professor Rudy Acuña from California arrived as a civil rights observer. Acuña recalls:

> Things were tense. They wouldn't let me stay in a motel because they thought I would be assassinated so we all stayed in the same house. All night long cars were circling the house with spotlights. I realized I only have to suffer this one night. Sister has to deal with this all the time. I thought, one of these days they will kill her.[34]

Criminal charges were never filed; however, Acuña and attorney Mark Smith, who represented the Abilene students, remained with the townspeople for several days. Their presence earned them the label of being "outside agitators" by the local law enforcement.[35]

A newly appointed bishop for San Angelo diocese began to scrutinize Ortega's involvement in community protests. Upon hearing that the bishop had visited the school board during the Abilene boycotts, Ortega took it upon herself to visit the bishop so that he could "hear the people's side of the story."[36] His refusal to meet with her was followed shortly by a letter to the bishop from a local priest. Ortega remembers painfully:

He said I was spreading hatred against white people. He would also say from the pulpit that I should be ashamed to wear panty hose! A group of priests along with the bishop decided I should be outsted from the San Angelo diocese. I was put on trial, found guilty, and I was not even present![37]

The efforts to discredit Ortega did not interfere with the long-lasting effects she had on many people. In reflecting on her impact historian Rudy Acuña shares:

I think she is a giant. She left a tremendous impression on me, as she was part of my political development. She showed me how people can rise to an incredible level. She was protesting the Church but was very much part of the Church. She is the only thing that kept me from being bitter toward the Church. She is a valiant woman, forcing a new paradigm.[38]

Ortega's dedication to her people and the Church did not stop with her expulsion from the San Angelo diocese. In the summer of 1970, with permission from Victoryknoll, Ortega traveled to the University of New Mexico to take summer coursework in Mexican American Studies and to take a respite from the turmoil. Her activism resumed upon her return to Texas.

Arriving in San Antonio at the end of summer, she contacted an old friend from her elementary school days, Edmundo Rodríguez, a parish priest. Fr. Rodríguez had helped to organize PADRES a year prior, and he expressed great enthusiasm and support for Ortega to do the same with Chicana sisters. The idea had been germinating in Ortega's thoughts for some time but, as she states, "the walkouts prevented me from doing anything about it."[39] The time had arrived for mobilizing!

Another Chicana sister, Gloria Gallardo, then residing in Houston, had the same idea for an organization. Fr. Rodríguez introduced the two, and they immediately understood each other's concerns. Gallardo grew up in a San Antonio barrio and joined a predominantly Irish American religious community, the Holy Ghost Sisters. Shortly after taking her vows, she and two other sisters worked as community organizers in San Antonio's Alazán Apache Courts, a barrio with "one of the roughest reputations in town."[40] In 1969, Fr. Patricio Flores asked Gallardo to assist him in Houston among the Chicano community.[41] Part of her assignment included being interim director for the Mexican American Education Council (MAEC), a local group seeking to assist in the educational concerns of Chicanos.

A vivid description of Gallardo at age thirty-two deserves mention, not only for its presentation of this impressive woman, but also because it provides an example of the "liberated style" chosen by many sisters in the early 1970s. Janice Law, a reporter for the *National Catholic Reporter*, wrote:

> She is a velvet-spoken, genteel nun . . . [who] carries her slightly portly, tall figure with grace, and her long, thick, dark hair is often drawn back softly from her face into a large rounded bun, held with a gold clasp, which matches her gold looped earrings. Long thick lashes shadow her large, darkly brown eyes set in her olive-skinned face. She smiles often. Very occasionally, "for official duties" she wears a nun's half veil on the back of her head but usually she wears tailored, simple street clothes of blues and browns.[42]

Certainly Gallardo's seemingly "genteel" manner did not inhibit her from demonstrating with picket signs, supporting school boycotts, and co-organizing the soon-to-be first national organization of Chicana Roman Catholic sisters.[43]

According to Ortega, Gallardo responded enthusiastically to her idea about an organization for Chicana sisters and immediately asked, "How can we work together? She invited me to live with her and her housemates in Houston. The next week I moved."[44] Victoryknoll's mother superior provided Ortega with travel funds, but no living expenses. Not quite knowing what to expect, she arrived in Houston with no return ticket. As the bus rolled in she thought, "My God, what am I going to be doing here?! Then I saw the newspaper with an article about school boycotts and Chicanos, and I knew that I belonged here!"[45] During the next several weeks Ortega assisted in more huelga schools, led rallies and fund-raising drives, attended court cases, and helped to develop the Mexican American Education Fund.[46] Amid all the activity she began recruiting for an organization of Chicana religious activists. With Gallardo sharing her salary from the Galveston–Houston diocese, the two women struggled to create their vision of a Church in support of Chicanos.

First National Conference: Goals and Challenges

In anticipation of the first meeting of Las Hermanas, Ortega and Gallardo contacted bishops throughout the country asking for the names of Mexican American sisters. While a few bishops responded, most refused to cooperate, reflecting an institutional disregard for the concerns of Latina/o Catholics. Unwilling to give up, the organizers contacted the mother superiors in charge of the various religious communities and were supplied with several names. Ortega also attended a national religious education conference in Houston to meet with the Missionary Congregation of Divine Providence (MCDP), a religious order founded for Mexican American sisters. Ortega recalls:

> I went to the conference with no money, only a bag of fruit to snack on. I was so daring! An inner force was moving me! I met Guadalupe Partida, who invited me to stay in her room. Four of us shared the room. I slept on the floor very comfortably. They invited me to breakfast and they were very interested in what I had to say. They called themselves Mexican Americans. As your identity became stronger, you called yourself a Chicana.[47]

The end result totaled fifty predominantly Chicana sisters representing twenty religious congregations and eight states (California, New Mexico, Colorado, Arizona, Iowa, Illinois, Kansas, and Texas) arriving in Houston. They came together not quite knowing what to expect. According to Ortega, the three days were "full of joy beyond all expectations! . . . we experienced a true feeling of *hermandad*."[48]

While fifty women in attendance might seem like a small number, religious life for women at the time still placed very restrictive limits on travel other than for spiritual retreats. According to Yolanda Tarango, "just the fact that these women strategized to get there was tremendous. Some went with their superiors as they were not trusted."[49] Catalina Fresquez, CCVI, and Blanca Rosa Rodríguez, CCVI, were among those who found it difficult to attend on their own. Fresquez remembers:

> We almost did not get permission to go. The superior general said it would be divisive, that it would tear the congregation apart. The only reason we finally got permission was that we suggested she

come with us. The mother superior and one of the counselors went with us.[50]

Coming together as Chicana sisters proved to be an emotionally charged event. Teresita Basso reflects:

> It was a turning point in my life. I had never known there were so many Hispanic sisters, or the pain of so many of them. I personally had never been discriminated against by my superiors but as I heard these women who had been in religious life for twenty years . . . they spoke with a lot of hurt from not being understood or encouraged in their education, hurt from not being allowed to go back into their own communities to work . . . but they also expressed a real sense of hope, of faith to go forward . . . to make the Church aware of the Hispanic reality.[51]

The women welcomed the opportunity to share their experiences as Chicanas in Euroamerican-dominated institutions. Their stories revealed the trauma that many of them underwent even as they committed themselves to the Church. María de Jesús Ybarra shared the following example taking place even after Vatican Council II:

> One sister was a daughter of farmworkers. She was working along the route that her parents traveled to pick the fields. She did not allow her parents to stop and visit her because she was ashamed of them. She told me, "I lived in fear for constant years that my order would discover that I was Mexican."[52]

Others shared feelings of being held to a higher standard than the white sisters or not being chosen to hold leadership positions, particularly if they were of dark complexion.[53] Sharing their stories enabled the women to recognize the similarities, identify the elements of oppression, and "realize it was not just my order or my life but that we were in a widespread situation. In the coming together we raised each other's consciousness."[54] Carmelita Espinoza, who at first did not want to go, found the meeting to be "a rebirth for all of us!"[55] Exposure to the modern styles of some of the sisters broadened their self-understanding. While some of the nuns arrived in full habit, others wore modest street wear and stylish haircuts. Theresa Basso remembers being shocked at the openness and vitality of many of the women. They experienced firsthand

how the personal is political *and* communal, a central characteristic of Chicana feminist thought.

Despite the tremendous pain that many of the sisters experienced in religious life, they understood their potential to effect change. "We belonged to different religious groups that were
power bases."[56] Acknowledging their unique resources as Spanish-
speaking religious women, they quickly identified their individual
and collective purpose: "to enable each other to work more effectively among and with the Spanish Speaking People of God in
bringing about social justice and a truly Christian peace."[57]

The first three-day meeting in Houston had the support of official representatives of the Church hierarchy, a welcome by Bishop
Morkovsky of the Galveston–Houston diocese, a keynote address
by Bishop Patricio Flores, and an address of full support by Fr.
Ralph Ruiz, the national chairman of PADRES.[58] A maríachi
Mass, dancing, the showing of *Yo Soy Joaquin,* and a presentation
on the Crusade for Justice by Carmelita Espinoza provided a cultural and political perspective. The presence of Chicano clergy reveals the respect that both Ortega and Gallardo had for PADRES,
whom Ortega credits as "inspiring" her to organize Chicana sisters. They also understood the significance of recognition from the
hierarchy, convincing them to invite the bishops. The inclusion of
cultural and political programming indicates that from its inception, Las Hermanas took responsibility for educating its members
on developments in the Chicano movement and for reclaiming a
cultural heritage.

Four specific projects were identified as the most effective ways
to achieve their purpose of service for social justice. First, team
ministry involved two to five sisters trained in the fields of education, health, social work, and religious education who would
travel to Chicano communities underserved by the Church. Second, "sensitizing teams" would educate their Euroamerican peers
in religious congregations on the cultural and social realities of
Spanish-speaking communities. Third, a central religious formation center would offer young Chicanas their basic formation in
preparation for religious life. Providing the right "*ambiente* which
they could relate [to]" would encourage more vocations and pre-
vent the cultural alienation experienced by so many Chicanas.
Fourth, an information clearinghouse would create a communication network among the members for consciousness-raising, lead-

ership development, employment opportunities, support, and collaboration.

These projects shed light on the multiple roles that the women
envisioned for themselves: as ministers immersed in the social context of la Raza, as bridges between Spanish-speaking communities
and Euroamerican ministers, as teachers to their white peers, as
mentors to potential Chicana sisters, and as collaborators in self-
education and leadership development. Las Hermanas set out to
carve their place among Catholic leadership by engaging in social
justice issues and confronting the legacy of cultural ignorance and
discrimination in the Church.

Naming and Identity

The name *Las Hermanas* with the motto *Unidas en Acción y Oración* [United in Action and Prayer] was chosen enthusiastically by
all. The emphasis on prayer held a primary place for Ortega. She
explains:

> I wanted the motto right away. We couldn't do anything without
> prayer. Without it we would be like empty tombs. I also called the
> Carmelite contemplative sisters in Houston and I asked them to
> pray for us. They were a part of Las Hermanas from its concep-
> tion.[59]

The importance of prayer and spirituality distinguished Las
Hermanas from other Chicana organizations forming in the
1970s. This emphasis eventually contributed to a U.S. Latina feminist theology articulated by members of Las Hermanas.

In reflecting on their choice of name, Las Hermanas, representatives wrote:

> We could have chosen such names as *Las Madres, Las Relgiosas His-
> panas*, or *Las Monjitas Revolucionarias*, etc. but we did not. Our ti-
> tle signifies the common vision and purpose of the first members.
> In our native language, the term "sisters" means much more than
> a blood relationship. Its more profound meaning is a relationship
> of sisterhood which demands a certain identity with, and sharing
> of the total self with the whole of humanity.[60]

Contrary to the use of the term *sisterhood* in the broader feminist movement, which presumed homogeneity or a female white

middle-class experience as the norm, Las Hermanas's use of the term presumed diversity within the group and made room for it.[61] The diversity of Latino cultures and women within Las Hermanas reinforced a shared vision of liberation for oppressed communities, of cultural reclamation for themselves, and of leadership development in a Eurocentric, male-dominated Church. Just as networks of "fictive kinships"[62] had sustained Mexicanas and Latinas historically during the harsh times of migrations and settlements, the bond of sisterhood would sustain Las Hermanas over the years to come.

Rosamaría Elías, MSBT, the first Puerto Rican to join Las Hermanas, recruited other Latina sisters such as María Iglesias and Dominga Zapata. The participation of these women reflected a commitment to solidarity among Latinas that the founding Chicanas envisioned for the organization. Elías recalls, "The Chicanas gave us such a warm welcome, they really wanted us there. I remember feeling so important. They were hugging me and I really felt at home."[63] A strong sense of being sisters and being rooted in the people's struggle, as well as the confidence that the Chicanas projected attracted Latinas. Carmen Villegas, a Puerto Rican laywoman, recalls, "I admired the Mexican American women because they were so clear about what they wanted. I felt a very strong sense of unity."[64] Tess Browne, OSF, originally from Trinidad, found the native-born women of Las Hermanas extremely helpful, as "they understood how this country worked more than I did."[65] María Iglesias, of Cuban and Puerto Rican ancestry, describes the cross-pollination that took place among the women. "In building solidarity with the women, we also built solidarity with each other's causes and we gained from each other a real solid focus that we needed to be advocates for our people."[66] Over the years Chicanas would remain the majority of Las Hermanas, but the influence and leadership of Latinas would shape the organization significantly.

Their need to show self-determination in the face of the hegemony of religious orders led to a decision to limit full membership with voting rights to "NATIVE Spanish-speaking sisters, Puerto Ricans, Cubans, Mexicans, Spaniards, Mexican-Americans, and any other Latin Americans."[67] The few Anglo sisters who had been ministering in Spanish-speaking communities either chose not to return or remained as associate members with limited privileges. Teresita Basso recalls: "There were some Anglo sisters who were very hurt by this decision and never came back, but we felt that this organization was going to allow us to develop our own leadership abilities. That would not happen if the Anglo sisters had the vote."[68] The decision to limit voting rights based on ethnicity did not pass easily and remained a controversial issue for several years. Carmelita Espinoza remembers, "I almost pulled out because Anglo sisters were going to have a vote. Every year this seemed to be an issue. I felt like it was wasting our time."[69]

A follow-up letter soon after the Houston meeting clarified the need to be exclusionary: "at this particular time there is a greater need to help ourselves with our own self-identity problem and to better establish ourselves among La Raza."[70] The "identity problem" referred to the historical pressure to assimilate and divest themselves of their culture upon entering religious life. Las Hermanas members recognized they had to reclaim their identities on their own terms and in their own space.

One of the most decisive moments for Las Hermanas took place during the first gathering in Houston. With financial support from PADRES, the organization sent Xiomara Maderos, ODN, along with six members of PADRES to study at the first session of El Instituto Pastoral Latinoamericano (IPLA) in Quito, Ecuador. Sponsored by CELAM, the Latin American equivalent to the National Conference of Catholic Bishops, the pastoral program offered training in the praxis of liberation theology. Realizing that they lacked experience in working in Chicano communities and the absence of such courses in the United States made study in Latin America essential. Other members of Las Hermanas also traveled to Quito the following year. María de Jesús Ybarra, Gregoria Ortega, and Carmelita Espinoza comprised the first Hermanas team to study at IPLA in early 1972.[71]

Some of the women had a difficult time receiving permission from their superiors to study in Latin America. María de Jesús Ybarra recalls that it took her three hours to convince her superiors. In their questioning of her commitment to the congregation, Ybarra realized that her desire to work with her people was seriously threatened.[72] Ultimately she received permission. The trip transformed her ministry. Upon her return from Latin America, Ybarra requested a placement in religious education in Yakima, Washington, among migrant workers. She shares, "I realized that my religious community must help me achieve my goal of serving my people."[73] Ybarra eventually transferred to another congregation, the Tacoma Dominicans, who fully supported her ministry in Washington.

The Houston conference ended with enthusiastic support for the proposed projects, the election of two national officers (Gallardo as president and Ortega as vice-president), six consultants, and several coordinators for fourteen states. Gallardo filed incorporation papers shortly after. Las Hermanas began its journey as the first national organization of Chicana/Latina Roman Catholic religious activists. As the first national president, Gallardo stated, "We are finally on our way to REAL ACTION! . . . *Adelante con La Raza y su hermana en La Causa* (Go forward with the race and your sister in the cause)."[74]

State coordinators lost no time in recruiting potential members. As previously stated, by September 1971, a total of 900 Spanish-speaking sisters representing twenty-five states as well as Mexico and parts of Latin America had been contacted.[75] State conferences in California, Texas, and Colorado gave Las Hermanas "wider and better exposure, to organize better in each state, and to become better acquainted with the local problems so that some action might be taken."[76] The first issue of the newsletter, *Informes*, edited by Gallardo, circulated on 19 September 1971, and that same month Gallardo addressed the Conference of Major Superiors of Women Religious in Atlanta, Georgia. Describing her reception, Gallardo stated, "*Hermanas, hemos ganado otra victoria!* (Sisters, we have won another victory). I met most of your superiors and their response was the same—positive and enthusiastic and hopeful!"[77]

Despite this initial, positive reaction to Las Hermanas, relationships often became strained as individual sisters challenged their religious communities. According to *La Historia de Las Hermanas*, "LCWR feared much that perhaps, the organization of *Las Hermanas* would eventually become a separate Hispanic religious congregation, thus taking away from their constituency."[78]

> For a few years some communities forbade their members from joining Las Hermanas. The implication was that when a sister went to the organization she became a rebel. She returned conscienticized and questioned every structure. A lot of rage erupted and there was nowhere to direct it except toward the institution . . .

Some religious orders felt it wasn't good because Las Hermanas made them too radical.[79]

Experiences varied, however, depending on one's religious community. Dominga Zapata, a Sister of the Society of Helpers, received academic and financial support for her graduate studies at Mundelein College in Chicago. She developed a program in "Hispanic ministry" along with her department chair, who "knew that the path of religious education for the Spanish-speaking had to be opened."[80] Zapata found additional intellectual and emotional support for completing her studies and developing the first religious education program for Latinos in the archdiocese of Chicago through the "sharing of pastoral concerns" with Las Hermanas.[81] Zapata, a Puerto Rican, describes the purpose of her ministry:

> We cannot remain silent through ministerial attempts which perpetuate the oppression of our people—liturgies celebrated in basements with poor lighting, bad translations, devoid of *celebration* of the Son of God; crisis responses to social and economic evils, geared to specific problems without analyzing their causes; pietistic programs oriented to "appeal to the masses." Our ministry must always have in view man [*sic*] fully alive![82]

Teresita Basso also received full support from her congregation, the Sisters of the Presentation of the Blessed Virgin Mary, to redirect her ministry to Chicano communities and complete a master's degree in Mexican American Studies at San Jose State College. In contrast, Ramona Jean Corrales remembers having her loyalties questioned. "They asked me, 'Are you a Chicana or a Victoryknoll sister?' I told them that they both have to work together."[83] Despite the varying responses to Las Hermanas, members remained faithful to their goals of bridging the spiritual and social needs of la raza. To allay some of the fears, the organization openly stated "that our goal was not to form a separate congregation but rather to unite in order to better serve our people."[84]

By the time of the next national assembly eight months later (25–27 November 1971) in Santa Fe, New Mexico, official membership had quadrupled, with close to 200 sisters attending.[85] Membership over the years has fluctuated depending on individual resources to attend meetings and pay dues, but as Yolanda Tarango and others have stated, "We consider all Latinas to be hermanas."[86] In the early 1990s, approximately 700 women belonged to the organization with an average of 200 attending the annual conferences, or *asembleas.*[87]

Fully developed proposals for team ministry, sensitizing teams (or *equipos de concientización*), and the formation center captured the attention of those present at the Santa Fe conference. Members saw themselves as "technical advisors and consultants" to ecclesial institutions and government agencies. As one such consultant, Mario (Lucie) Barron encouraged members to pursue degrees in Chicano and Puerto Rican Studies. "The Church must be made aware of and helped to understand the Chicano movement. It is about time they listened and began to be tutored by the few they have educated."[88] A clear sense of their role as participants in the Chicano movement within the church shaped the agenda for the equipos de concientización. Barron emphasized, "The Chicano movement seeks no more than what the Church desires for every human being."[89]

A deep concern for self-examination as "Chicana religious women" permeates the documents from this early period of the organization. The recognition that "Christian churches have made themselves guardians of the status quo to protect their existence, wealth, and assumed arthority [*sic*]" gives witness to Las Hermanas's critical self-reflection as members of the Church *and* the Chicano movement. A statement read at the Santa Fe conference outlines the process:

> The answer will be seen only if we confront ourselves by means of questions. We must first consider the role of the Church itself. The mission of the Church is to not only perceive the truth, but to do the truth. The second question: How is our role in the Church to be lived out? We must consider our own fields of competence, our cultural heritage, and other personal talents and qualifications. In other words we must decide where we could best serve as Chicana religious women.[90]

Critically analyzing their responsibility as Chicana religious leaders convinced many of the women to remain within their religious congregations, but on their own terms. According to Yolanda Tarango, "We decided we all needed to relearn Spanish and all of us were going to pressure our communities to work with Hispanics. You can imagine how that was accepted!"[91] For others, the contradictions of the Church proved too monumental. Tarango explains:

> The immediate result of coming together was that a lot of rage erupted and there was nowhere to direct it except toward the institution. The congregations were not able to absorb the anger and the militancy. As a result in those early years a lot of the women left their orders. It created an exodus and Las Hermanas got a bad reputation.[92]

The rage Tarango describes echoes the feelings the majority of Chicana/o activists felt toward the Catholic Church during the early 1970s as they developed a political and ethnic consciousness. Many considered the Church a persistent symbol of conquest and colonization and they negated a Catholic identity.[93] The experience of having professed religious vows to a "guilty" institution perhaps intensified the level of alienation felt by many Chicana nuns. Las Hermanas members realized that they "needed to be there for these women."[94] María Iglesias explains, "We had to accept the laywomen as equal members because some of the founders of the organization could no longer stay in their congregations who would not honor their desire to work among the poor. We couldn't turn our backs on them."[95]

While Latina laity could be members with full voting rights, they did not serve as national officers until 1976, when former sister Ramona Jean Corrales was elected. The decision to accept lay leadership was not without conflict. "It was painful because we knew we would polarize and lose people."[96] Moving to a fully inclusive membership automatically meant a change in identity for the organization. Some members felt that broadening membership rights to include lay leadership would diminish the organization's voice with supporters such as the LCWR. For some, like María de Jesús Ybarra, the move proved too radical and influenced her departure from the organization. "I felt like somebody took over the organization."[97]

Clericalism or dominating behavior that "rests on a claim to special religious expertise or ecclesial authority, based on role or status in the church"[98] not only influences ordained clergy. Clearly clericalism affected the cohesiveness of Las Hermanas during these early years. Yolanda Tarango reflects on its negative impact: "The sisters could talk about being oppressed as women, but some failed to look at how we oppress as clerics."[99] Despite the tremendous loss incurred with the departure of such key members as Ybarra, those remaining agreed that the move to a lay organization reflected a sign of vitality. As Teresita Basso says, "Las Hermanas's identity developed with the people."[100] Supporting former sisters and welcoming laywomen as leaders reinforced Las Hermanas's understanding of ministry based on shared power and egalitarian relations. This continues to remain a distinct characteristic of Las Hermanas.[101]

Finances

Recognizing its work as "monumental and ambitious, but necessary—indeed, a crying need" required Las Hermanas to assess the financial feasibility of its projects. Essential to its success would be the support from the superiors in charge of personnel decisions within each religious order. Aware that they had very little control over this area, the members strategized on funding possibilities. Requesting release time for one to three years would place a strain on religious communities in charge of schools, especially given the diminishing number of sisters. Working for Las Hermanas on a volunteer part-time basis as an "intercommunity endeavor" appeared as the immediate viable solution. Other ideas included federal grants, the Bishops' Campaign for Human Development (CHD), and diocesan funding. Finances, however, did not concern some of the leaders. Ortega states very clearly, "I separated myself from the money aspect. I never wanted to ask the Church for money. I wanted to make it on our own. It didn't seem right to ask them for money and then fight against them."[102] Teresita Basso concurs: "If we received money from a diocese we would have been beholden to them."[103] Other national leaders, however, sought financial support from their religious communities. Sylvia Sedillo received support from the Sisters of Loretto for three years during her term as a Las Hermanas national coordinator. María Iglesias also received partial funding from the Sisters of Charity during her leadership term.

Over the years Las Hermanas has received very minimal monies from the institutional Church and none from the CHD despite their commitment to grassroots communities. A proposal to the CHD for the ministry teams was denied in 1971, the same year that PADRES received support from the CHD. Support monies have come primarily from donations and nominal membership dues. Women religious congregations provided the bulk of financial support almost from the beginning. Financial statements dated December 1971 indicate a $1,800 contribution from dioceses, $1,034 from "other sources," and $40.00 each from individual women religious. One year later the majority of direct revenue came from the LCWR at $1,211 and a $2,238 in-kind contribution from the diocese of Galveston–Houston, most likely to cover release time for Gallardo, then-president of Las Hermanas. By 1976 LCWR donations had increased to an average of $6,500 and in subsequent years individual congregations such as the Sisters of Charity of New York and the Sisters of Loretto made significant contributions through in-kind salaries for national coordinators.[104] Not until 1979 under the leadership of Sister Sedillo did the organization begin to establish a more independent solid funding base with the purchase of certificates of deposits (CDs). Interest from the CDs supported organizational activities until the early 1990s.

With annual expenditures soon consuming the limited revenues, the projects envisioned in the early 1970s faced serious constraints. Reflecting on these financial circumstances, Basso observes, "With funding we might have been even more effective. If each coordinator had been freed up full-time and with funds . . . financially we have always been limping."[105] Las Hermanas, however, chose autonomy for the sake of direct service to their people. According to María Iglesias, "We did a lot of the work on our vacations or on our own discretion, we never asked. We operated on a shoestring. We didn't want to put our money into trappings like a national office with fancy furniture. We wanted to go directly to the people."[106] In light of the limited financial resources, the members pooled their skills and "kept going on the impetus, the dedication, and the faith of the women."[107] Optimism and courage overshadowed the financial constraints.

Changes in Leadership Structure

Immediately following the Hermanas team's return from Quito in 1972, the third annual Las Hermanas asemblea convened in Chicago, where the form of national governance took a radical turn. Influenced by the pastoral training at IPLA with its emphasis on shared responsibility, the membership voted to transform the traditional structure of leadership with a president and vice-president to a "team government concept." The team included three national coordinators holding equal status and power to represent the organization. Proponents of the team concept expressed being "tired of the traditional form of government in their congregations in which all the decisions and policies were made by the one superior."[108] They wanted to model a structure other than a hierarchy. Recognizing the diverse talents essential for national leadership also justified the team structure. One of the "IPLAistas," Carmelita Espinoza explained, "In this way, we would show the community in general, and the Hispanic community in particular, a new model, one that promotes creativity and co-responsibility in leadership."[109]

Moving to a collaborative model created significant conflict for some of the members, in particular the president, Gloria Gallardo. Despite her election to the first national team in Chicago along with Carmelita Espinoza and María de Jesús Ybarra, the change in status proved too disturbing for Gallardo. She resigned shortly after. Weathering the loss of one of the founders and a few others, the organization remained committed to the very model its members hoped to promote for Chicano/Latino ministry. The collective agency of the group prevailed. According to Yolanda Tarango, Las Hermanas exemplified team government for other national women's religious organizations including the LCWR, the National Association of Women Religious (NAWR), and Sisters Uniting.[110] She states, "They picked up the same model. Las Hermanas was the first and the idea came from Quito."[111]

In 1976, the organization also lost co-founder Gregoria Ortega. A change in Victoryknoll superiors convinced Ortega that it was time to leave religious life, as her community "no longer understood my vision of ministry."[112] Unfortunately her departure from religious life accompanied her departure from Las Hermanas, as she chose to spend the next period of her life uninvolved in the institutional Church. Gallardo also eventually left religious life in order to marry.

Before their decisions to live very private lives, Gallardo and Ortega had laid the foundation for an organization designed to support other Chicanas and Latinas in their ministerial commitments to el pueblo. The fact that the organization continued without the presence of its co-founders highlights the strength of the vision animating the group and its strong sense of decentralized power. Las Hermanas exemplifies the power of women's collective agency and underscores the potential of shared power and the equality of all members.

Widespread Support

National visibility came quickly for the first cohort of women gathering in Houston, Santa Fe, and Chicago. Lacking leadership experience was of minor significance as they set out on a course of self-education and on-the-job training. "We didn't have all the skills but we covered every meeting we could, voiced every position, shared with each other where we should be . . . we learned as we went!"[113] Propelling themselves into leadership roles, they slowly began to fill the historical vacuum of Chicana/Latina representation in the Church.

Even before Las Hermanas completed its first year of organizing it received the "full endorsement and support" from numerous national and international groups. The United States Catholic Conference/Division for the Spanish Speaking, PADRES, Leadership Conference of Women Religious, National Association of Women Religious, National Black Sisters Conference (NBSC), El Congreso Episcopal Latinoamericano, and the Mexican American Education Council supported the vision that Ortega and Gallardo first shared with the fifty nuns who gathered in Houston.

The years ahead provided many opportunities to prove members' resolve to remain united in sisterhood. Although financial constraints inhibited the full realization of the four goals set in Houston, Las Hermanas made significant inroads in its first decade of organizing. Its commitment to service brought members into core sites of justice-making, including the farm labor movement, the push for episcopal representation, the development of the first pastoral center for Chicano Catholics, issues of ecclessial labor exploitation, and theological production. In carving space for themselves in a Euroamerican-dominated Church, Las Hermanas's members relied on each other for information and support as they individually and collectively claimed their right to express a politicized spirituality. Ethnic identity, interethnic solidarity, shared leadership, women's agency, and the tenets of liberation theology shaped the group's consciousness early on.

3

Una Nueva Iglesia Latina

Activism and Alliances, 1971–1980

We shared our stories of pain and decided to have courage. We wanted to fight the battle, speak, and celebrate; live life with passion. We were all in this together, trying to support each other, work with each other, and walk with each other.
—Irene Muñoz, SHM, member of Las Hermanas

We must identify with the poor and the oppressed . . . By pooling experience, information and research we can arrive at informed and effective action. The solution lies in unity. —Las Hermanas

THE WOMEN attracted to Las Hermanas recognized the symbolic power they held as women religious and their access to authority, although limited, within the Church. They sought to use their power to broaden the ministerial role of the Church. Understanding themselves as agents of change for social justice reflected a transformation of the use of religious power within the Church. Each woman brought to the organization her particular Latina ethnicity, class, educational background, and ministerial skills. What they all shared was the determination to create a new way of "being church," or what María de Jesús Ybarra called "*la Nueva Iglesia Latina*."[1]

This chapter explores the major arenas of Las Hermanas activism during the 1970s. Among their early accomplishments can be noted the co-founding of MACC; the successful lobbying for more Chicano bishops; co-planning the first two historic national gatherings of Latino Catholics; monitoring the fair treatment of

Mexican nuns in the United States; and contributing to an emerging U.S. Latino theology. While most of the activism took place around issues of Latino empowerment in the Church, Las Hermanas also participated tremendously in the farm labor movement under César Chávez and Dolores Huerta. Participants understood their support for the farmworkers to be a central way to bring the Chicano movement into the Church and the Church into the Chicano movement.

Representing diverse regions of the United States, the women drawn to Las Hermanas shared certain experiences: working-class origins, Catholic education, and varying degrees of cultural alienation either in religious life or as lay members of the Church. Some of the women were fluent in Spanish and already involved in ministering to Spanish-speaking communities when they joined Las Hermanas, while the majority had been isolated from their ethnic communities. Collectively they understood the necessity to reclaim the Spanish language and learn how to minister to Latinos/as.

The Mexican American Cultural Center

Las Hermanas soon had the opportunity to pursue one of its most important goals, that of educating members and other ministers regarding the cultural and social realities of Spanish-speaking Catholics. Training ministers both religious and lay required special attention since seminaries and formation houses were ill-equipped to develop socially aware and culturally specific programs. Realizing its own limited resources, Las Hermanas chose to collaborate with PADRES on the development of the first Mexican American national pastoral institute. Under the leadership of PADRES member Fr. Virgilio Elizondo and with an initial grant of $5,000 from the Texas Catholic Conference of bishops, MACC opened in San Antonio in January 1972. Members of Las Hermanas and PADRES formed the first steering committee consisting of several bishops, priests, and laity.[2] According to María de Jesús Ybarra, "The idea was to have the same kind of institute in Quito, Peru, here in the U.S. Virgilio was very happy that we [Las Hermanas] wanted to come to MACC."[3] María de Jesús Ybarra, Consuelo Pacheco, and Carmen Montalvo were among the Hermanas who planned and conducted the first mini-pastoral training program for Euroamerican and Latino seminarians.[4] Immersion in the culture, music, art, history, and social action relevant to the Chicano experience shaped these new programs of preparation.[5] Las Hermanas members Mario (Lucie) Barron, Dolorita Martínez, and Carmelita Espinoza, and PADRES members also offered leadership training in Chicano communities.[6] Between Las Hermanas and PADRES, "there was always someone ready [at MACC] to teach, promote, recruit or give workshops in the barrios of the Southwest."[7] For the first time in the history of the Church, Chicanas and Chicanos designed the type of training religious leaders received.

MACC was designed with a twofold purpose: to empower the poor and to train religious leaders. Modeled after IPLA in Quito, Peru, and the East Asian Pastoral Institute in Manila, Las Hermanas helped shape MACC as a site for "empowering the poor so that they may be able to control and direct their own destinies."[8] According to Fr. Juan Romero, who served on MACC's board of directors from 1972 to 1975, "We considered Las Hermanas and PADRES as co-founders."[9]

Latin American scholars and students taught and studied at MACC, providing an international character and solidifying alliances with Latin American liberation theologians.[10] A Spanish-language institute comprised one of the first programs at MACC to help Chicano priests and Chicana sisters relearn the language. Between 1974 and 1976 Sylvia Sedillo of Las Hermanas directed MACC's language institute. Sedillo held a master's degree in Spanish, and her previous teaching career prepared her for the administrative position at MACC.[11]

Initially MACC courses emphasized a critical socio-political analysis of U.S. society, the social justice teachings of the Church, and the pedagogy of liberation.[12] As the fifth anniversary booklet of MACC underscores, MACC took seriously the vision of empowering the poor:

> From language we went to the deeper question of education, economics and politics . . . Our people had to become familiar with the institutions that controlled their lives. . . . [MACC] had to be a center for organizing and speaking out against an economic system that enslaved our people.[13]

To ensure the presence of grassroots representatives, MACC's first board included members of the local community as well as ecclesial leadership.[14] In February 1973, a revision of MACC's bylaws ensured that PADRES, Las Hermanas, and the Office of the Secretariat for the Spanish-Speaking of the U.S. Catholic Conference of Bishops would "always be invited to have ex officio representation on the MACC Board of Directors."[15] The revision formally acknowledged MACC's development in close relationship to each of these organizations.

Sustaining the commitment to empower the poor proved difficult over time for MACC. The Vatican's coolness toward liberation theology combined with funding instability began to destabilize MACC's initial ambitions. Training Euroamerican ministers committed to working in Spanish-speaking communities evolved quickly into a reliable source of income for MACC. As this service took more of a primary focus, departing from the original goals of serving the poor, the issue of MACC's purpose soon became a point of contention among the staff and administration.[16] According to Yolanda Tarango, "We wanted MACC for the grassroots versus the institutional Church."[17] A report conducted by an outside evaluator, Management Design, Inc., offered several reasons why the majority of those serviced were non-Latino: more expendable resources of white clergy; the academic orientation of MACC; and MACC's own lack of recruitment efforts led to the divergence from its original goals.[18]

For Virgilio Elizondo, MACC's principal founder and president for its first fifteen years, the tension between the grassroots advocates and how MACC could survive financially required "a balancing act between what the bishops wanted and what members in PADRES and Las Hermanas demanded. I was walking a tightrope."[19] According to Elizondo, the ideological question of whom MACC should service remains open. Despite the challenges, after nearly thirty years MACC continues to train religious leaders for Latino pastoral ministry.[20] Las Hermanas no longer holds representation on MACC's board of directors. The current relationship between Las Hermanas and MACC will be addressed in Chapter 4.

Proyecto Mexico

With MACC underway, Las Hermanas proceeded with generating more leaders among the Spanish-speaking laity. After Gloria Gallardo resigned from the national leadership team in 1972, the remaining national coordinators, Carmelita Espinoza and María de Jesús Ybarra, needed housing and a site for the national office, as both had been living with Gallardo in Houston. Receiving release time from their religious communities to coordinate Las Hermanas offered no financial support for the tasks ahead. In October 1972, the national coordinators once again contacted the MCDP at Our Lady of the Lake University in San Antonio about using their facilities.[21] Renting a room and borrowing a typewriter during the evenings allowed Espinoza and Ybarra to continue to publish *Informes* and to expand recruitment efforts. Their vision proved too radical for their hosts, however, and after one month they were asked to leave the MCDP facilities. Ybarra recalls:

> The superior of the house said we were a very controversial group, too radical and that we were not good for the other sisters. We had no car and no money. Somehow we ended up in an empty house with no blankets and no food. It was the first time in my life that I cried for being hungry. For three days we had only coffee.[22]

Lacking support from their own religious communities and living in poverty only strengthened their resolve to make the Church accountable to Chicanos. With a vehicle borrowed from Pablo Ciddio y Abeyta, the Southwest regional coordinator of the Secretariat for the Spanish-speaking Apostolate, the women forged ahead with their vision to activate leadership among la raza.[23] Ybarra and Espinoza soon initiated Proyecto Mexico, a two-year project challenging exploitative employment practices against Mexican sisters in the United States by Church-related institutions, including seminaries and Catholic colleges.

The reality that Mexican sisters provided a source of cheap labor in the Church came to the attention of Las Hermanas through members of the Movimiento Familiar Cristiano (MFC).[24] According to Ybarra, Protestant women connected to MFC became aware of the situation while on retreat at a seminary in Chicago and they immediately contacted Las Hermanas. Ybarra and Espinoza wasted no time and notified a progressive network of priests and sisters in Mexico, the Latin American Conference of Major Superiors of Men and Women (CIRM), to collaborate on a plan of action. Their goal was to determine the number of Mexican sisters working as domestics at a time when Spanish-speaking religious were sorely needed in ministerial roles in the United States. With the CIRM in accordance, Ybarra took on the challenge of visiting some of the sites. She recalls a particularly poignant example of the conditions some of these sisters faced:

> I visited the seminary in Chicago. The sisters were living underground in the basement with no windows. There was a ramp going up to the kitchen. One sister told me that she had been at the seminary since she was fifteen years old and that she had never gone to Confession in Spanish. She desperately wanted spiritual direction! When the director of the seminary found out I was talking to the young sisters about studying, I was told to leave. [25]

Upset by what Ybarra and Espinoza encountered, Las Hermanas started raising funds for scholarships to help the domestic-bound sisters. Some of the sisters from Mexico had been trained as nurses or teachers but had to curtail their education because of the financial demands of their religious communities. Working as domestics in the United States provided a meager but stable income for the Mexican orders. [26] Harsh economic factors in Mexico that continually convince Mexican laborers to migrate north have obviously impacted women religious as well.

By September 1974, with the help of the CIRM, a total of fifty-nine sites including seminaries, colleges, rectories, retreat centers, and parishes had been identified as employing Mexican women religious as domestics. [27] Concern over these women's meager wages, virtual isolation from seminary staff and surrounding Latino communities, and the urgent need for Spanish-speaking ministers convinced Las Hermanas to contact several bishops throughout the United States for scholarship monies. They proposed scholarships at $2,200 each for one year of study at MACC. Courses offered at MACC would train the Mexican sisters in pastoral ministry among U.S. Latinos by familiarizing them with Chicano history and culture, and the reality of being bicultural in an Anglo-dominated society. Proyecto Mexico included the commitment that the sponsored sister would be employed in Chicano ministry projects. All the bishops who responded stated "they had no funds." [28] Clearly the plight of Mexican women religious and the ministerial needs of Chicano communities were not a priority for the bishops. Rather than give up, Las Hermanas turned to the next level of logical support. The LCWR responded with a $6,540 contribution, enabling three sisters to attend training at

MACC.[29] Despite minimal support from the institutional church, Las Hermanas remained in the forefront of holding the Church accountable to its Spanish-speaking constituency.

Resistance to the project, however, came not only from U.S. bishops and priests, but from the mother superiors of several Mexican religious communities and from some of the Mexican sisters themselves. Wanting "to remain loyal to the bishops"[30] prevented Mexican congregations from supporting the project while some of the sisters declared that they "embraced domestic work as a definition of their vocation."[31] They accepted their work as vital to the financial support of their congregations.

Ultimately, Proyecto Mexico assisted in educating further only four sisters, yet in the process alliances and relationships crystallized between Las Hermanas and its Mexican counterparts. As Las Hermanas educated its own religious congregations on the plight of Mexican sisters, it broadened the discourse around racism, women, and justice in the Church. As Tess Browne, OFM, stated, "Religious congregations had not been thinking about that area of justice before Las Hermanas brought it to light."[32] Proyecto Mexico also initiated Las Hermanas's long-term commitment to raise scholarship funds for Latinas in need of financial assistance for education. Scholarship funds averaged $4,000 per year well into the 1980s. Laywomen received the majority of the educational assistance, reflecting Las Hermanas's commitment to leadership development for all Latinas.[33]

Survey on Church Accountability

Before Proyecto Mexico came to a close, Las Hermanas carried out another national survey, this time on the existing Latino pastoral ministry offices in the United States. In April 1974, Ybarra and Espinoza conducted a month-long visitation to "various offices for the Spanish-speaking apostolate . . . in order to have an up-to-date picture of the services being rendered to our people both in the social services and in spiritual formation."[34] Ybarra recalls their journey:

> Carmelita asked her order [the Good Shepherds] to borrow a Ford Pinto they had. From San Antonio we drove to Chicago, then New York. We finally ended up in New Orleans. We wanted to see the

Hispanic offices, to see what they were doing. We also recruited Hermanas along the way. We had no "official" power. We took notes, talked to the people. Everywhere we stopped it was the same. There were no Spanish Masses, services were held in the church basements or the Spanish-speaking were not allowed to enter the main church.[35]

Upon returning to San Antonio, the sisters separated, with Espinoza driving the Pinto to the Midwest and Ybarra traveling by bus to the Northwest to continue the survey. By the time they were done, they had "covered the country."[36]

The results revealed a dramatic lack of service to Latino Catholics, an overwhelming presence of Euroamericans as directors for existing Latino ministry programs, a lack of authority held by those in charge, and a "prevailing mentality that the Hispano apostolate was a necessary evil rather than an integrative part of the total life of the Church."[37] Ybarra and Espinoza sent a letter to the U.S. bishops dated 27 May 1974 outlining the abuses they had witnessed with recommendations for the development of "indigenous lay leadership with no other 'job' than to the apostolate to the Hispano"[38] Ybarra recalls that only one bishop responded saying, "I did not know I had any Hispanics in my dioceses."[39]

Such disregard for Latinos convinced Las Hermanas to continue the push for Latino/a leadership in the Church. Its self-appointed surveys demonstrate the tactic of these women to seize power rather than passively waiting to receive it. They used their authority as women religious to expose the conditions and circumstances facing Latina/o Catholics that the Church hierarchy refused to confront. Such a proactive stance demanded recognition. Las Hermanas's next step required collaboration with PADRES.

The Appointment of Chicano Bishops

Las Hermanas joined PADRES in the push for more Chicano bishops although it did not see this as its primary purpose. Their decision to assist PADRES in the fight for more bishops resulted from their awareness that la raza needed representation in the policy-making arena of the Church. Desiring higher institutional status did not shape the aspirations of Las Hermanas. "From the very first meeting our purpose was to get out into the community. This is related to how we saw power. For the men, power was getting into the structures. For the women, power was participating in the liberative actions of the folks."[40] Their gender and status as laity within the Church also quelled any ambitions for institutional elevation. Although Las Hermanas would push for women's ordination in the immediate years ahead, its distance from the hierarchical structure ultimately worked to its advantage. Members realized they "had little to lose," giving them a greater sense of autonomy.[41]

By 1974 the Catholic hierarchy began appointing a few more Chicanos to the episcopacy. On 10 April 1974, Gilbert Chávez was appointed to the rank of auxiliary bishop of the diocese of San Diego. Members of Las Hermanas and PADRES had lobbied for two years prior to his appointment. Representatives from both organizations met with the Vatican's Apostolic Delegate, Rev. Jean Jadot, and PADRES submitted a resolution to the National Federation of Priests Council, identifying necessary qualifications for a Chicano bishop along with a list of twenty-one nominees.[42] A few months after Chávez's appointment, Roberto Sánchez accepted the honor of archbishop of Santa Fe, the first Latino archbishop in the country. Chávez, Sánchez, and Patricio Flores, the first Chicano bishop appointed in 1970, were all members of PADRES. Fr. Juan Romero stated, "PADRES made a lot of noise and did some effective politicking as we learned about the system and process for the selection of bishops."[43] In reality the strategic collaboration of PADRES and Las Hermanas began to take effect as Latino Catholics emerged as a powerful force demanding full representation.[44] Ybarra recalls some of the lobbying that took place and the strategies they implemented:

> PADRES called a meeting about the appointment of a Chicano archbishop to Santa Fe and Sedillo's office was in danger of closing. Edmundo Rodríguez, Virgilio Elizondo, Carmelita Espinoza, and myself met with some of the bishops. Our strategy was that I would be the soft-spoken sister in secular clothes, and Carmelita would wear a habit but be very radical. They were not expecting it! Carmelita pounded on the desk, "The church is not helping the people . . . it takes too many years to get a priest while the Protestants can get one quicker with good training! The Church is neglecting the Mexicans!" Well, the bishops kept Sedillo's office and they named a Chicano archbishop in Santa Fe. It was a joint effort of Las Hermanas and PADRES.[45]

Four years later, demands for representation would again be challenged. The newly created San Bernardino diocese with a 65 percent Chicano Catholic population offered the church a prime opportunity to appoint another Chicano bishop. But the selection of a Euroamerican, Fr. Phillip Straling, was a blow to progress. Las Hermanas and PADRES collectively protested the misguided action. Following two years of lobbying, they expressed their outrage and indignation. A collective letter to the Apostolic Delegate of the United States, Rev. Jean Jadot, communicated their anger and astonishment:

> We are appalled that the caliber of Hispano bishops and priests has been deemed too inferior to serve their own people . . . The refusal to act upon [our] requests is to invite the accusation of continuing racism and systematic exclusion in leadership positions . . . in the Church . . . Such a continuing policy of systematic exclusion tempts traditionally faithful people to severe and drastic measures. [46]

The letter included four demands to rectify the lack of "recognition and respect": episcopal representation in dioceses where Chicanos/Latinos comprise at least 50 percent of the population; the voice of the local people taken into consideration during the selection process; the appointment of Chicano/Latino vicars to dioceses with a large percentage of Latino Catholics; and the consideration of potential bishops from the ranks of religious orders. [47]

In addition to sending the letter, both organizations requested a meeting with four California bishops and a separate meeting with the Apostolic Delegate. [48] Sara Murrieta and Juan Romero took a primary role in coordinating the bishops' meeting, which included a committee of nineteen PADRES and Las Hermanas representatives. [49] On 19 November 1978, at the Mount Carmel Retreat House in Riverside, California, the committee gathered with a clear agenda in hand. The delegation outlined its four demands. Responses from the bishops ranged from "there were no qualified candidates available" to a willingness to consider nominations from religious orders, representing a considerable advancement for the pool of Chicano candidates. [50] The plea for community participation in the selection process fell on unsympathetic ears, but the bishops did agree to consider the appointment of Chicano vicars to dioceses with heavy concentrations of Latino Catholics. [51]

Other protests against Bishop Straling's appointment occurred independently of the PADRES–Las Hermanas delegation. Earlier community rallies and demonstrations on 6 November 1978, in Riverside, resulted in the appearance of the "police armed with rifles, guns and full riot gear."[52] Understandably, this action outraged the community.

The collaboration between Chicana and Latina sisters and Chicano priests in the 1970s reflects an era of intense activity and optimism. In the words of Carmelita Espinoza, "It was a real decade of conversion and change!"[53] Latina/o Catholics were truly coming of age as these women and men struggled to empower themselves as leaders and their communities as subjects in a sanctified institution. The right time had arrived for a very visible national gathering of Latino Catholics.

First and Second Encuentro Nacional Hispano De Pastoral

Preceding the appointments of Chávez and Sánchez, the First National Hispanic Pastoral encuentro, or structured gathering, convened in June 1972 at Trinity College in Washington, D.C., with members of PADRES and Las Hermanas present. The idea for a national encuentro among Spanish-speaking leaders of the Church came from Edgar Beltrán, a Latin American priest and educator who was working with Pablo Sedillo in the Division for the Spanish Speaking of the U.S. Catholic Conference in Washington, D.C. Beltrán suggested an encuentro as a way for Latinos to discuss their concerns on a national level. The emerging Latino/a leadership in the Church, both lay and religious, would mobilize, dialogue, and move "from a negative lament to positive strength, knowing that they were capable of contributing to the historic change in the church and in society."[54] Mobilizing, however, would first require the venting of much anger at the Church. According to Moisés Sandoval, "the encuentro became a vehicle to confront the Church."[55]

This historic first encuentro brought together 250 representatives and only a few bishops. After three days participants produced seventy-eight demands to the NCCB. Some of the more progressive demands included the prioritization of base communities at the parish level, the ordination of women as deacons, married priests, and seminary training to include cultural education.[56] In time only a few of the demands were met, such as the appointment of more Latino bishops and Spanish as a required language for seminarians in dioceses with a large Latino population. Most significantly the first encuentro led to a second encuentro in 1977 followed by a third encuentro in 1985.[57] II Encuentro and III Encuentro increased in size, indicating the growing strength of Latino Catholics. Encuentro IV in 2000 focused on a multicultural Church and was very much influenced by the leadership of Latino Catholics.

Las Hermanas played a pivotal role in pushing for the II Encuentro, with members taking leadership positions. María Iglesias facilitated the national coordinating committee, Margarita Castañeda represented the New York diocese, María de Jesús Ybarra represented the Northwest, and Rosa Martha Zárate assisted with liturgical music.[58] According to Iglesias, "We demanded in the name of Las Hermanas that there be a 50/50 share of leadership between men and women at the second encuentro."[59] Five hundred delegates, 700 observers, and thirty-four predominantly Euroamerican bishops attended, showing the growing activism among laity and the increased endorsement of the hierarchy. According to Castañeda, the encuentros intended for "all involved to hear the voices of Hispanic people across the country."[60]

Meeting in small base communities at the local parish and diocesan levels prior to the II Encuentro ensured that the voices of grassroots people would be heard. Representatives from various regions spoke on their specific concerns. With participants coming from across the nation, including numerous farmworkers from California and Washington, the meeting hall at Trinity College could not handle the unexpected turnout.

> It was a wonderful experience to see so many Hispanics. The bishops present were in a listening mode. It was totally chaotic. Fr. Roger Mahony and I were trying to impose Robert's rules of order. Forget it! People needed to be heard. Everyone raised their issues, farmworkers, the youth. It was the Spirit alive and well moving among the people![61]

When it came time to celebrate the Eucharist, participants marched from Trinity College to the National Shrine of the Immaculate Conception, and proceeded into the main part of the church. Castañeda recalls, "I remember Virgilio Elizondo saying to me, 'We finally made it out of the basement of the church!' This was a symbolic move to celebrate Mass in the main church of the national cathedral!"[62] Latino Catholics were finally moving toward first-class status in the Church.

Following three days of many chaotic deliberations, priorities for a final document emerged. Concern for the ordination of women found expression in what might be called coded language. In the final report, in the section on lay ministers, participants concluded that vocations must be sought without distinctions based on gender, race, age, or social class. Final conclusions stated, "we ask that equal consideration be given to women for ministries in the community."[63] According to Castañeda, "Just to raise the consciousness of the bishops to the fact that women were second-class citizens in the Church was a tremendous accomplishment."[64]

The II Encuentro again emphasized the need to establish small base communities, to eliminate economic and social injustices, and to affirm Latino cultures in religious education.[65] According to the *Proceedings of the II Encuentro:*

> This signaled a change in the Church: from a silent Church to one that is prophetic. From a vertical Church to one of dialogue and communion. This process may well appear in history as the major step taken up to this moment by the Hispanic sector of the Church in the United States before the country and the world.[66]

Five years later the NCCB would state in their pastoral letter, "We recognize the Hispanic community among us as a blessing from God."[67] The encuentros helped to reverse more than a century of viewing Mexican American and Latino Catholics as a problem.[68] Las Hermanas's role in this change of consciousness cannot be underestimated.[69]

Las Hermanas did not limit its demands for justice to the Church. Its accomplishments in the early 1970s, including I Encuentro and II Encuentro, MACC, Proyecto Mexico, the appointment of bishops, and national surveys, only encouraged participants to keep up the momentum of building *una nueva iglesia Latina* beyond the boundaries of the institutional Church. Their commitment to social justice and the Chicano movement naturally brought them into the farm labor struggle with the UFWA.

The Farm Labor Movement

Las Hermanas can be counted among the "scores of priests, nuns, ministers and church members [who] donated time, money, facilities, and energies to the farm workers' cause."[70] Their support for collective bargaining rights and fair wages upheld Catholic social teaching first declared in 1891 by Pope Leo XIII in the encyclical letter, *The Condition of Workers* (*Rerum novarum*), and later confirmed by the papacy in the 1930s and 1960s.[71]

Despite the legacy of support for workers' rights within Catholic teachings, the U.S. Catholic bishops failed to offer their official support during the initial years of farmworker organizing under César Chávez and Dolores Huerta. That many of the growers contributed substantial funds to the Church determined the bishops' unwillingness to support farmworkers.[72] In addition, the federal National Labor Relations Act (1935), popularly known as the Wagner Act, excluded agricultural workers in its provisions guaranteeing workers the right to organize. Thus, the Catholic hierarchy was not legally bound to support the farmworkers. The Church's resistance, however, would weaken by the end of the 1960s.[73]

While mainline Protestant churches played a major role in the farmworker struggle during the mid-1960s, the U.S. Catholic hierarchy still had not issued an official statement or pastoral letter supporting the farmworkers. Each Catholic bishop could essentially determine his own diocese's position on farmworkers.[74] The move toward increased collective action on the part of the Catholic bishops turned decisively in 1969 when Chávez asked the NCCB to support the California grape boycott begun four years earlier. In response to Chávez's request, the bishops offered to act as a mediating body between the growers and workers in lieu of a statement supporting the boycott. According to "labor priest" George Higgins, if the bishops had followed Catholic social teaching they would have supported the boycott without reservation.[75] The decision to mediate occurred after an international and now "legendary" boycott against all California table grapes.[76] Union representatives coordinated boycott activity throughout the country and a national consciousness arose regarding the farmworker struggle in California.[77]

At the suggestion of the NCCB, an ad hoc committee on farm labor formed under the direction of Bishop Joseph Donnelly of Hartford, Connecticut. The committee included Archbishop Manning of Los Angeles, Bishop Donohoe of Stockton, Bishop Humberto Medeiros of Brownsville, and Bishop Walter Curtis of Bridgeport, Connecticut.[78] Beginning in January 1970, the committee met in "a seemingly endless series of meetings with growers up and down the valleys of California, individually and in groups, as well as with Chávez and his people."[79] After convincing the growers that they were there to help the parties negotiate contracts rather than to take sides, the growers indicated a willingness to meet the demands of the farmworkers "as long as the bishops' committee sat in on the meetings."[80]

In April 1970, the committee facilitated the signing of a contract with Lionel Steinberg, the largest table grape grower of Coachella Valley. And by July at least three-quarters of California's grape growers agreed to collective bargaining with the United Farm Workers Organizing Committee.[81] Never before in the history of U.S. agriculture had labor managed such a victory.[82] The committee of Catholic bishops played no small role in this historical success, as did the numerous priests, sisters, and Protestant ministers and laity who accompanied the farmworkers on their ardous journey for labor rights. Gregoria Ortega remembers "the triumphant feeling as I witnessed Chávez and the growers signing the contracts."[83]

The monumental gains achieved by the union were short-lived. During the next three years the UFW battled Teamster "sweetheart contracts" signed with lettuce growers in the Salinas Valley of California.[84] The UFW temporarily moved union headquarters to Salinas and began organizing a strike. And by April 1973, the majority of Coachella Valley table grape growers refused to renew their contracts with the UFW, signing with the Teamsters instead. Grape growers in the San Joaquin Valley followed suit, leading to a strike and a renewed national boycott.[85] It appeared that the entire California agricultural industry was slipping away from the UFW.

The summer of 1973 witnessed one of the most violent periods of UFW history. Teamsters arrived in Coachella Valley hired especially to intimidate and physically harm UFW strikers.[86] By August the strike moved north to San Joaquin Valley, where sheriff deputies turned violent and "became the union's enemy."[87] Mass

Participants at the third Las Hermanas national conference in Lake Forest, Illinois. Conference theme "Leadership." Las Hermanas Archives.

Las Hermanas member Rosa Martha Zárate singing at a student protest at UCLA, 1992. Author's personal collection.

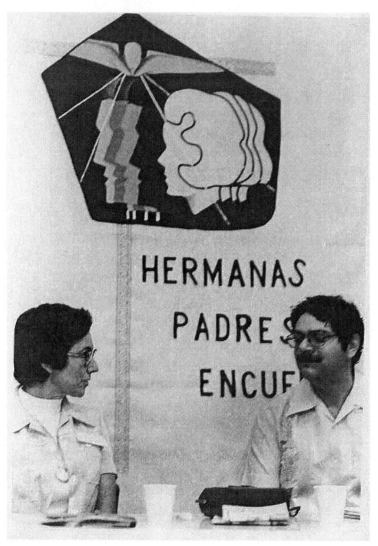

The 1978 Las Hermanas and PADRES joint conference in Las Cruces, New Mexico. Conference theme "Partnership in Ministy." Las Hermanas Archives.

Ada María Isasi-Díaz preaching the gospel at the 1978 Las Hermanas and PADRES joint conference. Las Hermanas Archives.

Las Hermanas member Tess Browne conducting a workshop on the injustices toward farm laborers at the Las Hermanas national conference in 1981 at St. Mary's College, Notre Dame, Indiana. Las Hermanas Archives.

Las Hermanas leading a prayerful protest in front of the national cathedral following the adversary vote towards women in full ministerial roles at the third Encuentro National Hispano de Pastoral in Washington, D.C., 1985. Las Hermanas Archives.

Agricultural laborers attending a Las Hermanas conference. Las Hermanas Archives.

A liturgical altar arranged by members of Las Hermanas. Las Hermanas Archives.

The regularly scheduled Saturday night dance at a Las Hermanas national conference. Las Hermanas Archives.

Las Hermanas national board members in 1987. Las Hermanas Archives.

arrests totaling 3,500 UFW supporters, including sixty to seventy priests, sisters, and religious brothers, took place.[88] Among those jailed were Juan Romero and Raul Luna of PADRES.[89] Being imprisoned for thirteen days for "illegal assembly and failure to disperse the picket line" did not deter these religious leaders from publicly supporting the farmworkers. A call for support reached Las Hermanas in August 1973 as members prepared for their fourth annual conference in Los Angeles. María de Jesús Ybarra recalls:

> César called and wanted us to go on the picket line during our conference. We felt that if the younger sisters went their superiors would never allow them to attend another conference again. We decided that I would go. I said I would go to jail also along with PADRES. César said no, he wanted me to preach at the Masses in the labor camps. He thought that if the priests were in jail, then they would not hurt the people. We invited the other sisters to go but they were not told to go.[90]

Ultimately a delegation of sisters representing Las Hermanas arrived in Parlier, California. They understood that they might be arrested and jailed for violating an injunction limiting picketing. According to the *Los Angeles Times*, the "decision to go north was not approved until after some delicate discussion and assurances to one another that those who stayed were not being criticized."[91] Those joining Ybarra included Gregoria Ortega, Mary Jo Arredondo, Clarita Trujillo, Juanita Flores, Teresita Basso, and Ramona Jean Corrales.

Time spent on the picket line turned quickly into two weeks for some of the hermanas. "We picketed, slept on linoleum floors, got up at 4:00 A.M., and ate no breakfast. We walked, prayed, and sang as the police with their dogs watched us."[92] Ybarra served as a captain on the picket line, made a citizen's arrest of an abusive police officer, ministered to the strikers, and even accompanied singer Joan Baez in providing moral support to those picketing. Ybarra witnessed so much violence that she became convinced that "the only reason I slept was due to the Holy Spirit watching over me."[93] When Las Hermanas and PADRES joined forces with numerous other religious supporters, both Protestant and Catholic, it enabled Chávez to say that summer, "Never have we had more support from the Churches."[94]

By mid-August, because of two fatalities and tremendous bloodshed, Chávez called off the strike.[95] With the violence hurting union morale and strike funds running low, Chávez called an end to the grape strike in the fall of 1973, yet increased the national boycott of nonunion grapes, lettuce, and Gallo wines, made by the nation's largest wine maker.

Las Hermanas could be found on the picket line in many parts of the country. Several members worked on a part-time basis for the UFW or volunteered after their regular work hours.[96] For Ramona Jean Corrales, Clarita Trujillo, and Lucy Martínez, the picketing of a Colorado Springs Safeway market in 1973 led to their arrests.[97] After posting bond they returned to Safeway to resume picketing against the sale of nonunion lettuce. By the afternoon a second group, again including Trujillo, Corrales, and Martínez, were arrested for "unlawful use of private property: stopping customers with leaflets and conversation." Corrales remembers with humor, "Well, the judge gave us what we wanted. He publicly told us to stay away from Safeway!"[98]

It grew increasingly evident that farmworkers and their supporters needed legislation protecting their right to organize. Lobbying for farm labor protection proved to be a monumental task. A migratory workforce had special needs such as protection for organizers, protection from threats of firing, and of utmost importance, protection for a farmworker's right to secondary boycotts, the union's most effective tool against growers. Lengthy negotiations with growers, politicians, and the union ultimately resulted in the passage of the Agricultural Labor Relations Act (ALRA) in 1975, a historic piece of legislation granting farmworkers protection. The law provided funding for a government "watchdog" agency, the Agricultural Labor Relations Board (ALRB), to oversee grower compliance with union elections and contracts. Fresno's auxiliary bishop, Roger Mahony, served as the board's first chairman. The UFW appeared successful in its long battle for legal protection.

However, after one year of substantial funding, the labor board ran into insurmountable obstacles as growers and Teamsters resisted compliance, accused the board of biased decisions, and lobbied for its defunding. In response the UFW gathered support for Proposition 14, a California measure to guarantee permanent funding for the board and to add provisions for the ALRA in the state constitution. To the dismay of the UFW, Proposition 14 failed by a substantial margin. Refusing to give up, Chávez continued to pressure legislators to fulfill the legal requirements of the board. Numerous broken contracts, grower resistance to union representation, and an increasingly politically conservative climate made the ARLB ineffective.[99]

The organizing efforts of the UFW required a vast amount of people power, both volunteer and minimally paid staff. Chávez reached out for support from religious groups. In 1974 at a meeting of the NAWR in St. Louis, Chávez requested that the organization employ one sister who could recruit other sisters to the farmworker movement. Pat Drydyk, a Franciscan sister, fulfilled the request and eventually became a staff member of the National Farm Worker Ministry (NFWM), an ecumenical organization supporting the unionizing of farmworkers.[100] Drydyk's recruitment efforts led her to Tess Browne, another Franciscan and Las Hermanas member. Browne's commitment to the rights of farmworkers quickly evolved into a full-time career.

When the UFW closed its boycott office in Milwaukee in 1975 to reassign staff to the fields in California, Browne was asked to work full-time as the boycott director for the state of Wisconsin through her position at the Justice and Peace Center (JPC) in Milwaukee.[101] As director of the Wisconsin boycott, Browne garnered the support of religious and secular groups, picketed, and persevered through numerous days in court as Gallo tried to get an injunction against picketing.

After serving on the NFWM board from 1975 to 1978, Browne relocated to Texas, where she served as director of the National Farm Worker Service Center in San Juan. Appointed in 1981 by the UFW as citizen advocates before the Texas legislature, Sister Browne and Sister Carol Ann Messina lobbied successfully for legislation to abolish *el cortito,* the short-handled hoe previously outlawed by California's State Supreme Court in 1975.[102] This twenty-four-inch long farming tool required workers to stoop for numerous hours, causing debilitating back problems and premature arthritis. Browne reflected on the legislative battle: "We wanted workers' compensation or unemployment benefits to be the top priority. The workers said el cortito is the first priority, the right to stand upright, to work with dignity. That taught me much."[103] Browne, who served as "a major force testifying at committee and House hearings on behalf of the workers,"[104] continues to serve on the board of the NFWM. Browne kicked off a UFW statewide march and rally in Watsonville, California, in 1997 in support of strawberry pickers.[105]

Support for farmworker rights consistently found a home with Las Hermanas as members such as Tess Browne, Teresita Basso, Pauline Apodaca, Irene Muñoz, Consuelo Covarrubias, and Mario (Lucie) Barron kept the national organization informed and involved. The exchange of information between regional representatives enabled the membership to keep abreast of rapid changes in the farmworker struggle nationwide. "We learned from each other, built solidarity, and recognized that we needed to be advocates."[106] Labor rights received attention consistently at Las Hermanas national conferences and executive board meetings, reflecting one of the most frequently discussed topics.[107] Sixty percent of *Informes*, the organizational newsletter, between 1971 and 1996 publicized information about the UFW, the Farm Labor Organizing Committee (FLOC), and other labor struggles such as the 1978 boycott on JP Stevens products.[108]

Advocating for the rights of farmworkers influenced Las Hermanas's interactions with their religious communities. Las Hermanas's willingness to challenge others on justice for farmworkers reflected its commitment to bring the struggles of la raza into arenas often removed from the realities of labor exploitation. Negotiating support often took much strategizing, "as many non-Latina sisters came from families of growers who perceived a different reality from the farm laborers."[109] As examples of the strategies used by Las Hermanas, in 1975 during a NAWR conference at the University of San Francisco, Mario (Lucie) Barron identified nonunion lettuce in the cafeteria. Barron and other hermanas organized a walkout and picket line against the university.[110] That same year, at the first Women's Ordination Conference in Detroit, Las Hermanas representatives asked the hosts to stop serving nonunion grapes and lettuce. At the sixth national Las Hermanas conference in 1976 convening at Loretto Heights College in Denver, Las Hermanas successfully demanded that the nonunion lettuce be removed from the college cafeteria.[111] While these might appear to be minor accomplishments in relation to picketing or striking, their resistance influenced an entire generation of women religious who, in turn, had tremendous power to sensitize Catholic laity and Catholic institutions.

In 1981 the issue remained on the agenda at the NAWR conference in San Antonio, where sixty members participated in an early morning picket and "prayer walk" through the city's produce row. They asked dockworkers to support the boycott of all United Brands products, including Chiquita bananas and lettuce.[112] Such organized efforts helped to keep the various boycotts strong, and as Tess Browne states, "grounded Las Hermanas in *la lucha*, in the struggles of el pueblo."[113]

Theological Discourse

By 1975 international theological discussions included the voice of Las Hermanas. Through the Theology of the Americas project sponsored by the Division of Latin America of the United States Catholic Conference and the Latin American Working Group of the National Council of Churches, Las Hermanas joined with theologians from North America and Latin America, PADRES, and other Christian activists committed to social change to begin a process of exploring the meaning of liberation theology for North America. Sergio Torres, a Chilean priest living in exile in the United States, directed this five-year project with the goal of articulating liberationist theologies from the multiple realities of distinct class, racial, and ethnic groups within the United States. Participants intended to "initiate a new way of doing theology based on the grassroots experiences of those who are oppressed by society's racism, sexism, classism and imperialism."[114] The original intent to bring Latin American liberationist clergy present at Medellín, Colombia, into dialogue with North American theologians quickly evolved into a broader coalition of academics, activists, and grassroots representatives.

Las Hermanas maintained diverse representation in Theology of the Americas through the participation of Chicanas, including Mario (Lucie) Barron, Margarita Castañeda, Yolanda Tarango, and Rosalina Ramírez. Puerto Rican representation included Dominga Zapata, Carmen Villegas, and María Iglesias. Ada María Isasi-Díaz presented a Cuban perspective.[115]

Convening in downtown Detroit in mid-August 1975 at the Sacred Heart Seminary, participants from more than fifty reflection groups throughout the country gathered to share their documents and working papers developed during the previous year.[116] Such a tremendous endeavor to bring together African American, Asian American, Native American, Latino/a, and Euroamerican men and women to reflect on their distinct realities inevitably resulted in serious tensions. Time constraints and "deficiencies in planning" scheduled simultaneous panels for the Native American, Asian American, and Latino groups. Resulting tensions produced a "Statement from the Coalition of U.S. Nonwhite Racial and National Minorities" challenging organizers on the silencing of nonwhites in the North American section, creating divisiveness and tokenism.[117]

Despite these difficulties, the "Chicano Reflection Group," including Las Hermanas and PADRES representatives, released a statement titled "The Chicano Struggle," which stressed the tension between the "American Catholic/Protestant ethics and the Indo-Hispanic cultural ethic of our Mexican ancestors."[118] Giving primacy to the latter, the participants defended their unique form of Catholicism enriched by their indigenous ancestry.

> Our Indian forefathers were a people very close to nature, and nature's unknown elements were our gods. Living in harmony with nature meant that the gods were pleased, and it meant *la madre tierra* needed *el dios de la lluvia y del sol* [the mother earth needed the god of the rain and the sun so as to give the harvest] so as to give us *la cosecha* which was necessary for living. A religious, cultural difference between the Chicano and the North American is evident in relation to nature. Our heritage has taught us to live in harmony with nature, whereas the Anglo-Saxon has conquered nature and has abused it to become a powerful nation.[119]

These cosmological/theological understandings provided a corrective to Euroamerican theologies that historically have ignored the religious *mestizaje* of Latinos. The effort undertaken by the Chicano Refection Group to bring an indigenous perspective to the Christian table challenged both Euroamerican and Latin American theologians. Not until the late 1980s would indigenous belief systems be addressed by other liberation theologians.[120] Las Her-

manas and PADRES were in the forefront of addressing the mestizaje now presumed foundational in U.S. Latino/a theologies.[121]

The Chicana/o theological reflections also recognized that the
outward expressions of Mexican Catholicism such as "*nuestras
medallas, altares, curaciones,* and *días de los santos, vivos y difuntos*"
(our meals, altars, cures, and saints' days, the living and the dead)
still exist despite the strong Hispanic and Anglo-Saxon religious
influences that would interpret these religious events as supersti-
tious."[122] Validating the significance of "popular religion" posed a
challenge to traditional European theologies that tend to view the
"unofficial" practices of the masses as merely folk religion. Identifying these popular religious expressions as core to the faith of
Mexicano/Chicano Catholics would become a central theme to
Chicano/Latino theology in subsequent years.[123] Las Hermanas
and PADRES set in motion a theological discourse relevant to
Chicano/a culture.

The vision of a Church in solidarity with the poor and oppressed shaped the discussions at Theology of the Americas.
However, the ethnic, class, and gender diversity present at Detroit prevented a single North American liberation theology from
emerging. According to participant and sociologist Gregory Baum,
"Throughout the conference it became clear that one should only
speak of liberation theologies in the plural."[124] In spite of the differences, Las Hermanas member Aurora Camacho de Schmidt observed the following:

> We realized that we were not alone in the struggle. We gained
> a basic sense of solidarity even if we could not agree. This was
> extremely important during the 1980s, during the height of civil
> war in parts of Latin America as the Christian right were gaining
> power. We represented the progressive and radical core of main-
> stream churches.[125]

The "Christian left" present at Detroit emphasized faith and its
ability to make change. According to Baum, "This faith was present with such a density that one could touch it with the hands."[126]
Faith, however, could not resolve differences regarding economic
and political solutions to the world's problems. While Latin American project leaders advocated socialism, the North American participants wanted to consider reforming capitalism.[127] Ultimately,

the participants formulated ideas for several theologies of liberation, taking seriously the different social, ethnic, and racial realities. In the process they wanted to "discover the historical relationship between their various emancipatory struggles and strained to
find a language that would not neutralize or suppress but rather
protect and strengthen the particularity of their struggles."[128]

As coordinator between 1978 and 1980 of the "Hispanic Project" within Theology of the Americas, Margarita Castañeda reflects:

> It was really an exciting time, as we were immersed in theology
> from all over the world and from the underside of society. It af-
> fected the shape of pastoral ministry among those committed to
> empowering small communities at the base or grassroots level. If
> we lose touch with the base and remain on the intellectual level
> we lose the reality of our people, from where we came and from
> where the real theology is going on. By interacting with *la mujer de
> la base*, that's where our theology comes from. We can't theologize
> in the sky.[129]

Numerous working relationships evolved out of Theology of
the Americas and many of the participants have produced significant theological works. In 1988 Ada María Isasi-Díaz and Yolanda
Tarango published *Hispanic Women: Prophetic Voice in the Church,*
the first book on U.S. Latinas "doing theology,"[130] an enterprise
that would later be named mujerista theology. Mujerista writings
enable the voices and experiences of grassroots Latinas to be heard
as theological constructs. Las Hermanas provided the seedbed for
mujerista theology,[131] and theological contributions of Las Hermanas members over the years, beginning with Theology of the
Americas, earned them recognition as leading spokespersons on
theology and spirituality from the perspective of U.S. Latinas.[132]

The first decade of Las Hermanas resulted in significant accomplishments for Chicano/Latino representation and visibility
in the Church. Las Hermanas's concern for lay leadership, ecclesial accountability, culturally sensitive ministries, and politically
grounded theologies reflected its vision of a Church relevant to
Chicano/Latino lives. Its growing feminist consciousness would
bring new challenges in the decades ahead. Experiencing interethnic sexism in its work with PADRES, marginalization at MACC,
silencing at the III Encuentro, and disappointment in its work on

the Women's Ordination Conference (WOC) persuaded Las Hermanas to refocus its goals specifically on empowerment for Latinas. The spiritual and social welfare of Latinas would occupy its priorities beginning in 1980. The following chapter will highlight the various situations and experiences that ultimately convinced Las Hermanas that "women never have been nor will be for many years, a priority for Hispanic ministry in the U.S."[133] In response to this realization, Las Hermanas continued to mobilize its collective strength to resist silencing and inequality.

4

The Challenge of Being Chicana/Latina, Catholic, and Feminist

Although some will tell you nothing is able to change. / Fight for a new world, fight for the truth . . . / Although it may seem that the steps you are walking are useless, you are making pathways that others will follow.
—*"Santa Maria del Camino"*[1]

VATICAN COUNCIL II and its call for adaptation to the modern world set the stage for women religious to contribute to modern American feminism. Las Hermanas articulated a feminist consciousness from its inception. National priorities set at the third annual conference specified that the organization would "initiate statements which would encourage the acceptance of women as active and valuable participants in Pastoral Ministry."[2] Although not yet a full call for women's ordination, Las Hermanas's emphasis on team ministry with priests, women religious, and laity ministering as equals chipped away at the familiar stereotype of nuns being obedient women under the authority of clergy. A *nueva iglesia Latina* would have to accept women as full participants. This chapter explores the feminist agenda developed by Las Hermanas and the challenges members faced in transforming a Church intent on excluding women and Chicanos/Latinos from full and equal participation. Their efforts would be twofold: influencing the institutional Church on the needs of Latinas and sustaining an autonomous women's organization where Latinas could openly discuss their personal and political lives.

Las Hermanas and PADRES

As women committed to their own empowerment and that of their ethnic communities, Las Hermanas faced particular gender struggles. Its initial decision to collaborate with Chicano clergy through PADRES meant confronting intercultural sexism as well as broader institutional barriers for women. Las Hermanas understood the profound impact of Catholicism, a patriarchal religion, on gender norms within Chicano/Latino cultures. The willingness of Las Hermanas members to cooperate with their male counterparts gave rise to particular challenges not experienced by other Catholic feminist groups. For example, the LCWR, the NAWR, and the Women's Ordination Conference (WOC) never had a peer group of clergy with which they collaborated and shared common goals, or as one PADRE member stated, "a common enemy," discrimination in the Church.

The shared vision of making the Church responsive to the needs of Chicano Catholics created a natural alliance between Las Hermanas and PADRES. Yet traditional gender expectations prevented their success at sustained collaboration.

The fact that Las Hermanas invited PADRES to its national conferences until the early 1980s suggests strongly that the strategy to empower Latinas within the Catholic Church included engaging their male counterparts in the dialogue. Las Hermanas understood that for patriarchy to be undermined those with ordained status must be influenced on the issues concerning Latinas. As Hermana Carmelita Espinoza said in the mid-1970s, "*Nuestros PADRES* still need to be challenged by our *pueblo* and by *la MUJER* . . . there is an influence in their thought patterns by our *granito de arena que ponemos en sus vidas* [grain of sand that we put into their lives]."[3] This awareness, combined with a "community-centered consciousness," provided the motivating factors for Las Hermanas to attempt collaborative leadership.

Las Hermanas encountered barriers similar to those faced by Chicana feminists active in the Chicano movement as discussed in Chapter 1. Male counterparts attempted to relegate women to traditional roles such as cooks and secretaries, while motherhood was espoused as a woman's full commitment to the movement. Unwilling to accept prescribed gender roles, many Chicanas formed their own organizations in order to concentrate on the concerns of women, such as welfare rights, job training, and health care, in addition to bringing a feminist perspective to the male-dominated organizations.[4] Historian Vicki Ruiz notes that "Feminists could be found at every pivotal event and in every major movement organization."[5]

Las Hermanas also faced traditional expectations. Ramona Jean Corrales explains: "The priests were used to having nuns take care of them, cooking in the seminaries. We didn't want to be helping them step up in the institution. We wanted to share power and leadership. We were making sure our collaboration was mutual."[6] Ensuring mutuality in a sanctified patriarchy required Las Hermanas to consistently challenge PADRES, which had much more invested in a male-dominated structure. Some PADRES held aspirations of achieving the status of bishop.

At the Las Hermanas Fourth National Conference held in Los Angeles the summer of 1973, discussion resulted in several conclusions to be communicated to PADRES. The lack of a "strong, supportive, *compromiso de riesgo* [commitment to risk]" on the part of PADRES toward the projects of LAS HERMANAS, led the women to feeling "held back" by the clerics.[7] They felt that "at times *HERMANAS* or the name of the organization were merely utilized rather than mutually sharing as a brother-sister organization." The assembly decided to maintain a "peaceful-coexistence" with PADRES "as long as this relationship [was] not an impediment to *trabajo de avanzada* [sic] *de Las Hermanas por la liberación auténtica de nuestra gente* [Las Hermanas's work in advancing the authentic liberation of our people]."[8] Rather than creating a fissure between the two organizations, the strategy of Las Hermanas focused on reconciliation and unity in order to ensure greater success at transforming the Church.

Discontent with its relationship with PADRES did not deter Las Hermanas from maintaining a visible presence among the emerging Chicano/a and Latino/a religious leadership. Las Hermanas continued to provide input into priestly formation programs. Members advised clergy and bishops regarding bilingual and bicultural seminary training. As examples, María de Jesús Ybarra met with PADRES members and Bishops Rauch and Bernardin at MACC in 1974 to discuss the need for Chicano Studies and Spanish-language classes in seminary programs.[9] Teresita Basso conducted a two-day workshop for deacons and seminarians titled "Unity and Pluralism within the Church," held at St. Patrick's Seminary in Menlo Park, California, in 1976. These contributions from Chicanas marked a turning point in formation programs for clergy. For the first time women with a feminist, cultural, and political perspective were advising future priests.

Las Hermanas's seat on the National Advisory Council (NAC) to the United States Catholic Conference-Secretariat for Hispanic Affairs placed Latinas at the core of advocating for Latino concerns with the bishops. The NAC played an instrumental role in the development of Hispanic Ministry offices throughout the nation, and in the development of the National Hispanic Pastoral Encuentros until its demise in 1990.[10]

By 1975 PADRES showed interest in reconciling with Las Hermanas. PADRES's fifth national congress in 1975 promoted the theme, "*La Raza Nueva y Nueva Esperanza*" [The New People and the New Hope].[11] The 130 participants, including eight Hermanas, heard from a variety of speakers, including Bishop-elect Roger Mahony and Las Hermanas National Coordinator Clarita Trujillo. After presenting Las Hermanas's priorities for the coming year, which emphasized support for the farmworkers and Proyecto Mexico, Trujillo challenged PADRES to consider seriously where women fit into the priests' agenda.[12] She spoke frankly in asking for their support of women's ordination[13] and pressed the issue of the lack of Latina representation on diocesan advisory councils, vocation commissions, and seminary review boards.[14] PADRES could influence bishops on the appointment of Latinas. Pursuing a collaborative posture, Trujillo concluded by assuring PADRES that her organization was once again willing to "work hand in hand with our brothers, the priests. We ask that you take seriously our agenda and at the same time we hope that the two organizations will carry the agenda of our pueblo forward."[15] A community-centered consciousness continued to inform Las Hermanas's activism but one not overshadowing its focus on women.

Calls for the recognition of women did not go unheard. Resolutions from the PADRES conference included renewed support for Las Hermanas. A press release following the conference stated, "In a gesture of fraternal support the *PADRES* made their own the recommendation of *Las Hermanas* that women should have a greater voice in decision making within the church."[16] While women's ordination did not receive explicit support, PADRES did resolve "to be open to the preparation of Hispanic women for the ministry of priestly orders" and to support the Equal Rights Amendment.[17] The following year, Fr. Roberto Peña reiterated a stance of solidarity in his presidential address at the PADRES national convention: "*La mujer* is as capable and as dedicated to the mission that we as PADRES have chosen."[18]

A renewed relationship between the two organizations proved timely. Shortly after the PADRES convention, the U.S. bishops called for a national gathering of representatives from across the nation to prioritize the concerns of American Catholics for a five-year pastoral plan.[19] Thirteen hundred people from Catholic communities across the nation attended the first Call to Action Conference, including 140 Latino and Latina delegates. Accepting the invitation to be heard by the larger Catholic Church, the Latino/a delegates "initiated an intense effort to unite so as to make an effective contribution to the dialogue."[20] Once again, solidarity was the chosen strategy for a strong presence.

Recommendations from the entire conference body shaped a far more progressive agenda than the U.S. bishops had envisioned. Advocating for women's ordination, married priests, birth control, and the acceptance of divorce convinced the bishops to cancel any further meetings. Not until the late 1980s would Call to Action convene again as an independent and member-supported organization of laypeople, progressive religious, and clergy.[21] According to María Inez Martínez, "the bishops got more than they bargained for."[22]

PADRES continued to strive for a working relationship with Las Hermanas. Fr. Juan Romero's suggestion for a joint national meeting materialized as PADRES desired "to become a not so clerical organization and to show by action [its] support of women in ministry."[23] Both organizations negotiated a conference theme of "partnership in ministry." Under the direction of PADRES members Edward Salazar, David García, Edmundo Rodríguez, Arturo Bañuelas, and Alberto Gallegos and Hermanas Alicia Salcido, Elisa Rodríguez, Yolanda Tarango, and Sylvia Sedillo, the first national PADRES/Las Hermanas conference convened on 14–17 August 1978, in Mesilla Park, New Mexico. Participants included

150 priests, religious women, laity, seminarians, and three bishops, together representing thirty-nine dioceses. The joint meeting marked a historical moment as the "first meeting of national Catholic organizations of priests and sisters gathering as equal partners."[24] As Juan Romero stated, the efforts for collaboration "came out of a history needing us to be mutually supportive."[25]

The conference provided a forum for those already practicing shared ministry to speak on its challenges and successes. Sister Jacinta Millán and Fr. Ricardo García, co-directors of the Centro Pastoral in San José, California, described how they shared equally in administrative responsibilities, preaching, public benedictions, and being present in the "*luchas* of our *gente*" (struggles of our people). They blessed each other simultaneously, providing a powerful symbol of equality that conference participants were encouraged to imitate in small discussion groups.[26] Mutuality in ministry could subvert the limitations of patriarchal religion.

Las Hermanas faciliated discussions on the difficulties of team ministry. Mixed feelings about collaboration were evident. For María Iglesias, the idea of partnership appeared irrelevant, "I've lost the desire to work with priests anymore—they always have to be number one. I don't even want boys to go to the seminary."[27] For seminarian Eduardo Hernández, "the fear of falling in love" created a barrier to discussing male-female relationships.[28] Several PADRES members responded defensively to the frankness of the women. Comments ranging from "It's part of the process of being militant," to "the 'good guys' become the targets of their hostility"[29] reflected a common reaction toward assertive women. Clearly all was not harmonious between the two organizations. In reflecting on the planning process, Teresita Basso remembers "how hard it was to get the PADRES team members to even follow through on their commitments for the conference."[30]

After three days of focusing on partnership in ministry, PADRES submitted an "Open Letter of Apology" to Las Hermanas. Admitting their failures, PADRES members asked for forgiveness "for those moments when we have failed to listen or to take you seriously."[31] For Fr. Balthasar Janacek, the letter and joint meeting was sending "a pacesetting message and a pattern for co-ministering in the Church."[32] Judging by the responses from several of the conference participants, the effort to equalize relationships proved effective. Fr. Ed Salazar commented, "We are becoming an 'adult' Church dealing with one another as equals," and Hermana Margarita Castañeda stated, "[it] was so good, it must be continued throughout the year in the regions."[33]

Following the Mesilla Park conference, the two organizations decided to publish a joint newsletter for a one-year trial period. With a $3,000 grant awarded to PADRES from the Jesuit Society Apostolic Fund, a co-editorial team published five issues of *Entre Nosotros-Informes de HERMANAS y PADRES* from the fall of 1978 to the fall of 1979.[34] A review of the issues addressed in the newsletters reflects the vitality of the joint effort. Ministry to the undocumented, alternative formation programs for Latinos/as, women's ordination, Latino theology, support for immigrant and farmworker rights, international and interracial dialogues indicate the high level of activity for PADRES and Las Hermanas during this one-year period.

PADRES and Women's Ordination

Las Hermanas members Ada María Isasi-Díaz, Sylvia Sedillo, and María Iglesias had collaborated with the WOC since its inception in 1975. They networked nationally with Catholic women to establish WOC chapters in different cities and organized an unprecedented joint statement among eight national sisters' organizations in response to Pope Paul VI's "Declaration on Women in the Ministerial Priesthood."[35] This papal letter, issued 15 October 1976, stated that women could not be ordained since they did not image the maleness of Christ. In response, the network, Sisters Uniting, under the leadership of Iglesias, rejected "the theological reasoning in equating the humanism of Jesus and the risen Christ with maleness."[36] They understood that divinity goes beyond male physiology. In reflecting on the WOC's decision to push for women's ordination rather than leave the Church, Isasi-Díaz stated, "We had no choice but to try and impact the institution, as it is an intrinsic part of our culture."[37]

Las Hermanas turned to PADRES for financial support in sending more Latina representation to the second national WOC in Baltimore. Although PADRES did not want to support the WOC directly, they willingly supported "the participation of grassroots Hispanic women in the WOC by donation to *Las Hermanas*."[38] With additional fund-raising efforts, Las Hermanas sponsored 200 grassroots Chicanas/Latinas, increasing the percentage of women of color attending the WOC in 1978.[39]

PADRES's unwillingness to explicitly support women's ordination reflected the patriarchal limitations its members accepted as clergy. As Clarita Trujillo stated, "PADRES simply had to measure their words, they were not as free to speak out."[40] Despite these constraints, PADRES made small but frequent financial contributions to Las Hermanas. According to one PADRES leader, "Among us could be found those with a real desire to work together with our sisters knowing constantly that we were forging new ground."[41]

A long-term collaboration between PADRES and Las Hermanas never materialized. An attitude of male dominance continued to plague PADRES, as individual members simply could not accept the Hermanas as equals.[42] Aspirations for upward mobility in the hierarchy of the Church for some PADRES prevented them from endorsing fully the equal status of women in the Church. As Clarita Trujillo pointed out, "They were in a very vulnerable position and we were strong women who did not mince our words."[43]

Relationships between individual members of Las Hermanas and PADRES varied. Clearly Las Hermanas found individual members truly supportive, although the clerical organization as a whole was too enmeshed in the trappings of a patriarchal Church and culture. PADRES's desire for institutional mobility and the contention that it would have more clout as a clerical organization limited the extent of PADRES's support for women.[44]

The gender conflict does not detract from the reality that Las Hermanas and PADRES led the Chicano/Latino movement for change within the Catholic Church. Their public presence as working partners was crucial to the overall goal of institutional accountability. Unfortunately, a serious break in these efforts occurred at MACC by 1979.

Las Hermanas and MACC

Since 1972 Las Hermanas and PADRES worked to establish MACC as the first national pastoral center for training in the religious and socio-political needs of Chicano/Latino Catholics. However, as feminist theory and theology informed the consciousness of Las Hermanas, its presence at MACC became problematic.

As director of the language institute from 1974 to 1976, Sylvia Sedillo standardized the use of inclusive language in the curriculum and liturgies. Interacting with the Latin American scholars at MACC gave Sedillo the opportunity to challenge them on gender issues, then absent in liberation theology. Sedillo recalls:

> Any time I heard about our people being oppressed, I would say, "As a woman, I feel it twice." Gustavo Gutiérrez used to tell me the issues I raised belonged to a white women's agenda. I would tell him, "But I am not white." I was not quiet about feminism at MACC.[45]

Sedillo agrees that Gutiérrez "did come around" in his use of inclusive language. She remembers proudly her attendance in 1980 at a lecture and liturgy in Lima, Peru, where Gutiérrez made a conscious effort to adopt liturgical language inclusive of men and women.[46]

Women at MACC experienced a double standard in relation to domestic responsibilities. Sedillo recalled a particularly poignant example. As the cook's day off approached, the female staff of MACC had to sign up for cooking duties. When Sedillo questioned the procedure, she was told that the male directors did not have time to cook! Her refusal to accept the prescribed gender role led to some of the men helping in the kitchen and also to a significant amount of tension. "It became very uncomfortable for me, very tense. If things had been more accepted I would have stayed longer. It was just too hard."[47] Other Hermanas vocal about feminist praxis found it hard to stay for long periods of time at MACC. According to Yolanda Tarango, "Many of us were fired or forced to leave."[48]

By 1979 the tensions between Las Hermanas and MACC became insurmountable. Having served on the board and faculty of MACC since its inception, Las Hermanas representative María Iglesias was quite shocked when MACC notified her that she was terminated from the board of directors.[49] When she asked for a written explanation, MACC's executive officer, Ricardo Ramírez, responded that a change in the bylaws now required the election of board members. This change coincided with the expiration of Iglesias's term; however, Ramírez stated that suggested nominations would be welcomed.[50] Las Hermanas representation on MACC's board was no longer guaranteed. Within one month of Ramírez's explanation, Las Hermanas nominated three women for MACC's board, Clarita Trujillo, Teresita Basso, and Carolyn López, all quite familiar with the history of MACC. Shortly after, Las Hermanas National Coordinator Margarita Castañeda received notification that "the board [of MACC] decided to maintain its present policy which does not allow for representation from any organization."[51] While individuals belonging to Las Hermanas could serve on the board, the organization would no longer have representation. Understandably, Las Hermanas felt the action to be underhanded and a tactic "to hand pick" board members.[52] After almost a decade of service to the center, Las Hermanas found themselves excluded from what they had helped build. Clarita Trujillo expresses the underlying dynamics: "If the women are strong and speak out they don't want to be heard. They sweat and build but do not get the credit. The easiest thing is to remove them."[53] Significantly, the dismissal followed Las Hermanas's unanimous board decision in August 1977 "to challenge MACC in its evaluations, personnel policies, openness to the poor, curriculum, programs and the implementing of the MACC philosophy."[54] Margarita Castañeda describes the impact that the rupture between Las Hermanas and MACC continues to have: "In the 1970s our level of consciousness was being raised that the Church was a male and hierarchical system we were engaged in. We were put down and even told that we were crazy! It was extremely disappointing. At this point it is like a divorce."[55] Despite the difficulties at MACC, individual Hermanas continued to offer their services as faculty, recognizing the impact they could have in the area of training. In 1983 Rosa Martha Zárate, María Carolina Flores, Jo Marie Arredondo, and María de Jesús Ybarra taught courses dealing with Latina spirituality, music, and leadership development. Las Hermanas members at MACC would not run into conflict with the administration again until 1985.

In 1983 Yolanda Tarango returned to MACC to direct its pastoral program. The importance of the center and its international stature convinced Tarango to attempt another visible presence of Las Hermanas at MACC. A literature series organized by Tarango the summer of 1984 included Chicana feminist writers Sandra Cisneros and Cherríe Moraga. Cisneros had recently relocated to San Antonio, and Tarango seized the opportunity to invite her to MACC. Moraga had just published *Loving in the War Years,* a

collection of writings exploring the political and personal meaning of being a Chicana lesbian. After the women read from their
works, several seminarians and priests studying at MACC raised
serious concern about lesbian issues being discussed at a Catholic
pastoral center.[56]

That same summer a group of women students from the Graduate Theological Union at Berkeley chose to study Spanish at
MACC. They brought with them their feminist understandings of
liturgy. Tarango joined in their planning a Eucharistic celebration
at MACC that included the traditional role for a priest, but with
increased participation for women. Again, this event "was highly
criticized" by unsympathetic seminarians and priests studying at
MACC.[57] Shortly after the Eucharist celebration, Tarango was
unexpectedly and without explanation terminated. She believes
strongly that the reaction by the clerics led to her dismissal from
the staff. When challenged, her superiors at MACC explained that
financial restraints required her to be terminated. Yet, after two
years of work Tarango had increased the enrollment of the pastoral program, "which generated the most funds at MACC."[58]
Tarango has never been given an adequate explanation for her
dismissal.

Since her departure from MACC, Tarango has co-founded Visitation House in San Antonio, a transitional residence for bat-
tered and homeless women and their children. She has directed an
adult religious education program for a six-parish cooperative, co-
authored *Hispanic Women: Prophetic Voice in the Church*, and written numerous articles on Latinas and spirituality.[59] She is currently
earning a doctorate in ministry from Austin Presbyterian Theological Seminary. According to Tarango, her "chief vocation is the education and liberation of women within the Catholic Church . . .
[where] laity, especially women, have always been treated as children."[60] Her experience at MACC has not deterred her from this
vocation.

Latina Feminists Confronting Sanctified Patriarchy

Las Hermanas and PADRES brought together very strong and
dedicated women and men. They joined forces not only in the
creation of a center for Chicano/Latino ministry, but in an entire
movement for change in the Catholic Church.

When asked why Latina feminists would bother with the Roman Catholic Church, Ada María Isasi-Díaz and Yolanda Tarango have responded: "The church sanctions—justifies—patriarchy in society by being itself a patriarchal structure . . . If the church were to denounce patriarchy, it would be an important moment in the process of the liberation of women."[61] Las Hermanas understood that it would take women to continually pressure the Church to transform its unjust doctrines and structure. Their commitment to the empowerment of grassroots Latinas, combined with their own faith in a God of justice, led Las Hermanas to continue its struggle against the sexism inherent in the Church's structure. The desire to remain within their religious tradition combined with a sense of entitlement compelled these women to stay.

Las Hermanas confronted the "patriarchy par excellence" in March 1985, when the United States Catholic Conference of Bishops convoked public hearings in Washington, D.C., on the concerns of women in the Church in order to formulate a pastoral letter. The bishops invited Las Hermanas representatives to speak on behalf of Latina Catholics. Hermanas members Beatriz Díaz-Taveras, Terry Garza, Ada María Isasi-Díaz, and Carmen Villegas seized the opportunity to educate the bishops on the social realities of Latinas. Villegas began her address to the committee of six bishops and eight women consultants by quoting the liberationist martyr, Msgr. Oscar Romero of El Salvador, "I am the voice of the voiceless."[62] Each woman then took her turn describing the specific struggles she faced. Díaz-Taveras spoke as a young single Catholic woman who received no education about her sexuality; Garza gave testimony as a divorced woman and mother who experienced alienation in the Church; and Villegas spoke for women who have lost their children to drugs and who lack pastoral counseling. Collectively they declared their "commitment to work in the church so that other Latinas would not experience the oppression they have lived in the church."[63] With a dramatic closing, they assured the bishops that Latinas would not be silenced. Each Hermana placed a stone in front of each bishop and said:

> We have asked for bread and you have given us stones. If you truly desire a reconciliation without repentance, place the stones on your altars when you celebrate the Eucharist and remember the His-

panic women who are fighting for the liberation of our people and for our own liberation.[64]

The experience of challenging the authority figures of the institutional Church proved extremely empowering for the women:

> The bishops were very rude to us when we entered the room. After our presentation they said to us, "Why are you in the church?" I replied, "We stay to fight!" When we were done, we left and embraced each other and cried. Since we were little girls we had been trained not to question the bastions of power in the church. It was very empowering![65]

Las Hermanas played a significant role in dismantling the patriarchal endeavor to speak for women. Over the next several months, Catholic women across the country criticized the bishops, who ultimately abandoned their intent to write a pastoral letter about and for women.[66]

Las Hermanas and the III Encuentro

The mid-1980s witnessed Las Hermanas pushing further for a Latino Catholic commitment to the equal status of women. In 1983 the United States Catholic Conference of Bishops approved the pastoral letter, *The Hispanic Presence: Challenge and Commitment.* The document called for a third encuentro and the writing of a national pastoral plan for Latino ministry.[67] Since Latino/a laity and religious leaders had convoked the two previous encuentros, the third encuentro marked formal episcopal recognition of the Latino Catholic presence. Las Hermanas, however, criticized the bishops' call for another encuentro, as the recommendations from the II Encuentro had yet to be implemented.[68] Some members also criticized an encuentro "under the watchful eyes of dozens of U.S. bishops."[69] While institutional validation might appear as advancement in the struggle for recognition and respect, for some it meant closer scrutiny that would diminish the voices of grassroots communities. Thus, the members of Las Hermanas taking leadership in the III Encuentro did so as individuals and not as representatives of the organization. Nonetheless, their consciousness as Hermanas influenced their participation.

With two years to prepare, members of Las Hermanas and PADRES, and directors of the regional pastoral offices, organized the encuentro first on a local level in parishes throughout the country. Hermanas Consuelo Tovar, Elisa Rodríguez, Olga Villa, Dolorita Martínez, Carmen Villegas, María de Jesús Ybarra, Rosa Martha Zárate, and Dominga Zapata assumed pivotal roles in the planning and implementation of the III Encuentro. Juan Romero of PADRES undertook the responsibilities of national coordinator and Consuelo Tovar of Las Hermanas accepted the position of national chairperson.[70] As members of either the Executive Committee or the National Promotion Team, each representative organized the participation of an entire state and/or region.

National Chairperson Consuelo Tovar grew up in San Antonio, where she worked closely with Communities Organized for Public Service (COPS).[71] She applied her organizing experience with COPS to the encuentro process. Her commitment to community participation led Tovar to say, "many of the bishops who called for it may not quite realize what they have by the tail."[72] Elisa Rodríguez, who organized Oklahoma and Texas, describes the process the women undertook:

> We met first with the bishops to obtain the authority to organize in his diocese. As many had called for it they couldn't turn us away. Then we met with the parish priests. Most of them challenged us. They said it would be a waste of our time. But if we had the bishop's approval we went ahead and organized the parish. We worked very hard with the grassroots laity. We were mostly sisters and laywomen.[73]

National Coordinator Juan Romero remarked on the "Impressive leadership abilities" demonstrated by the Hermanas.[74] The commitment to grassroots community participation motivated their activism.

The encuentro process modeled a participatory and egalitarian Church, characteristics marking a unique contribution of Latinos/as to the wider Church. Influenced by the comunidades eclesiales de base of Latin America but contextualized for U.S. Latino realities, small grassroots networks developed to transform a hierarchical model of church. These small church groups could address and act upon their social realities guided by Christian faith.[75] Thirty thousand Latinos participated in comunidades eclesiales de base across the nation in preparation for the III Encuentro. Facilitators made a concerted effort to hear the voices of Latinos alienated from the institutional Church. Priorities took shape around youth ministry, leadership formation, culturally relevant training for pastoral workers, and a greater role of the Church in the social realities of Latinos. Delegates from each region presented these priorities at the national encuentro. The model required collaboration and critical reflection on every level.[76]

Approximately 1,200 delegates representing 133 dioceses attended the III Encuentro in August 1985 in Washington, D.C. Most witnessed a radically different way of what it means to be church.[77] An international team under the direction of Fr. José Marins and Sister Teolide Trevisán of Brazil and Sister Carolee Chanona of Belize coordinated the on-site national process. In addition, a national team consisting of Fr. George Crespín, a Chicano; María Luisa Gastón, a Cuban American laywoman; and Fr. Domingo Rodríguez, a Puerto Rican, worked closely with the Latin Americans.[78]

Three days before the third encuentro convened, Las Hermanas held its annual conference in Washington, D.C., entitled, "*Hacia El Tercer Encuentro*" [Toward the III Encuentro]. Recognizing the importance of the III *Encuentro* in setting the agenda for Latino/a Catholics in the next century, Las Hermanas sought "to contribute the perspective of *la mujer Hispana* to the process."[79] According to Ada María Isasi-Díaz, "We did not think that a radical perspective was going to be present."[80] At regional meetings prior to the Las Hermanas conference in D.C., members solicited the opinions of Latina Catholics across the United States on issues ranging from domestic violence, sexual abuse, dual wage systems, and the exclusion of women from the priesthood.[81] Following these regional meetings Las Hermanas reported:

> We constitute the majority of the lowest level of the economic scale of this society; we suffer the highest percentage of domestic violence at the hands of our husbands, lovers, fathers and even sons; a high percentage of the women raped are Hispanic; we are the heads of family in a growing number of homes and are the only ones responsible for our children. Many of us have to work outside of the home where we receive only fifty-nine cents for every dollar that men receive for the same work. When we arrive home, we begin a second shift of work in the same day.[82]

According to data from 1980, Latinas earned less than Anglo women in the same occupations and predominated in clerical, factory, and service work.[83] In 1985, 23 percent of Latino families were headed by women, and 56 percent of these families lived below the poverty level.[84] Women of all races were vulnerable to violence at the hands of an intimate, yet women in families with incomes below the poverty line were more likely than other women to suffer violence at the hands of a family member.[85] Latinos experienced violent crimes, including rape, at a higher percentage (38.1 percent) than non-Latinos (30.5 percent).[86] Las Hermanas clearly intended that the concrete reality of Latinas be reflected in the national pastoral plan resulting from the III Encuentro.

Las Hermanas understood that the rapidly increasing Latino demographics in the United States (twenty million in 1985) and their growing majority in the Catholic Church amplified "the enormous responsibility on *la mujer Hispana* who have the responsibility as women and as mothers to provide sexual education and prenatal care, etc."[87] Their significance to the local church, as volunteer committee members, as religious educators for youth, and as the primary transmitters of the faith in their families, justified their demands for equal status. "The Church praises the woman but does not permit us to fully participate in its ministry, excluding us not only from the priesthood but from the permanent diaconate."[88]

By the time the bishops convoked the III Encuentro, many of the women in attendance had discussed in-depth, through the support of Las Hermanas, the socioeconomic and religious reality of Latinas. The III Encuentro included very politicized women, women who participated as voting delegates, staff, press, musicians, and invited guests.[89]

In the actual proceedings of this encuentro, a vote by consensus approved several progressive pastoral guidelines based on the priorities of the regional groups.[90] The initial proposed guidelines, however, did not mention women. It was only after the first session at the encuentro that discussion groups submitted a guideline on women. For many in the voting body, the wording of the guideline implied women's ordination: "We as Hispanic people want to follow a thrust that values and promotes women *at all levels* in the Church and in society."[91] Although at least 70 percent of the delegates voted in favor of the guideline, those facilitating the process rejected the final tally due to a lack of full consensus.[92] For facilitator María Luisa Gastón, the decision was a judgment call. "We had to be true to a process that had agreed upon a show of consensus."[93] For Las Hermanas, reconciling the difference between the majority victory and a consensus proved problematic. According to Isasi-Díaz, "It was never explained that consensus meant 100 percent agreement, which was never reached on any vote!"[94]

Ensuing pandemonium led to outright protest. "It was a very telling moment. We felt we had won a vote and it had been taken away . . . a tremendous injustice had been done."[95] After an intense explosion of anger and disbelief, several women convened a brief strategy meeting. The next morning an estimated 500 women demonstrated outside of the national cathedral. They chose to say the rosary as they marched, incorporating prayers of justice for women between the decades of the rosary.[96] Carmen Villegas, who led the prayers, explained their action:

> There were some women who wanted to take more radical action, like covering all the female statues in the national cathedral. That would have only turned people against us for any possible revisions. I asked them to remember how much support we did have, and that the majority voted for us.[97]

Following the demonstration, the entire encuentro reconvened in small groups to discuss how to revise the guideline. According to Gastón, five halls of approximately 250 people each met. These large groups were divided into smaller groups to ensure that everyone's voice would be heard.

The body eventually approved the following revision: "We as Hispanic people wish to follow a thrust of valuing and promoting women, recognizing her equality and dignity, and her role in the Church, the family, and society."[98] This more general statement about women satisfied those fearful of women's ordination. It also alludes to prescribed gender roles and assumes a woman's place in the home.

The conflict over ordination did not come as a complete surprise to some of the clergy attending. Juan Romero pointed out that an event convoked by the bishops could not support anything implying women's ordination.[99] Two bishops during the encuentro confirmed this as they "warned delegates of Vatican opposition."[100]

In retrospect, María Luisa Gastón, now an active member of Las Hermanas, wishes she had participated in the process of reflection held by the organization prior to the encuentro. "If I had been imbued with their perspective I could have contributed that dimension to the planning and decision-making process of the facilitating team. We were all caught up in the process, yet I still believe we [the team] acted with integrity."[101]

Many of the original goals of Las Hermanas can be found in the final National Pastoral Plan, such as leadership formation, culturally sensitive vocation programs, the training of pastoral agents, and representation of "the voice of the people." The status of women, however, remained sorely ignored in the bishops' final drafts. According to Carmen Villegas, who attended a National Advisory Committee (NAC) meeting on the drafting of the national plan, "We do not have even a full page in the document, we are only a small part of the section of the family.[102] Clearly the bishops were most comfortable with women remaining at home.

The disappointment experienced at the III Encuentro did not deter Las Hermanas but deepened its members' resolve to move forward on a feminist agenda. In reflecting on the course of events, Las Hermanas coordinators stated, "[They] have affirmed us in strengthening our commitment to work tirelessly for justice both in the Church and society, especially for women.[103] Under the leadership of Yolanda Tarango, María Teresa Garza, and Carmen Villages following the III Encuentro, the organization continued in its advisory capacity to the United States Catholic Conference-Secretariat for Hispanic Affairs, increased its involvement with international and national women's organizations, and distributed more information on the collective patterns of oppression facing women worldwide.[104] Las Hermanas groups at the local level increased following the III Encuentro, particularly in the Northeast including East Harlem, Paterson, New Jersey, Brooklyn, the West Bronx, and West Manhattan. These small local groups met once a month to discuss women's personal and neighborhood concerns. Meetings also included prayer and ritual celebration of womanhood.[105]

By January 1986, Las Hermanas drafted specific proposals addressed to the U.S. bishops concerning the participation of the "la mujer hispana" in the church. Las Hermanas requested a commitment of resources for Latinas to develop programs on issues of sexuality, social political realities, and religion.[106] Emphasizing the need "to reclaim our sexuality as an integral part of being women," Las Hermanas challenged the bishops to denounce domestic violence from the pulpit and to instruct Latino priests "to stop advising women to suffer silently all types of abuse and infidelity . . . for the good of their children."[107]

A 1989 revision in the *Constitution and Statutes of Las Hermanas* claried further the decision to advocate specifically for the rights of Latinas: "The expressed priority of the organization is the promotion of the Hispanic woman. *Las Hermanas* will develop their work both in the Church and in society."[108]

Las Hermanas renewed its commitment to the self-determination of Latinas within and beyond the boundaries of the institutional Church. The ecclesial power structure, however, often found ways to undermine the advancements that individual Hermanas made, even at the expense of the larger Chicano/Latino Catholic community. The following experiences of Sara Murrieta and Rosa Martha Zárate exemplify the obstacles placed in the paths of strong and vocal women and highlights further the gender politics in the Church.

Gender Politics: The Cases of Sara Murrieta and Rosa Martha Zárate

Sister Sara Murrieta, a Chicana from the Los Angeles area, and Sister Rosa Martha Zárate, a Mexicana/Chicana originally from Guadalajara, Mexico, successfully administered pastoral programs, making San Diego and San Bernardino "hotbeds" for new developments in Chicano ministry. In 1973 Zárate began organizing comunidades eclesiales de base and schools of ministry in the San Diego diocese. A year later, Murrieta began an eleven-year term as director of the Padre Hidalgo Center located in Barrio Logan, a Chicano community in San Diego.

The Padre Hidalgo Center served as headquarters for the Roman Catholic Community Services. The center offered legal assistance, leadership training, English-language classes, job training, and parenting classes to a large Chicano/Mexicano community. The center also served as an early site for Latin American liberation theologians and pastoral workers to share their knowledge and experiences with U.S. Latino Catholics. According to Zárate, "Liberation theology was teaching us to go beyond prayer."[109] A school of ministry offered "integral education" to prepare Chicano laity for involvement in their community and the Church.[110]

Initially under the leadership of Fr. Juan Hurtado, the center opened in 1972 as a response to the challenges raised by Católicos por la Raza in San Diego. Several Chicano priests, including Patricio and Manuel Guillen, Juan Hurtado, Peter Luque, Adolfo Chávez, and Gilbert Chávez, suggested the center as a concrete way for the Church to strengthen its services to Chicanos.[111] The appointment of Sara Murrieta as director of the center in 1974, by the second Chicano bishop, Gilbert Chávez, marked a twofold step forward. Chávez's commitment to Chicanos and the poor and oppressed showed in Murrieta's appointment.[112] In Murrieta's words, "One of the oppressed groups in the Catholic Church is the women . . . and by naming me to this position, Msgr. Chávez has demonstrated that he means what he says."[113]

Under the leadership of Murrieta and a staff of twelve, the center expanded its programs targeting Chicanas and Mexicanas for job training. The center collaborated with Organización Femenil, and with government funding the Spanish Speaking Women's Training Program prepared women for employment in clerical and managerial positions. Over a ten-year period, 900 women graduated with viable employment opportunities in companies such as Pacific Telephone, Bank of America, and San Diego Gas & Electric. Often, the program was a stepping stone for women to pursue advanced education.[114] Besides job training, Murrieta led the center in the development of leaders for the community and the Church. "It was a place where we convoked the community and where many people went for consciousness-raising. It was a new paradigm of church."[115]

Involvement in direct community action characterized Murrieta's leadership. In 1981, the Chicano community newspaper, *La Prensa*, acknowledged her commitments:

> Her religion is manifested in her actions in the barrios, in the streets of our Chicano communities . . . helping those who need it the most has propelled Sister Sara Murrieta into a leadership role in our community that no Priest, Bishop, or Cardinal could possibly have. . . . We honor her for it."[116]

The communities' gratitude for an active religious leader threatened the Church hierarchy. The public role that Murrieta achieved and the new paradigm of church she and her staff created ultimately led to her displacement from the institutional Church.

In late February 1983, Murrieta received a telephone call from Bishop Chávez notifying her that starting 1 March 1983, there would be two co-directors for the Padre Hidalgo Center. Enrique Méndez, a native of Puebla, Mexico, would share the administration of the center.[117] Murrieta's responsibilities would be limited to finance and maintenance, assisting the women's employment program, job referrals, and immigration referral assistance, areas that would keep her close to the center. Méndez, assisted by Fr. Luis Bernal, would be organizing a ministry program to federal, county, and city jails in the diocese, developing a service program to undocumented workers, and coordinating the documentation for a Pastoral Plan for Hispanics.[118] Méndez, who had worked as a pastoral specialist at the center for ten years, felt very saddened by the reassignments. "I saw that it was very hard for Sister Sara to accept any limitations on her work with the community."[119] Murrieta remained at the center until 29 July 1983, when she resigned after eleven years of service.

Displacement did not deter Murrieta from continuing her work with the community. In September 1983, she marched with 500 Chicanos, including the Committee on Chicano Rights, El Centro Cultural de la Raza, the Lawyers Guild, and the Mexican American Political Association, to protest the proposed Simpson–Mazzoli Immigration bill.[120] As the marchers waited in vain for the approval of the local priest, Murrieta took matters into her own hands and blessed them as they departed.[121] Her action did not go unrecognized by the local press. La Prensa acknowledged Murrieta as the "only Catholic insider who supported La Marcha wholeheartedly . . . other priests left much to be desired in the matter of guts, integrity, and support of people."[122]

Murrieta's resignation can be understood within the broader efforts of the Vatican to monitor powerful women *and* the spread of liberation theology. With the 1984 publication of "Instruction on Certain Aspects of the 'Theology of Liberation,'" the papacy hindered worldwide progress of an institutionalized preferential option for the poor. Murrieta's political vision of the Church and her courage to go beyond prescribed gender roles threatened the power structure of a Church operating with clear boundaries of authority and established economic alliances. According to Murrieta, the limitations sapped the energy fermenting in the local Chicano/Latino Church. She explains: "If they had allowed us to continue, we would have changed the economic and power structure of the Church just as sisters had changed the educational system in previous years. This was too threatening."[123]

Murrieta believes that if the momentum among the religious leaders had not been curtailed, her work and that of other women and a few priests would have radically changed the model of the U.S. Church, at least on the local level. Liberation theology essentially demands that the Church change sides, from supporting the interests of the wealthy to supporting the interests of the poor. According to Lilia López, who assisted Murrieta in the administration of the Hidalgo Center, "It was Sara's political vision that the bishop could not support. We were strong women helping the people."[124] López also had to leave the Hidalgo Center two years after Murrieta. The funding for the job-training program was not renewed. Murrieta has remained a woman religious to the present day primarily due to the affirmation received from her religious order, the Community of the Holy Spirit. She now administers health education programs in the Los Angeles area.

During the time that Murrieta directed the center, Sister Rosa Martha Zárate worked as the first coordinator of the Office of Religious Education for the Spanish Speaking in the diocese of San Diego. Zárate and Murrieta collaborated on a model of team ministry that Bishop Chávez specifically called for shortly after his own appointment. Convening for a week-long retreat in San Diego, Chávez and his team worked out a *Plan Pastoral* calling for the establishment of comunidades eclesiales de base and schools of ministry to train lay leaders throughout the diocese.[125] According to Fr. Patricio Guillen, who participated in the retreat, Bishop Chávez wanted the schools of ministry "because even if we do have comunidades de base, if the people are not educated, they will not really be in charge of this. It will continue to be paternalistic."[126]

Enduring the criticism of her religious community, yet with the approval of Bishop Chávez, Zárate set out to organize comunidades eclesiales de base throughout the diocese, which at the time covered San Diego, Imperial Valley, Riverside, and San Bernardino counties.[127] With no support staff and few resources, Zárate had her work cut out for her. Latinos comprised 52 percent of the approximately 400,000 Catholics in a diocese spread out over 160 parishes.[128] In comparison, a diocesan staff of eight attended to the needs of Euroamerican Catholics.[129] No services existed specifically for African American or Asian American Catholics. Zárate remembers, "I was working very hard, organizing the people. I would drive from Calexico to Coachella Valley, Barstow, Victorville, San Bernardino, and Ontario. All the leadership was emerging from the comunidades eclesiales de base."[130]

Informed by liberation theology, Zárate's vision for the small Christian communities expanded the traditional meaning of catechism or religious education. Comunidades eclesiales de base could educate entire families on their social reality, promote viable solutions, and enable self-determination. Participants could help renovate the Church on all levels. By 1976 Rosa Martha organized twenty-seven comunidades eclesiales de base throughout the diocese.[131] In addition, she shared in the teaching responsibilities for the schools of ministry that sought to provide theological training for grassroots communities. Fundamental to the training was the belief and experience that the people create church. A new paradigm of church was in the making, "*una iglesia popular*" (a church of the people).[132]

In 1978 when the San Bernardino diocese formed, Zárate became coordinator of the Department of Religious Education for the Spanish Speaking (Departamento de Evangelización y Catequises Hispana, DECH) along with Fr. Patricio Guillen. Under their leadership the DECH sought to address social injustice as well as the spiritual needs of Latino Catholics. Zárate continued her work with the small church communities, organized additional schools of ministry, developed youth groups and choirs, coordinated a diocesan pastoral plan for Latino ministry, and developed the first national guidelines for the certification of Spanish-speaking catechists.[133] Prior to the certification process, Latinas provided religious education to children after school, yet received no official recognition or validation from the institutional Church.

By 1985 forty-five comunidades eclesiales de base existed in the San Bernardino diocese, involving families, businesses, parishes, and neighborhoods; five pastoral centers had been established.[134] Participants ranged from sixty-year-old Eliseo Viyera, who focused on assistance to farmworkers, to eighteen-year-old Carmen Adame, who helped Zárate organize young adult choirs.[135] When the III Encuentro convened in 1985, the San Bernardino diocese was "far advanced of most dioceses in its Hispanic ministry."[136]

More conservative elements in the Church soon attacked the work of Sister Zárate and Fr. Guillen. The DECH appeared too revolutionary for those clergy unwilling to accept the ramifications of liberation theology, for example, communities grasping their own power. By July 1985 several pastors branded both Zárate and Guillen "communists" and demanded an investigation of the DECH administration.[137] Rumors brought into question Zárate's status as a woman religious.[138]

A blue ribbon commission selected by Bishop Straling reviewed the complaints and found no evidence for the accusations. They recommended that the bishop affirm "the good work DECH has accomplished to date."[139] Despite the recommendation, "negotiations" to resolve the dispute took place, none of which permitted Zárate to speak on her own behalf.[140]

> The political orientation of the base communities frightened these priests. They were our allies until we got too close to their parishes and they began to see the effects of the base communities. I was told I had too much influence in their parishes. I was found guilty without being present or being able to defend myself.[141]

Even though the diocesan pastoral plan called for the establishment of base communities, the effectiveness in politicizing the people proved too threatening to the status quo.

In 1986 Bishop Straling asked for the dismissal of Zárate and pressured Guillen for a voluntary resignation. A newly created Hispanic Ministry Board and Advisory Committee on Hispanic Affairs would oversee the work of the DECH in the future. Following a six-month sabbatical, Zárate could return to work in a parish of the diocese, and Guillen could work full-time for PADRES.[142]

The promise of continued employment in the Church never materialized. Parish pastor Fr. Luque denied Zárate her job when she returned from her sabbatical, and PADRES could not provide full-time employment for Guillen. After a long period of depression, Zárate filed probably the first civil lawsuit against a Roman Catholic diocese and bishop. Charging wrongful termination and defamation of character, Zárate sued the diocese for $1.5 million. Her religious community in Mexico notified her that she was being expelled, despite her unwillingness to break her commitment as a woman religious. Zárate never signed the letter of expulsion and continues to consider herself a religious sister. In her words, "I have nothing against being a sister, I am just not submissive or a nice little sister who is going to obey all the rules."[143]

In 1992 Zárate lost the lawsuit based on the determination that "the case had to do with internal Church affairs."[144] In retrospect, Fr. Guillen observed that

> Sister Zárate experienced more than anyone else the greater brunt of the rejection on the part of the Church. We learned that the Church can never, as an institutionalized entity, really embrace the [people's] movements because it is too much a part of the problem.[145]

This harsh realization has only strengthened Zárate and Guillen to continue their work among the community, but on their own terms.

Zárate and Guillen currently co-direct CALPULLI, a network of small base communities in San Bernardino, California. Modeled after the communal ideals of Mesoamerican indigenous communities, CALPULLI seeks empowerment for the poor through neighborhood organizing. CALPULLI offers English-language instruction, immigrant rights counseling, and health care education. Fundamental to CALPULLI is an integration of Christian faith and Mesoamerican indigenous spirituality. This mestizaje expresses a theology based on a God of justice rooted in the land and symbols of native Mesoamerican ancestors. In 1992 CALPULLI helped to sponsor the Peace and Dignity Journey, a spiritual run from Alaska to Argentina, commemorating 500 years of resistance by the native peoples of the entire continent.

Zárate involves herself directly with the indigenous movements for human rights in the United States and Latin America. She has served as a human rights observer to the Zapatista movement in Chiapas, Mexico, and she aids indigenous women in that state in developing textile cooperatives. She also helps to organize retired Mexican laborers in their suit against the U.S. and Mexican governments for the loss of wages during the bracero program in the 1940s and 1950s. Zarate coordinates chapters of Alizanza Braceroproa in San Bernardino and in Ameca, Jalisco, traveling extensively to strengthen support for the thousands of workers denied their earned wages. Amid all her commitments Zárate continues to compose, sing, and record *nueva canción*, reflecting her ongoing courage and stamina to fight against injustice.[146] For example, her singing provided moral support to the Zapatistas in 1995 at their international conference on neo-liberalism in Chiapas.

The experiences of Rosa Martha Zárate and Sara Murrieta exemplify the barriers placed in the path of women who dare to put into reality a model of church where the poor and oppressed have a voice. Their efforts placed them "between service to our own people, and the demands and expectations of the official church; between developing our own leadership and thereby threatening the established leadership."[147] Tragically, their stories are not isolated cases. The same year that Murrieta received her reassignment, Sister Alicia Salcido was fired from the San Diego diocese and two other women left the Padre Hidalgo Center.[148] As Zárate lost her position at the DECH, Sister Elisa Rodríguez received only a few days' notification to cease operation of the Southwest office for the Spanish-speaking housed at MACC in San Antonio.[149] In 1986 *Informes* stated that "each year we hear of an increasing number of Hispanic women who are 'dismissed' from their current ministry positions. Rarely is this due to incompetence."[150] Murrieta likened the exodus of women to the dissipation of King Arthur and his round table. "It was like Camelot, it is now all gone. By getting rid of the women, they got rid of the ferment, the energy that was building."[151] Rather than allow the institution to squash their spirits and confidence, the leaders of Las Hermanas reminded the women that

> the story of *Las Hermanas* is one of *mujeres valientes*—"courageous women who simply do what needs to be done at every level of society." Let us then enter the New Year with a strong sense of our collective strength. Let us use it to transform the world. *Adelante!*[152]

Collectively Las Hermanas members once again renewed their willingness to face the challenges confronting them as Latina Catholic feminists.

Las Hermanas and the Women-Church Movement

Besides battling for self-determination as Latinas in the Church, Las Hermanas took on the challenge of confronting the Women-

Church movement on its own patterns of ethnic/racial exclusion. The Women-Church movement grew out of the WOC and presented a broad-based effort of predominantly Euroamerican Catholics committed to creating church through a feminist lens.[153] Las Hermanas tirelessly brought the issue of race to the dialogue. A brief history of Las Hermanas's involvement with the Women-Church movement will help to explain its decision to withdraw in the early 1990s.[154]

Las Hermanas participated in the WOC from its inception in 1975, when 1,200 women gathered in Detroit for the "Women in Future Priesthood Now—A Call to Action" conference to discuss women's ordination in the Roman Catholic Church.[155] Las Hermanas immediately saw the need to challenge the WOC on its practices of ethnic/racial exclusion. Refusing "co-optation into a predetermined agenda of the dominant cultural group," Las Hermanas advised the WOC to address the particular realities of Latino communities and the perspective of *mujeres de la base*.[156] María Iglesias explains:

> We were never advocating for women to be ordained in the present clerical structure because for Hispanics it was not lifegiving. We didn't even have men priests. We realized though that if the Anglo women were ordained they would most likely be assigned to Hispanic parishes. We realized that we had to influence them.[157]

As participants in the WOC, Las Hermanas joined with several other Catholic pro-women groups to form the Women of the Church Coalition (WCC).[158] In the light of the Vatican's hardening position against women's ordination, members of the WCC decided not only to focus on ordination, but also to dialogue on building autonomous "feminist communities of faith and praxis."[159] As plans for a third WOC national meeting disintegrated, Las Hermanas, along with several members of the WCC, decided in 1983 to sponsor the first national Woman Church Conference, "From Generation to Generation: Woman Church Speaks." The agenda focused on feminist models of church and issues of justice and spirituality. In the conference statement titled "From Hispanic Women," Las Hermanas representatives spoke forcefully: "Hispanic understandings, customs, history . . . spirituality must be an intrinsic part of WOMAN CHURCH [as well as] the active participation of our black, indigenous and Asian

American sisters."[160] Las Hermanas members Ada María Isasi-Díaz, Margarita Castañeda, Aurora Camacho de Schmidt, Yolanda Tarango, and Carmen Rios spoke to the 2,000 women in attendance.[161] Soon after this successful gathering in Chicago, the members of the WCC decided to reformalize their coalition under the name Women-Church Convergence.[162] Las Hermanas remained a member of the convergence; however, as plans evolved for a second national conference in 1987, the issue of racial and ethnic inclusivity in the WCC was still not being taken seriously. Unfortunately, this resulted in intense conflict. As the only woman of color on the program committee for the 1987 conference, Ada María Isasi-Díaz recruited two other women, Terry Hamilton and Altagracia Perez Maceira, to assist her in bringing nonwhite perspectives to the planning process.[163] By March 1987, however, the three women felt compelled to resign from their positions due to the inability of the larger planning group to take seriously their concerns as women of color. Their entire program proposal had been rejected. In a letter informing the Las Hermanas national coordinators, Isasi-Díaz wrote:

> We believe this group [Women-Church Conference Planners] does not understand that women of color have the right to contribute to the norm. Our ideas are welcomed only insofar as they can be accommodated within the framework that the women of the dominant culture have set.[164]

Unwilling to serve as "tokens," yet believing in the importance of the Women-Church movement, Las Hermanas chose to retain its membership in the Convergence but withdrew from active participation in the planning of 1987 WCC.[165]

In a subsequent effort to broaden the perspective of the WCC, Las Hermanas and the NARW collaborated in planning the 1993 WCC conference in Albuquerque. Members of both organizations worked hard to provide diverse representation of women, including not only Latinas but African Americans, Asian Americans, Native Americans, lesbians, and Euroamericans. Tess Browne, Mary Peter Bruce, Annette Hernández, and María Elena del Valle worked on the Program Committee. In addition, a joint NAWR–Las Hermanas gathering convened during the conference for "celebration and cross-cultural exchange" at the Laguna Tribal Pueblo Center in Laguna, New Mexico.[166] Despite these efforts, the WCC conference ended with women of color voicing strongly their concerns over inadequate representation, the disregard for sufficient Spanish translations, and a lack of facilitators.[167] The small percentage of women of color felt exploited and overworked.[168] Furthermore, their suggestions for diversifying the program did not end up in the actual conference.[169] In retrospect, Annette Hernández stated, "We felt at times excluded, not respected, our language not honored."[170]

Following the third WCC national meeting in 1993, both Las Hermanas and the NARW opted out of membership in the WCC because of its inability to become more racially and ethnically inclusive.[171] Both the NARW and Las Hermanas felt that the absence of a significant percentage of women of color had gone on too long.[172] Frustration with the WCC's unwillingness "to link racism with sexism and see them as two ways in which patriarchy continues to oppress" led both organizations to dissolve their relationship with the WCC.[173] The pressure placed on the WCC to diversify its leadership met resistance as some WCC members felt that the idea of Women-Church should first expand organically "into non-Euroamerican communities so that groups . . . in these communities could be represented on the board, [then] there would be authentic diversity."[174] The lack of outreach and the failure to include diverse ethnic/racial women in organizational planning appear to have been insurmountable obstacles for the WCC. In 1997 the WCC remained more monocultural than in the previous two decades.[175]

The battle waged in the WCC against silencing the voices of women of color is a familiar one for Latinas involved in predominantly white feminist organizations. The second wave of American feminism witnessed numerous women of color attempting to build coalitions with Euroamerican feminists, only to encounter arrogance, discrimination, and a set agenda separating racism from gender oppression.[176] It is primarily through autonomous feminist organizations led by women of color that Chicanas/Latinas, and most women of color, have been able to address their distinct struggles as working-class women of racial/ethnic minority groups.[177] The relationship between Las Hermanas and the NARW, however, offered a unique example where coalition work can be productive.

Las Hermanas continued to articulate the concerns of Latinas in other women's religious organizations. For example, in 1987 at the national LCWR, Yolanda Tarango challenged "the membership to not merely incorporate *hermanas* into their ranks, but to accept Latinas as a transformative presence within the organization."[178] As a result of the organizing efforts of Las Hermanas, members have achieved leadership positions within several women's religious communities. For example, Yolanda Tarango has served on the executive council of Sisters of the Incarnate Word. Margarita Castañeda serves on the council of the Congregation of Notre Dame, and Lucy Regalado has been president of Our Lady of Victory Missionary Sisters since 1992. Dolorita Martínez has served in leadership in the Sisters of St. Dominic of Grand Rapids, Michigan, and Linda Chávez has been provincial of the Sisters of Charity of Columbus, Ohio. Teresita Basso provides consulting services to Sisters of the Presentation of the Blessed Virgin Mary even though she has left that religious community. In 1992 Anita de Luna assumed the presidency of the LCWR, marking the first time a Latina filled the position.[179] Their presence in the decision-making level of religious communities is a direct result of the challenges that Las Hermanas raised to religious life. Their now visible leadership stands in sharp contrast to the earlier years when Chicana and Latina sisters did not even have the right to work in their respective ethnic communities.

As Latina Catholic feminists, members of Las Hermanas confronted the barriers placed in the pathway of women of color not satisfied with subservient roles in society and the Church. Unequal status, silencing, and dismissal marked only some of the hurdles they encountered. Through perseverance, determination, and collective strength, Las Hermanas took numerous courageous stands to represent the "voice of the voiceless." As Latinas, they stood in solidarity with the poor and with women in order to transform the elitist alliances of the Church. Though not always successful, they confronted the sexism within the structures of sanctified ecclesial authority. They not only confronted the patterns of exclusion within the institution, but also within the broader feminist movement. Las Hermanas met the challenge of being Latina Catholic feminists.

While their efforts sought to transform the institutional Church, they worked simultaneously to transform the personal lives of Latinas. A multifaceted agenda focusing on education, support, leadership development, spirituality, and advocacy for Latinas enabled Las Hermanas to influence laity, sisters, priests, and even bishops.[180] In the process, Las Hermanas articulated a Latina feminist spirituality and a theology based on justice and trust in a divine presence *and* in each other as Hermanas. Their spirituality enabled them to sustain their commitment to the poor and to women despite tremendous obstacles. The following chapter explores the particular spiritual praxis of Las Hermanas.

5

Transformative Struggle

The Spirituality and Theology of Las Hermanas

Al viento nadie lo para	*No one can stop the wind,*
al mar nadie lo encadena	*no one can chain the sea;*
las mujeres solidarias	*women in solidarity*
son fuego que nadie apaga.	*are a fire that no one can put out.*
Lucha, poder, esperanza	*Struggle, power, hope,*
sea consigna en la batalla	*the battle continues*
por rescatar la justicia	*to rescue justice,*
nuestra HERMANA aprisionada.	*our imprisoned sister.*[1]

—*Rosa Martha Zárate, "Lucha, Poder, Esperanza"*

COMMUNITY EMPOWERMENT and women's self-determination had held priority for Las Hermanas since its inception; however, after two decades of work, what the members had encountered was chiefly "the indifference of the church towards women."[2] This painful reality persuaded members that their energies would be most effective if they focused specifically on empowering grassroots Latinas. Beginning in 1980, this decision shaped more directly the themes of the national conferences, the topics discussed in *Informes,* and the mission of the organization. Signs of this shift had occurred earlier in 1976 at the Sixth National Conference, when Las Hermanas had invited renowned theologian Gustavo Gutiérrez from Peru to speak on the distinct characteristics of Latin American liberation theology. While Las Hermanas highly respected the work of Gutiérrez, they did not presume that he could speak from women's experience. Rather than ask Gutiérrez to be the keynote speaker, Las Hermanas members delivered presentations throughout the four-day conference that the liberation theologian responded to. María Iglesias led a discussion titled "The Role of Women in the Church," and Teresita Basso presented her work on "What It Means to be a Chicana, Latina Woman." This format emphasized Las Hermanas's recognition that "while theologians and pastoral agents could be their allies, it was up to Hispanic women to articulate their own experience and pursue theological reflection on it."[3]

Las Hermanas understood that women and community are not mutually exclusive; the empowerment of women is directly tied to the empowerment of Latino communities. When women are free, so will a community be free, but Las Hermanas's increased attention on women signaled its disillusionment with transforming the patriarchal Church structure. The feminist focus resulted in educational conferences, theological writings, newsletters, women-centered rituals, and creative artistic works. In the process, Las Hermanas expressed and articulated a spirituality and a theology both rooted in Mexican/Cuban/Puerto Rican Catholic faith and shaped by the experiences of Latina feminists. This chapter explores the spirituality and theology of Las Hermanas, eventually named mujerista theology. It also considers the weakening of the organization by the mid-1980s, as well as the resolve of its members not to let their vision of an autonomous Latina Catholic organization fade.

Spirituality of Transformative Struggle

While spirituality often eludes definition, my use of the term emphasizes the multiple ways people relate to the world around them, to their source of life or their Creator, and to themselves.[4] For the majority of Latinas, relating to the world involves struggle. The struggle might be against economic oppression that affects all other areas of one's life, including health, education, family, and political representation. The struggle might also be one of cultural survival, or how Latinas sustain their dignity and self-esteem in a society that continues to stereotype, exploit, ridicule, and marginalize them. For women struggling not only to survive but also to prosper spiritually, culturally, and economically, the manner in which they engage in this struggle becomes key to understanding their spirituality. Engaging in struggle in a transformative manner rather than in a passive victim mode appears fundamental to the spirituality of Las Hermanas. Embracing struggle in order to make justice a reality is viewed as life-giving.[5] Keeping in mind class differences,

> Hispanic women do not envision themselves apart from the struggle. The challenge is in transforming that struggle so that it has not only a redeeming but an energizing effect . . . The transformation of [struggle] is critical for the liberation of Hispanic women . . . for assuming control over one's life . . . *La vida es la lucha*, implies the struggle we must embrace and learn to love in order to survive in the present and envision life with dignity in the future.[6]

Vital to embracing struggle as life-giving is a deep faith in a divine presence that desires justice for el pueblo and for women. This "sense of the divine" illuminates the manner in which members of Las Hermanas respond to struggle. As Isasi-Díaz and Tarango point out, this "sense of the divine in their lives . . . gives them strength for the struggle—a struggle that is not part of life but life itself."[7] Furthermore, faith in women's creativity, supportive relationships, and intuitive and cognitive abilities enable Las Hermanas to express a spirituality and theology beyond the boundaries of the institutional Church.

Mujerista Theology

An overview of the theology emerging from Las Hermanas helps us obtain a deeper grasp of the underlying spirituality. The first articulation in 1988 of what would later be termed mujerista theology is now over fifteen years old and continues to offer insight into the theological praxis of Latina Catholic feminists. Although the contributors to mujerista theology chose specifically not to use the term *feminist*, they did not deny a feminist vision and praxis. As Chicana feminists had experienced in the Chicano movement, feminist concerns within the initial stages of Latin American liberation theology were either ignored or dismissed for being white women's issues and divisive to the movement.[8] On the other hand, a Chicana feminist critique of racism and classism often left them marginalized and ignored in the white feminist movement.[9] The

Chicana and Latina theologians in Las Hermanas in the late 1980s had experienced this same marginalization in Latino church communities and thus chose to rename Hispanic women's liberation theology mujerista theology in order to "identify the specificity of our struggle without separating us from our communities."[10]

In an effort to select a name that would help "us identify one another in the trenches as we fight for our survival within Hispanic communities and the U.S. society at large,"[11] *feministas Hispanas* turned to the music of their cultures and chose the term *mujer.* "In love songs as well as in protest songs we are simply called *mujer*—woman."[12] Inspired by music written by Rosa Martha Zárate, as well as other Latinas, mujeristas signify "women who make a preferential option for Latina women, for our struggle for liberation."[13] Zárate's *Cántico de Mujer* describes what it means to be a mujerista:

> Mujer que se libera
> Dios se solidariza con me causa,
> me consagra portavoz de la esperanza . . .
> ¡DICHOSA MUJER LA QUE SABE SER FIEL AL QUEHACER DE IMPLANTAR
>   LA JUSTICIA Y LA PAZ!
> ¡BENDITA SERÁ LA MUJER QUE HACE OPCIÓN POR LA CAUSA DE DIOS,
>   POR LA LEY DEL AMOR! . . .
> Nos llamas a gestar en nuestro vientre mujeres y hombres nuevos,
>   pueblo fuerte
> Nos unges servidoras, profestisas, testigos de tu amor que nos
>   redime . . . Espada de dos filos sea mi canto pregón de un
>   Evangelio libertario.[14]

> [A woman who liberates herself—
> God is in solidarity with my cause,
> and consecrates me as a proclaimer of hope—
> Fortunate woman who knows how to be faithful to the task of
>   making justice and peace flourish!
> Blessed is the woman who makes the option for God's cause for the
>   law of love!
> We are called to gestate in our wombs new women and new men, a
>   strong people.
> We are anointed by God as servants, prophets, and witnesses
>   of redemption . . . My song will hold a two-edged sword, a
>   proclamation of the gospel of liberation.]

Yolanda Tarango and Ada María Isasi-Díaz co-authored the first publication articulating a U.S. Latina feminist theology, titled *Hispanic Women: Prophetic Voice in the Church*. The two theologians synthesized the religious understandings of grassroots Latinas following several small group retreats organized by members of Las Hermanas. According to Tarango, Las Hermanas provided "a real link" and "the seedbed" for the production of mujerista theology. Financial support from numerous women's religious congregations, individuals, and organizations, including the Center of Concern, Quixote Center, National Assembly of Religious Women, and the National Coalition of American Nuns, enabled the authors to dialogue with Latinas in various parts of the country.[15] Isasi-Díaz elaborates further on the influence of Las Hermanas:

> When I returned from pastoral work in Peru in 1976, I met Yolanda through Call to Action. She introduced me to Las Hermanas and from them came my induction into the U.S. Hispanic/Latino world. I had been out of the country for several years and away from the struggles of Latinos in this country. Las Hermanas became the matrix in which I thought about gender analysis and the relationship between racism and sexism. The ethos of the organization, *la lucha* for the people from a women's perspective, motivated us to begin to elaborate a theology . . . I was able to meet with Hermanas members and their contacts in small groups and listen to their understandings of God. Las Hermanas is a very significant part of what we call mujerista theology.[16]

Sylvia Vasquez, a former member of the organization, comments on the role that Las Hermanas and mujerista theology played in her own educational and spiritual development:

> The work of Ada María and Yolanda has been to extrapolate what goes on in Las Hermanas and put it into theological language . . . our ability to articulate our experience of God. This has far-reaching implications. It helped me to understand that theology is everybody's. Mujerista theology affirmed and validated me; it freed me.[17]

When Isasi-Díaz further developed the theology in her second book, *En la lucha: Elaborating a mujersita theology* (1993), she returned to several of the women connected to Las Hermanas whom she and Tarango had interviewed.

Influenced by Latin American liberation theology, these Latina theologians emphasize "doing theology" as a praxis versus solely an intellectual exercise.[18] As feminist theologians, they challenge traditional theology that ignores the experiences and perceptions of women, particularly women of color. Tarango and Isasi-Díaz place theological authority in the hands of grassroots Latinas whose faith and lived experience inform their beliefs and actions. The goal of this theological enterprise is to maintain Latino/a cultural values but with a commitment to the struggle against sexism in all its manifestations, and to reach "not equality but liberation"[19] from the socio-political-economic oppression that Latinas experience.

A four-part methodology intrinsic to this theology includes "telling our stories, analyzing, liturgizing, and strategizing."[20] These interrelated "parts" describe *how* the transformation of struggle takes place. Through "telling our stories," Latinas engage in a process of self-reflection that gives importance to their experiences, reveals shared experiences, and leads to the recognition that the "personal is political" or that structural forces impact not only individuals but also communities. Analysis requires a deeper inquiry beyond the obvious into the forces of oppression in order to make the connections between its different manifestations. Liturgizing enables Latinas to design "how best to represent the divine"[21] in their lives and negates the sense of unworthiness or absence often experienced in patriarchal rituals. Strategizing seeks to find ways emerging from the community to change oppressive structures by transforming a domineering use of power into an enabling and creative use of power-"all in the context of a community and its common good."[22] This process also provides the structure for all Las Hermanas's national conferences.

These parts do not operate in isolation but intertwine in developing critical consciousness and praxis among these Latinas. Praxis, or "critical, reflective action based on and dealing with questions of ultimate meaning,"[23] means to act in the world out of a commitment to the liberation of Latinas and other oppressed communities. According to Tarango and Isasi-Díaz,

Hispanic Women protesting the lack of city services in the South Bronx, emptying a bag of trash on the desk of the city official who could order the garbage picked up more frequently in the area where the women live-that is doing Hispanic Women's Liberation Theology.[24]

The struggle for liberation, or transformative struggle, means not only striving for individual self-determination, but also for the ability to survive and prosper physically, economically, and culturally as active agents in making justice a reality for all.

Transformative struggle requires a redefinition of power that Las Hermanas has addressed consistently at its national conferences, in its women-centered rituals, newsletters, public speeches, protests, and mujerista theology. What Mary Fainsod Katzenstein calls "feminist discursive politics" helps to explain the significance of these activities. Katzenstein applies feminist discursive politics to the activism of American Catholic feminists beginning in the 1970s. She states:

> [Discursive politics] is the politics of meaning making. It is discursive in that it seeks to reinterpret, reformulate, rethink, and rewrite the norms and practices of society and the state. It is about cognition. Its premise is that conceptual changes directly bear on material ones. Discursive politics relies heavily but not exclusively on language. Its vehicle is both speech and print—conversations, debate, conferences, essays, stories newsletters, books.[25]

Feminist discursive politics articulates a counter-discourse to the status quo that excludes women in primary spheres of influence. It challenges the way people think, talk, and act upon deeply held beliefs by emphasizing perspectives privileging women's experiences and voices. In the process, culture is re-created. Las Hermanas engages in feminist discursive politics and in the process re-creates Chicano/Latino culture privileging the voices of women.

National Conferences

Las Hermanas's focus on women sharpened at the eleventh annual assembly held in northern California at the University of Santa Clara in 1980. Under the title "Mujeres Hispanas en la Iglesia," approximately 200 women listened to presentations followed by discussions on female sexuality. They grappled with changing gender roles for Latinas in family, church, and society within the context of Latina socioeconomic realties. The theme, women as agents of change, shaped the workshops beginning with scriptural readings highlighting the sacred and prophetic roles of women in the bible and in daily life. Small group discussions enabled grassroots participants "to enter into an analysis of our situation as Hispanic women, in whatever capacity we find ourselves."[26] For many women it was their first time away from family and domestic responsibilities. Discussions centered on the self-acceptance of women's bodies. According to Margarita Castañeda,

> We focused on the many myths attached to women's bodies and the different aspects of a woman's life cycle. The grassroots women at the conference responded enthusiastically. What resulted is the women realizing that men do not have a right to abuse a woman's body, and that now they could go home and talk to their daughters about their bodies. Traditionally, Latina mothers have not talked with their *hijas.*[27]

While open dialogue may seem like a minor step in the process of empowerment for Latinas, the traditional legacy of silence regarding female sexuality has led to dire consequences. Latinas currently have the highest teenage pregnancy rate among all women in the United States.[28] The consciousness-raising and educational work of Las Hermanas as well as the safe space for dialogue it provides stands in sharp contrast to the restrictive teachings of the Church on matters of gender and sexuality. In this context, feminist discursive politics clearly affects cognitive changes that influence the behavior of Latinas and ultimately reshape culture. Open dialogue is the first step toward empowerment.

The positive responses to discussing sexuality convinced the national leaders to continue to focus on "women's sexuality as a source of spiritual power and individual growth."[29] Subsequent biennial conferences have emphasized the sacredness of women's bodies and have explored issues including domestic violence, reproductive rights, teenage pregnancy, and power relations.[30]

At the "quinceañera," or fifteen-year celebratory conference, in Denver in 1987, conference planners chose the theme "gift of being/ *nuestro don de ser*" to initiate dialogue on moral agency. Presentations and discussions underscored the ability of Latinas to make their own ethical and moral decisions regarding their bodies, particularly around reproductive rights. The conference created the space for Latina Catholics to debate moral choices. Understandably, the topic of abortion resulted in a conflicted yet fruitful discussion.

For Sister Veronica Méndez, discussing a woman's right to an abortion proved too disconcerting and ruptured her membership with Las Hermanas:

> When the discussion on abortion began it seemed like the women religious were the ones for it . . . I raised my hand and said, "Murder is not a choice!" Then other laywomen started telling their stories . . . It was interesting that a nun had to stand up and say that abortion was not right, because the other nuns were saying that one has to follow their own conscience.[31]

In contrast, the dialogue helped many laywomen to understand better the difficult choices women often make. Teresa Barajas explains:

> I have always been against abortion, but when I heard a young women talk about having a child when she was sixteen years old, and how she resented not having a choice . . . I began to see things differently. We often believe a certain way because other people want us to believe that way. Since I heard that girl speak, I can understand others' experiences better.[32]

Reproductive rights clearly deserve attention for grassroots Latina Catholics who often find themselves subject to poor advice under the guise of "spiritual counseling." Isasi-Díaz shared a poignant example of what one woman experienced. "A mother of twelve children had a confessional screen slammed in her face due to confessing that she had had a tubal ligation!"[33] The work of Las Hermanas provides a counter-discourse to such demeaning and oppressive actions toward women.

Besides reproductive rights, the women also wanted to know more about how to discuss sexuality with their daughters and the kind of moral guidelines they should provide. According to Isasi-Díaz, "they did not want their daughters to undergo similar experiences that they had had as young women."[34] Las Hermanas provided the conditions for women to ask questions freely and to receive culturally specific advice from their peers.

The explicit focus on women required a revised constitution and in 1989 the National Coordinating Team approved the following:

> The purpose of *Las Hermanas* is the development of leadership among Hispanic women, with a view to the needs of all members of the Hispanic community. The expressed priority of the organization is the promotion of the Hispanic woman. *Las Hermanas* will develop their work both in the Church and in society.[35]

Diverging from the initial purpose of "more effective and active service to the Hispanic people" to one more specifically for women did not lessen the commitment to Chicano/Latino communities, but sharpened the focus on the challenges facing women as agents of change in the wider community.[36]

Recognizing the great need and positive response to discuss ethical and moral choices encouraged the national leadership team to stabilize the precarious financial base and overextended leadership of the organization. In 1989, the national office relocated to San Antonio at Our Lady of the Lake University at the Center for Women, in office space donated by the university and the Missionary Sisters of Divine Providence.[37] Grant monies supported a part-time administrator, Sylvia Vásquez, a member of Las Hermanas. Vásquez managed the difficulties of keeping the national organization afloat with few resources and she encountered "too many women who didn't want Las Hermanas to fail."[38]

The stabilizing efforts and renewed energy were evident at the 1989 national assembly in San Antonio, Texas, under the theme, "La Mujer Hispana: Lucha, Poder y Esperanza" [The Hispanic Woman: Struggle, Power, and Hope]. Struggle, power, and hope characterized the almost two decades of mobilizing that had brought Las Hermanas to this point. The 200 women gathered included "*Chicanas, Puertoriqueñas, Cubanas, Centroamericanas, Mexicanas, Suramericanas,* artists, singers, *campesinas,* housewives, *estudiantes,* educators, younger, older, *abuelitas.*"[39] Seventy-four new members represented the largest increase in membership ever experienced at a national conference since 1971. The national board increased its size from three to seven members, representing a mixture of laity and women religious.[40]

The issue of power and the need to redefine power held primary attention at the 1989 assembly. Speakers such as Rosie Castro, founding member of the Hispanic Women's Network of Texas and a longtime Chicana activist, and María Antonietta Berriozábal, San Antonio City Council member and founder of Hispanas Unidas, discussed how power can be utilized for self-determination and leadership in Latino communities. Defining power as enablement, creativity, and the ability to act rather than control and dominate set the framework for the participants to examine their own concepts of power; how they use their power in their daily lives; and what social forces including religion attempt to keep women powerless.[41]

The portrayal of power as coming from within the individual, existing between companions in the struggle for liberation, and emerging from the desire to make a difference in one's life gave the women a deep sense of their own personal power.[42] Conference participant Teresa Barajas describes the impact that redefining power had on her life:

> For me and I believe for many of us, the conference opened up a wider perspective of the meaning of the word *poder*. I saw in many of us that the word awakened a fear . . . because we have always associated it with oppression, violence, and absolute control . . . that many of us have experienced since we were little . . . We learned that power is something very good in us if we know how to use it . . . We also saw that we often use our power without even knowing it.[43]

Many of the grassroots women attending the conference were away from their husbands and their children for the first time. Many of them shared stories of abuse due to the actions of priests, bosses, husbands, children, and the government. But as Rosa Martha Zárate pointed out, "these women also shared experiences of resistance, of struggle, of liberation. This was an assembly of hope!"[44] Discussing issues of power, machismo, and the limitations of traditional gender roles imbued many of the women with the knowledge that they were not alone in the struggle for liberation. As one participant remarked, "Together we have the ability to plan and act—therefore WE HAVE POWER."[45]

The national and regional Las Hermanas conferences are perhaps the most significant activity of the organization since 1980. The termination of projects including Proyecto Mexico, active mobilizing of the UFW, representation on the board of MACC, and the NAC to the Secretariat for Hispanic Affairs has diminished the institutional visibility of Las Hermanas over the past twenty years.[46] However, the more "inward" focus chosen by Las Hermanas has proven effective for the process of consciousnessraising among Latinas. Biennial national conferences and annual regional retreats educate many women who normally lack the opportunities to meet, discuss, and analyze their experiences.[47] "Every time we come together a significant number of grassroots women attend. It means a lot to these women to feel free to talk. It is a means of sustenance for them."[48]

Women, like Dolores Florez, feel deeply empowered by their involvement with Las Hermanas.

> I was a battered wife for twenty-four years. I was coming out of it when I met Las Hermanas but I was afraid. I felt like a divorced women with a big D on her back. When I went to a Las Hermanas meeting, I realized that I was not alone. There were women who had raised children alone, who didn't have a college education but held down jobs, or women who had been in abusive relationships. There were so many things I could identify with. There was a special bonding of being Hispanic spiritual women. I loved it.[49]

The process of consciousness-raising through self-reflection and dialogue facilitates a transformative process for the women.

Mujerista Ritual

Mujerista liturgies are women-centered communal rituals created by Las Hermanas that take place at the national conferences and regional retreats. These rituals contribute immensely to the consciousness-raising process of Latinas as women take control over expressing and symbolizing their religious understandings. Mujerista liturgies express most visibly women's religious agency.

These rituals evolved out of the struggle over whether or not to celebrate Mass as part of the conference schedule. Catholic women are prohibited from consecrating the bread and wine for Eucharist, thus requiring the presence of a male priest, which many of the women found disempowering.[50] Sylvia Sedillo was one of the first members to ask, "Why are we continuing to do this? We need to be leading our own prayers!"[51] By 1985, Las Hermanas asserted its ability to shape its own liturgical services, "born out of Hispanic women's determination to be self-defining women."[52] According to Isasi-Díaz, the liturgies "celebrate in an autochthonous way who we are, our struggles, our preferred future, and our belief in the divine, in Jesus as a friend and *compañero* in the struggle."[53] While Jesus holds divine status in mujerista rituals, the naming and symbolizing of divine and saintly females also holds a primary place. As an example, a Las Hermanas communal altar might include multiple images of Our Lady of Guadalupe, as well as Nuestra Señora de la Caridad del Cobre, images of women saints, and photographs of female relatives and friends, both living and deceased.[54] While some members hold more devotion to male images of the divine, mujerista rituals privilege female symbols and inclusive language, but they do not exclude male representations.

To meet the needs of those women wanting a traditional Mass, conference coordinators for several years announced the times for Sunday services in a nearby church. Being sensitive to grassroots Latinas who attend church services, the planners of mujerista liturgies have never forced the rituals as a replacement for the Mass, but rather, seek to "enable the participants to develop and experience new forms of liturgical expressions."[55] In recent years a traditional Eucharistic liturgy with a male priest has taken place the final morning of the conference and a mujerista ritual the day before.[56]

A description and analysis of the communal ritual closing the 1989 conference provides a selected example of some of the principal elements of these new forms of liturgical expressions. Titled "Reclamando Nuestro Poder," the ritual was designed primarily by María Antonietta Berriozábal and Ada María Isasi-Díaz, in consultation with numerous other Hermanas.[57] Drawing on the home altar tradition of many Latinas, the participants created a communal altar in the center of the ritual space to claim and mark the gathering area as sacred. Pictures and statues of significant and saintly women important to the lives of the participants comprised the altar along with candles representing offerings to the divine and the spiritual presence of each woman. Bread, milk, honey, and dates symbolizing the sustenance needed for the struggle ahead as they claimed their power completed the offerings. Milk represented the life-sustaining power of women's bodies. The honey and milk recalled the journey of the early Israelites to the promised land, affirming the goal of Latina liberation. Dates had been brought to

the altar by farmworker women from California and contributed
to the symbolic need for sustenance.

Gathering in a circle around the altar emphasized egalitarian
relationships and the unity of the "community of faith struggling
for liberation."[58] The oral tradition of Latinas found expression
through "dialogic" preaching of the gospel and the *nueva canción*
of Rosa Martha Zárate, which included "Lucha, Poder y Esperanza," "Profetiza," and "Cántico de Mujer." These songs emphasized the challenges facing the women to construct a new reality
based on justice. The preaching included multiple voices to avoid
a "single interpretation of the biblical text but rather to enable each
one present to do her own articulation."[59]

The entire community participated at different points in the ritual either by calling out the names of powerful women, invoking
the divine, naming moments of power in their own lives, sharing in the preaching, or approaching the altar and blessing the
offerings. All the women participated in blessing one another using words of their own choosing. As Isasi-Díaz states, "we want
our liturgies to provide opportunity for as many women as possible to have an active role in sacred rituals in order to counter
their exclusion from approaching the altar during worship in their
churches."[60]

The language, symbols, and actions in the liturgy reflect the cultural, political, and feminist sensibilities of the women. The liturgy
created "a counter discourse in response to the words, rituals, and
symbols that emanate from the Vatican."[61] This is evident in the
following excerpts of the opening prayer and the blessing prayer.
Several women read the latter as they blessed the bread and other
symbols of sustenance:

> Opening Prayer:
> > The power to give life;
> > The power of being vulnerable without being weak;
> > The power of believing in a better future;
> > The power of changing oppressive situations;
> > The power to face difficult circumstances;
> > The power of not giving up;
> > The power of loving and claiming the need for love;
> > The power of crying;
> > The power that is ours because we are women.[62]

Blessing Prayer:
> The power of the seed from which the wheat grows.
> The power of the earth nurtures the seed and makes it
> flourish.
> The power of the sun that gives warmth and light to the
> wheat.
> The power of the *campesinas, campesinos*, who care for and
> harvest the wheat. . . .
> The power of this community which in breaking this bread
> renews its commitment to the people who struggle for
> their liberation. . . .
> . . . come and eat joyfully, with the resolution and
> understanding that we will continue in the struggle
> and that God will always sustain us if we sustain one
> another.[63]

Empowerment for women, solidarity, and commitment to liberation are uncommon themes in traditional Catholic services. While Las Hermanas does not identify its rituals as Eucharistic celebrations, they clearly celebrate the presence of the sacred amid the community of women gathered. According to Isasi-Díaz, "We do not get mired in the discussion of whether it is Eucharist or not."[64]

Liturgical dance provides another dimension to the counter-discourse emanating from Las Hermanas. For example, performance artist, educator, and choreographer Rosa Ramírez Guerrero brings a level of embodied spirituality to many of the liturgical celebrations.[65] While prayerful dance in Catholic ritual developed as a result of Vatican Council II liturgical changes, it was still not common in Catholic churches during the 1970s. Las Hermanas began incorporating dance into their rituals in 1978 at the joint Las Hermanas–PADRES conference. Dance as a prayerful expression merges the physical with the spiritual and deconstructs traditional Western boundaries that separate the body from the sacred. As in all expressions of popular religiosity, when people decide for themselves what images, rituals, and myths give expression to their deepest values, they ultimately express "a language of defiance and ultimate resistance."[66] Carmen Villegas explains the impact of women leading ritual:

> It is powerful seeing women lead us to God. Showing women that
> we don't have to follow the traditional prayers, that we can praise
> God with our bodies, with the pictures of our grandmothers, or

with what we have. For so long "the right way" to pray has been imposed on us.[67]

In mujerista liturgies, feminist values and a shared historical project of personal and social change find expression. Through the ritual actions and symbols, the women design a sacred environment that sanctifies and legitimizes their ability to shape religious practices that reflect their particular social, cultural, and political concerns. In the creative process, they construct a "redemptive reinterpretation of the hegemonic order."[68] The Catholic Mass with its strict gender roles, austere use of symbols, and silence regarding the everyday struggles of Latinas becomes relativized. The mujerista ritual itself becomes a political act as it stands "as a critique and a denunciation of institutional liturgies, which whether consciously or not, function mainly to maintain the good order of patriarchy."[69]

Enedina Vásquez-Casarez, who attended a Las Hermanas conference for the first time in 1989, shared the following comments about the impact the communal ritual had on her:

> It was taking part in something very important. I had never felt capable of anointing someone. After that weekend, I felt that yes, I could do this. I could touch you with this oil. It is within me to do this. It gave me a sense of being good inside, capable of sharing my feelings and embracing someone else and saying, "we are good." I am no longer the wrong gender to do this.[70]

While seemingly in conflict with traditional Catholic practice, mujerista liturgies actually carry out two principles advanced in the Constitution on the Sacred Liturgy of Vatican Council II. As Isasi-Díaz points out, mujerista liturgies "first . . . communicate God's presence and celebrate the identity of the people gathered; second, as symbolic activity [it] brings about an experience of individual and communal transformation."[71] As such, mujerista liturgies do not contradict Catholic tradition but rather provide a deeper or fuller expression of Latina religiosity. Mujerista liturgies continue the historical legacy of Latino Catholics, male and female, who "viewed their own interpretations of Catholicism as integral parts of their cultural life"[72] and, in the context of Las Hermanas, their political life.

My own participation in mujerista rituals in 1997 in New York and 1999 in Denver gave me a deep sense of how these women envision the divine in their lives as a transformative presence, one fully present but not exclusively in the image of women. The theme of the 1997 conference, "Celebrating 25 years of Las Hermanas," included a ritual designed primarily by Carmen Villegas and Sister Juanita Morales in consultation with numerous other hermanas. Again drawing on the home altar tradition, the participants created a communal altar to mark the gathering area as sacred. Pictures and statues of holy and empowering women adorned the altar along with candles representing the spiritual essence of each woman present.

Sitting in a circle around the altar emphasized egalitarian relationships and the unity of the women present. Rosa Marta Zárate serenaded the group with her music of liberation. One of the facilitators passed out pieces of colored paper and asked the participants to write on them words describing experiences or persons that limit their self-determination. The women then joined their pieces of paper, forming a long paper chain. Standing in a circle and holding the paper chain enabled the women to visualize the shared experience of bondage. As each woman called out her personal oppression she broke the chain and symbolically destroyed its source. The women then turned to each other and blessed one another using words of their own choosing. Prayer, reflection, and action imbued the participants with a sense of their own power to voice and release oppressions, and ultimately heal themselves and others.

The women-centered ritual at the 1999 conference held in Denver also instilled an awareness of the healing abilities of Latinas across generations in the women. After creating the ritual space, elder women were asked to come forward and bless the water to be used in the ritual. The elders then blessed younger women. Each woman in turn then blessed another woman with words of choice. Once again, Latinas experienced their own actions as avenues to the sacred, an experience not possible in male dominated liturgy.

The total experience of a Las Hermanas conference including self-reflection, dialogue, and ritual has sparked poetry, music, film, and performance art. Enedina Casarez Vásquez, an artist, writer, and teacher from San Antonio, returned from her first Las Hermanas conference in 1989 and decided to form a writing group for Chicana poets. Naming themselves Mujeres Grandes, they have since published two anthologies of poetry and continue to meet regularly to discuss their writings.[73] According to English professor Juanita Luna Lawhn of San Antonio College and a participant in Mujeres Grandes, "The pieces talk about empowerment, the empowerment of the individual by the use of the word and about the woman who is a doer, a woman who "breezes in / Making her presence known."[74]

Following is an excerpt of a poem entitled "She Spoke of Paradigms and My Mind Snapped," by Casarez Vásquez, indicating the effect that Las Hermanas and Mujeres Grandes have had on her life:

> So, with this encounter,
> these *mujeres grandes*
> Made me feel fulfilled
> Knowing that paradigms
> Exist in the mind of the viewer
> That it is more important
> That one know one's interpretation of self
> In order to break all paradigms
> And realize the self
> And let the others talk
> *El ejemplo que yo vi, ese sere yo.*
> To dare to be different
> Intelligent, Self sufficient, Hungry, Passionate, Beautiful, Driven,
>   Aggressive, And in love.
> For they need me, And I need them,
> and we know each other.[75]

The author's expression of self-reflection and self-determination speaks strongly to the support for transformative struggle within Las Hermanas. Other Las Hermanas members such as Flor Lovato, Margie Domingo, Tess Browne, María Jesus Robles, and Rosie Castro also write poetry inspired by their involvement with the organization. The following selection by Rosie Castro written in honor of Yolanda Tarango's election to the General Council of her religious order in 1990 provides an example of the support offered to Latinas as they forge new paths:

> As her journey embarked we knew we could not travel the broken road for her nor run ahead to warn her what lay around each corner. But we were committed to always being stationed by the path

to offer sustenance and respite when she sought it, to walk with her or carry her if the need arose.[76]

In 1990 actress Ruby Nelda Perez performed "La Guadalupe Camina," a piece written and produced by media artist Beverly Sánchez-Padilla. This play and the subsequent film depict the life of Rosa Martha Zárate from her childhood to her dismissal by the San Bernardino archdiocese and expulsion from her religious community. The media production communicated powerfully the obstacles placed in the path of a woman attempting to live her faith based on service to impoverished Mexicano and Chicano communities.[77] The songs of protest and hope written by Zárate have enriched the conferences and liturgies of Las Hermanas and have become symbolic of the creative political acts emerging from the organization.

Finances and Leadership

Despite the impact that the organization made on the personal transformations of numerous Latinas, financial difficulties plagued the organization during the 1990s. The twentieth anniversary commemorated in Albuquerque was a time of both celebration and sobering news. National Coordinator Yolanda Tarango reported that expenses for 1989 to 1991 had been drawn from the principal rather than the interest of their certificate of deposit.[78] "We consider that very serious because the interest from that investment is an important source for the future support of the office."[79] As the only coordinator since 1989, due to the lack of volunteers for national leadership, Tarango expressed a serious concern over the ability of the organization to survive much longer.

Strategies to increase financial resources and national visibility included asking members to pay their dues and subscription fees to *Informes*, to recruit new members, and to increase the visibility of Las Hermanas by referring to the organization at the meetings and conferences that members attend. A goal of 400 paid members by 1992 and 1,000 paid members by 1995 was set.[80] In addition, a new category of membership, Corporate Membership for Religious Communities, at $200 per year was created.

Las Hermanas knew quite well that Latinos would constitute nearly the majority of the U.S. Catholic Church by the year 2000.

Recognizing the role that Latinas had to continue to take in shaping the treatment of Latino/a Catholics energized their discussions despite the dismal financial status.[81] According to María Inez Martínez, "We just kept going. I tell myself, it is God's work and if She wants it to continue, She is going to do something."[82]

With the 1991 election of two new national coordinators, María Carolina Flores and Annette Hernández, Las Hermanas moved hopefully, yet precariously, into the 1990s. Tarango maintained primary responsibility for editing and publishing *Informes*,[83] and Flores began archiving the papers of Las Hermanas into a national repository at Our Lady of the Lake University in San Antonio. Working full-time as special collections librarian and archivist at the university, however, did not leave Flores much time to organize Las Hermanas on a national level. Moreover, Hernández failed to fulfill her term, further weakening the organization.

In 1993, the national coordinating team stabilized with the election of Dolores Florez and Rocio Talfur-Salgado and the re-election of María Carolina Flores. Talfur-Salgado did not serve a full term due to health problems, again weakening the national leadership.

Even amid these difficulties, Las Hermanas managed to convene successful conferences in 1993 at Ft. Meyers, Florida, and in 1995 at McAllen, Texas. Discourse around moral agency and sexuality continued at both of the gatherings. Information on domestic violence and sexual abuse within social institutions broadened the discussions to consider how a woman's sexuality is objectified and violated. Psychologists, school counselors, doctors, and social workers led the discussions, which enabled many of the women to examine the different forms of violence present in their own lives.

Of utmost significance is the safe space created by the Las Hermanas conferences. The accepting and affirming environment enabled those participants who suffered as victims of violence and other forms of oppression to share their painful stories. According to one participant,

> This theme invited much participation as the majority of us realized the lack of openness and information that predominates across generations on the topics of sexuality, women, and *la cultura*. We shared concerns about how to improve our lifestyles and the responsibilities we have as Hispanic women.[84]

In addition to dialogue, mujerista rituals provided healing for the women who shared their previously silenced stories. Isasi-Díaz describes one such ritual:

> We sat on the floor around a huge basin of water that was surrounded by candles, stones, flowers, pictures of dear ones, dead and alive, and numerous holy cards . . . After some moments of silence and a gathering song, the enablers of the liturgy invited us to take a stone and place it in the water, mentioning at the same time, if we so desired, a hurt from which we wanted to be cured. For over forty-five minutes the women named their hurts and asked for healing . . . they could say aloud what some of them had not dared to verbalize even to themselves . . . these women empowered each other, nudged each other into articulating their pain.[85]

Through support, listening, and "telling their stories," common struggles are revealed, as well as hopes and dreams for a better future. Claiming space, claiming one's voice previously rendered silent, remains central to the struggle for self-determination, the essence of discursive politics and oppositional consciousness.

As Las Hermanas moved forward into the mid-1990s, the persistent lack of resources heightened concerns over the ability of the organization to survive. The goal of 400 paid members by 1993 had not materialized. With only 140 paid members and seven corporate members, National Coordinator María Carolina Flores reluctantly asked the looming question, "Do we still need Las Hermanas?"[86] A survey sent to approximately 700 readers of Informes confirmed the continuing need for the organization. The desire to keep the organization alive prevailed. In 1995 members reelected Dolores Florez from Colorado and elected Lucy Ortiz from Florida to the national coordinating team. For the first time in the history of Las Hermanas, the national coordinating team was completely represented by laywomen.

The question to include non-Catholic women had arisen earlier in the organization's history, as many of the members no longer participated in the institutional Church. Over the years, with the increasing disenfranchisement of women in the Church, it had become accepted that Las Hermanas provides space for women who identify as Roman Catholic, as well as for those who loosely identify as Catholic. Members have decided to maintain their identity as an organization registered in the National Catholic Directory, but will not exclude women active in other churches.

Under the leadership of Florez and Ortiz and a six-member board of predominantly laywomen, Las Hermanas ventured into the second half of the 1990s. Surviving under a precarious financial situation did not alter the women's belief in the organization. Sheer will and an unwillingness to let go characterized their defense against a losing financial battle. Paying their own travel expenses to attend national board meetings reflected their commitment and resolve to keep Las Hermanas active.[87] With archival records in order, donated office space, and the hiring of a part-time office administrator, the national leaders regained hope for longevity. By early 1997, however, Las Hermanas could no longer afford an office administrator, and the need to relocate the office loomed on the horizon.

While a weak financial base caused most of the difficulties, several members interviewed expressed frustration over a vacuum in leadership, a lack of commitment from dues-paying members, and/or a lack of a specific national agenda other than annual conferences and the publication of *Informes*. An absence of a full national coordinating team of three members during the mid-1980s and 1990s meant only a few women kept the organization afloat. For example, Yolanda Tarango and Carmen Villegas comprised the national team for three consecutive years (1985–88) and Tarango served as sole coordinator for two additional years (1989–90). Under her capable leadership, along with the assistance of the national boards, the organization maintained national visibility as they moved toward the new millennium.

Into the Twenty-first Century

For a few longtime members, the lack of a radical political vision shaping the agenda of Las Hermanas for the twenty-first century causes concern. In their opinion, the early political activism deeply influenced by liberation theology and the Chicano movement had faded. According to Rosa Martha Zárate, "We don't have a political analysis or a concrete vision of the kind of society we want to create. We need a critique of liberal capitalism."[88] While justice remains an integral part of the organizational goals, concrete ways to achieve justice on a broad scale have become more elusive in the past decade.

Among the different opinions lies the awareness that the organization will never return to what it was like in the 1970s. The aging of many original members calls for "new blood, younger blood with fresh ideas" to contribute to future directions.[89] Most of the women interviewed agreed that the organization must reevaluate itself in order to advance in the twenty-first century. As Ada María Isasi-Díaz points out:

> The activism of today is different than [in] the 1960s and 1970s. The way to solve problems in the 1960s was a demonstration, a sit-in. Now the power of confrontation tactics has been taken away. We have to figure out how to organize in a highly industrialized country, in a Church where authority has become even more centralized.[90]

The leadership team took the challenge to heart and in late July 2001, 200 women from across the nation traveled to El Paso, Texas, to decide once again on the future of Las Hermanas. Participants listened to several of the founding members retell the history of the organization and their own personal growth through leadership roles.[91] A newer member with years of organizing experience, Sister Paula González, then delivered a dynamic analysis of organizational strategies in light of the reality of aging members.[92] After lengthy small group discussions, the entire body voted to restructure according to a network model. Revitalization would come from the action and prayer emanating from local or regional Las Hermanas groups. A National Coordinating Team made up of one representative from each local group would replace the existing three-member team. The level of action and the size of the new team would depend on the vitality of local groups rather than on the effort of a national team. The biennial asembleas would continue to take place and provide the opportunity for all members to gather, to make policy decisions, "to share and celebrate being *unidas en acción y oración.*"[93] Fund-raising by Linda Chavez would make the hiring of a part-time executive secretary possible for the year ahead. Members also approved a revised mission statement and goals:

> *Las Hermanas*–USA is a network of women's groups united to empower themselves and others to participate actively in prophetic, loving transformation of Church and society through sharing riches of Hispanic culture, language, spirituality and traditions.

Goals: To promote continual growth in self-respect, dignity, healing, and mutual support among Hispanic women. To promote activities that educate and develop leadership and participatory skills directed toward justice, peace, and the integrity of creation.[94]

Women, culture, empowerment, shared leadership, solidarity, education, justice, and spirituality remain hallmarks of Las Hermanas for the twenty-first century.

Under an increasingly conservative papacy and growing economic disparity in the United States, the need for Las Hermanas as a critical voice of dissension remains high. Immigrant-bashing, affirmative action censures, antibilingual legislation, and unfair wage differentials are but a few of the ongoing attempts to halt Latina/o self-determination. Many of the issues facing the Church of the 1970s continue to concern Latino Catholics in the new millennium. Underrepresentation, insensitive ministries, inadequate services, and limitations on women stifle the Church from effective ministry.

The decision of Las Hermanas to remain a decentralized, autonomous organization for women only allows freedom to create a new form of being church. This new form is necessary for Latinas needing more than what the "official" Church allows or offers. Las Hermanas's commitment to a woman's sphere in which religious and moral agency can be discussed and exercised, to living in the intersection between religion and politics, and to the strong sense of sisterhood among its members has contributed to the longevity of the organization. The lack of substantial financial resources, however, continues to poise serious obstacles. Yet, Las Hermanas offers a legacy to Chicanas and Latinas, forging paths toward greater self-realization for themselves and their communities. The struggle continues and transformation remains the ongoing challenge.

Conclusion

LAS HERMANAS organized during the tremendous so-
cial upheaval of the late 1960s and early 1970s. The influence of
the civil rights movements, Latin American liberation theology,
feminism, and the modernization of the Roman Catholic Church
coalesced to set in motion a struggle for Chicana and Latina recognition and authority in the Church structure. The mobilizing of
the first fifty women in 1971 quickly grew to hundreds that resulted in a grassroots movement for change. Combining forces
with PADRES initiated the forging of a path for a critical mass
of Latino/a religious leaders in a Euroamerican-dominated church
hierarchy. Rejecting any limitations on how it might challenge the
Church's inherent racism and sexism, Las Hermanas chose financial independence from the Church and a leadership model based
on shared power. While the decision for autonomy has no doubt
limited its financial resources and thus effectiveness, at the same
time autonomy has ensured its survival.

The early accomplishments of Las Hermanas included the co-
development of MACC, Proyecto Mexico, lobbying for the appointment of Chicano bishops, assisting in the planning and leadership of the I and II Encuentros Nacional Hispano De Pastoral,
contributing to an emerging Chicano and U.S. Latino/a theology,
and involvement in the Chicano student and farm labor movement. This activism planted the seeds for Latino/a leadership in
the Church and created a long-lasting momentum for change.

Confronting the inevitable gender conflict in a sanctified patriarchy only strengthened Las Hermanas's resolve to struggle for

gender equality. Tension in its collaboration with PADRES, its dismissal from the board of MACC, the marginalization of women at the III Encuentro Nacional Hispano De Pastoral, the dismissals of individual members from leadership positions, and estrangement in the Women-Church movement convinced Las Hermanas to focus primarily on empowerment for grassroots Latinas as it entered its second decade. Convinced that the Church was ultimately unwilling to promote fully the dignity of women generated an urgency in enhancing the moral agency of Latinas.

Turning to their own spiritual resources, Las Hermanas has become a site for the production of a Latina feminist theology. Mujerista theology elevates the religious understandings of Latinas for the goal of making justice a reality. It is a political theology that rejects unjust structures and actions as the "will of God." It is a theology that values the moral agency of women. Las Hermanas has made tremendous strides in advancing the self-understanding of grassroots Latinas who are often denied the opportunity to hear their own voices and imagine their own futures.

Las Hermanas's ability to create a space for Latinas to raise critical issues regarding women, religion, and justice has not been mirrored by any other national organization of Latinas in the United States. While other national organizations exist, such as the Mexican American Women's National Association (MANA) and Mujeres Activas En Letras y Cambio Social (MALCS), their focus does not address the intersection of gender, politics, and religion.[1] The distinct mixture of spirituality and justice that Las Hermanas is known for marks its contribution to the strategies of ethnic, gender, and class struggles. The spiritual basis of Las Hermanas combined with its feminist consciousness offers a counter-discourse to the patriarchal hegemony of the Roman Catholic Church. As Yolanda Tarango states, "All of our experiences with the official Church and social institutions create the urgency to say, 'no, we have a different perspective and we are going to give it a public voice.'"[2] As Latinas continue to find a safe place and opportunities for leadership development within Las Hermanas, they experience the power of "being church" beyond the boundaries of the institution.

Many of the issues that Las Hermanas first challenged in 1971 continue to plague the Roman Catholic Church. As the Latino Catholic population continues to grow and comprise the majority in many U.S. dioceses, adequate responses seem to elude the institution. According to one Latino pastoral agent, "The most difficult thing is this transition from minority to majority. No one knows how to manage that change. Until now it's been the Hispanics, the poor, who have had to adapt, not those in power."[3] Las Hermanas member María Luisa Gastón concurs that little is given in the way of "affirming, commissioning, giving authority and importance to Hispanics so they can have a sense of, 'I am doing this.'"[4] Recent layoffs and closure of the Offices of Hispanic Ministry in the Los Angeles archdiocese, where Latinos comprise 70 percent of the archdiocese, exemplify the systemic problems that remain for Latinos in the Church.[5] With the persistent vacuum in institutionalized Latino/a leadership and inadequate funding for the remaining programs, the Church is not addressing the culturally specific and social needs of its largest population. Furthermore, the differences between Latino immigrant and Latino native-born populations are ignored. The "Hispanic ministry" pastoral programs that do exist most often cater to a monolingual Spanish-speaking, first-generation population and emphasize evangelization at the expense of broader socio-political and economic concerns. While disenfranchised immigrants clearly need and deserve the support of the Catholic Church, the bicultural, bilingual, or often monolingual English-speaking Chicano/Latino remains ignored. As an example, Spanish-language Masses are now commonplace where Latinos comprise a significant portion of a parish community, yet services for a bicultural and English-speaking Chicano/a remain nearly nonexistent. The end result is that many Chicanos and native-born Latinos feel marginalized because they do not relate to services geared toward Euroamerican populations, nor do they feel comfortable in a solely Spanish-speaking environment. Several leading Chicano theologians and pastoral leaders shared with me their frustration that "Hispanic ministry means immigrant ministry."[6] Programs often fail to address the spectrum of Latinos whose experiences differ depending on numerous variants, including generation, class, ethnicity, nativity, language, gender, and sexual and political orientation. While some local parishes might be more successful at ministering to a diverse Latino population, the Church as a whole falls short and continues to restrict the leadership of women.

Las Hermanas's ability to address the concerns of progressive Latina Catholics, both native and immigrant, relativizes for its members the Church's limitations. Clearly, the organization succeeds at addressing bicultural and bilingual realities by respecting language preferences, class, and cultural diversity in its activities. The prophetic role that Las Hermanas has taken in breaking the barriers between women religious and laity is needed now more than ever as the failure of patriarchal power and authority of the institutional Church reveals itself. The numerous sexual abuses committed between clergy and young laity indicate the serious consequences that result from clericalism and its unchecked power. Las Hermanas has consistently modeled egalitarian relationships in order to supplant the dysfunction and violence of hierarchal/kyriarchal domination.[7] Las Hermanas counteracts the centralization of authority. The shared leadership of women religious and laywomen particularly in the area of ritual prove the vitality of shared ministry and an inclusive model of church.

Whether or not Las Hermanas can continue to overcome financial constraints will be seen in the coming years. A new structure with an emphasis on regional networks places increased responsibility on local groups of Las Hermanas rather than on a national team of leaders. The 2003 conference in southern California showed an increase in new members, and plans for the next national conference in 2005 in San Antonio, Texas, are underway.

The history of Las Hermanas reveals the importance of grass-roots organizing in the context of institutional marginalization and institutional limitations. Despite the ongoing inadequacies of the Church, the collective effort on the part of these Chicana and Latina Catholics set in motion a wave of change in how the Church would recognize the now near majority of U.S. Catholics. Las Hermanas offers a legacy to women seeking religious and political agency in a Church and a society that continues to marginalize them. At the center of this legacy lies the critical, creative, and prophetic voices of Chicanas and Latinas inspired by their faith based on justice.

Appendix: Acronyms

ACHTUS— Academy of Catholic Hispanic Theologians of the United States
ALRA—Agricultural Labor Relations Act
ALRB—Agricultural Labor Relations Board
AWA—Agricultural Workers Association
AWOC—Agricultural Workers Organizing Committee
CACM—Central American Common Market
CASA—Centro de Acción Social Autónomo
CCVI—Sisters of Charity of the Incarnate Word
CDP—Congregation of Divine Providence
CELAM—Congreso Episcopal Latinoamericano (Latin American Conference of Bishops)
CHD—[Bishops'] Campaign for Human Development
CIRM—Conference of Major Superiors of Men and Women
CNBB—National Conference of Brazilian Bishops
CND—Congregation of Notre Dame
COPS—Communities Organized for Public Service
CPRL—Católicos Por La Raza
CSJ—Sisters of St. Joseph of Carondelet
CSO—Community Service Organization
DECH—Department of Religious Education for the Spanish Speaking
EICC—Educational Issues Coordinating Committee
EVO—East Valleys Organization
FLOC—Farm Labor Organizing Committee
IHM—Sisters of the Immaculate Heart of Mary
IPLA—El Instituto Pastoral Latinoamericano
JPC—Justice and Peace Center
LCWR—Leadership Conference of Women Religious

LHS—Las Hermanas Collection, Mexican American Studies Department, Our Lady of the Lake University, San Antonio, Texas
LRUP—La Raza Unida Party
LULAC—League of United Latin American Citizens
MACC—Mexican American Cultural Center
MAEC—Mexican American Education Council
MALCS—Mujeres Activas En Letras y Cambio Social
MALDEF—Mexican American Legal Defense and Educational Fund
MANA—Mexican American Women's National Association
MASO—Mexican American Student Organization
MCDP—Missionary Congregation of Divine Providence
MEB—Movement for Grassroots Education
MEChA—El Movimiento Estudantil Chicano de Aztlán
MFC—Movimiento Familiar Cristiano
MSBT—Missionary Servants of the Most Blessed Trinity
NAC—National Advisory Council
NAWR—National Association of Women Religious
NBSC—National Black Sisters' Conference.
NCCB—National Conference of Catholic Bishops
NCCUSA—National Council of Churches of Christ in the USA
NCR—National Catholic Reporter
NFWA—National Farm Workers Association
NFWM—National Farm Workers Ministry
OLVN—Our Lady of Victoryknoll
OSF—Sisters of St. Francis
OSS—Office for the Spanish Speaking
PADRES—Padres Asociados para Derechos, Religiosos, Educativos y Sociales
PBVM—Presentation of the Blessed Virgin Mary
SC—Sisters of Charity of St. Vincent DePaul of New York
SCOC—South Central Organizing Committee
SEPI—Southeast Pastoral Institute
SHM—Sisters of the Humility of Mary
SL—Sisters of Loretto
UFW—United Farm Workers
UFWA—United Farm Workers of America
UFWOC—United Farm Workers Organizing Committee
UMAS—United Mexican American Students
UNO—United Neighborhood Organization
USCC—United States Catholic Conference
USCCB—United States Conference of Catholic Bishops
WCC—Women of the Church Coalition
WOC—Women's Ordination Conference

Notes

Introduction

1. *Women religious* is used interchangeably with *sisters* in the litera-ture. *Sisters* refers to women in apostolic congregations. While popular vernacular often uses the term *nuns*, this refers to women in cloistered contemplative orders. I will use *women religious* and *sisters* interchange-ably. Laywomen joined Las Hermanas by 1975, and in 1979 they pre-dominated the membership. This will be further explored in Chapter 2. Women religious are also considered as laity in the hierarchical structure of the Church, but are not commonly identified by this term. *Laity* or *laywomen* refers to Catholics who do not take any religious vows but are members of the Catholic faith by baptism.

2. The terms *Chicano* and *Mexican American* are used when referring specifically to persons of Mexican ancestry residing in the United States on a permanent basis. *Chicano* implies political awareness and ethnic pride and became widely used during the civil rights struggles of the 1960s and 1970s. *Chicana* is used when referring to women. The term *Latino* is used to identify the women and men of Latin American descent. *Latina* is used when referring specifically to women. It is an umbrella term that does not do justice to the diversity and complexity of specific Latino groups but implies a stance of solidarity with marginalized peoples of Latin American descent. *Hispanic* was coined by the U.S. government during the Nixon administration to homogenize the diversity of complex ethnic groups. It is a term that gives primacy only to the Spanish heritage of Latinos while ignoring the indigenous and African heritages. The term *Hispanic* will appear in the text only when quoting the use of the term. Las Hermanas used the terms *Chicano* and *Chicana* in their early doc-uments as well as the term *Spanish-speaking* persons. In the 1980s the organization began using *Hispanic*, as did the wider Church. Discussion

on terminology took place at the 2001 conference. Regional preferences from Colorado and New York prevailed and *Hispanic* remained the chosen term for its mission statement. Individual members use a variety of terms for individual self-identity.

3. For an analysis on Chicana/Latina working-class feminism, see Mary Pardo, "Doing It for the Kids: Mexican American Community Activists, Border Feminists?" in *Feminist Organizations: Harvest of the New Women's Movement,* ed. Myra Marx Ferree and Patricia Yancey Martin (Philadelphia: Temple University Press, 1995); see also Sonia Saldívar Hull, *Feminism on the Border: Chicana Gender Politics and Literature* (Berkeley: University of California Press, 2000).

4. In Spanish, the terms *comadre* and *comadrazgo* refer to a type of relationship where the women involved consider each other to be close confidantes and supporters as one's own mother or sister ideally is.

5. Chapter 2 explains further the relationship between Chicanas and Latinas in the organization.

6. I define grass roots as persons and/or communities at the lower end of the economic ladder who have limited formal education. Many of the current members are grassroots women accompanied by a significant number of middle-class/professional women.

7. Raza theology was named by the participants in Theology of the Americas project discussed in Chapter 3.

8. Tess Browne, OSF, interview conducted by author, 20 May 1997. (*Note*: All interviews in this book were conducted by the author.)

9. Catalina Fresquez, CCVI, interview conducted by author, 13 May 1997.

10. Vicki L. Ruiz, *From Out of the Shadows: Mexican Women in Twentieth-Century America* (New York: Oxford University Press, 1998), 100.

11. Ibid.

12. Mary Pardo, *Mexican American Women Activists: Identity and Resistance in two Los Angeles Communities* (Philadelphia: Temple University Press, 1998), 6.

13. Ada María Isasi-Díaz and Yolanda Tarango, *Hispanic Women: Prophetic Voice in the Church* (San Francisco: Harper and Row, 1988). Supporters are identified in Chapter 5.

14. Ministering can encompass a wide variety of responsibilities, including pastoral counseling, religious education, parish community organizing, leading para-liturgical services, and visiting the sick. In the Catholic tradition, women are prohibited from presiding over Eucharistic liturgies, one of the central ministerial responsibilities of male priests.

15. María de Jesús Ybarra, OP, *El Quetzal Emplumece,* ed. Carmen Montalvo, OSB, and Leonardo Anguiano (San Antonio, Tex.: Mexican American Cultural Center, 1976), 293.

16. David Yoo discusses a similar influence of Marxism on activists within the Asian American movement as well as the rejection of religion due to the role it played in the colonization process of Asia. See "For Those Who Have Eyes to See: Religious Sightings in Asian America," *amerasia journal* 22, no. 1 (1996): xiv–xv.

17. Timothy Matovina has also done significant work on Las Hermanas and PADRES cited elsewhere in this text.

18. Aída Hurtado defines intragroup sexism to identify how male members impose gender subordination on women of their own ethnicity. See "The Politics of Sexuality in the Gender Subordination of Chicanas," in *Living Chicana Theory*, ed. Carla Trujillo (Berkeley: Third Woman Press, 1998), 384–85.

19. USCCB, "Encuentro and Mission: A Renewed Pastoral Framework for Hispanic Ministry" (Washington, D.C.: USCCB, 2002). NCCB/USCC Secretariat for Hispanic Affairs, "National Survey on Hispanic Ministry" (Washington, D.C.: NCCB/USCC Secretariat for Hispanic Affairs, 1990). According to the Secretariat of Hispanic Affairs in Washington, D.C., the following (arch)dioceses total over 50 percent Latino: Amarillo, Brownsville, Brooklyn, El Paso, Los Angeles, Las Cruces, Lubbock, Miami, Santa Fe, San Angelo, San Antonio, Tucson, and Yakima. Los Angeles represents the largest archdiocese in the United States, where Latinos total approximately 70 percent of the Catholic laity.

20. See as one example, "Budget Axe Falls in Los Angeles; Chancery Staff Faces Drastic Cuts," *National Catholic Reporter,* 27 September 2002.

21. "Hispanic Ministry at the Turn of the New Millennium," report of the Bishops' Committee on Hispanic Affairs (Washington, D.C.: NCCB, 1999). Cited in Gilbert R. Cadena and Lara Medina, "Liberation Theology and Social Change: Chicanas and Chicanos in the Catholic Church," in *Chicanos and Chicanas in Contemporary Society*, 2nd ed. (New York: Rowman & Littlefield, forthcoming).

22. Richard Schoenherr and Lawrence A. Young, *Full Pews, Empty Altars* (Madison: University of Wisconsin Press, 1993).

Chapter One: The Emergence of Las Hermanas

1. Gloria Gallardo, SHG, to prospective members, 20 October 1970, Las Hermanas Collection, Box 4, Mexican American Studies Department, Our Lady of the Lake University, San Antonio, Tex. All subsequent references to the Las Hermanas Collection will be designated as LHC, followed by the specific box number.

2. Circular letter to Las Hermanas, 21 April 1971.

3. Carmelita Espinoza, RGS, and María de Jesús Ybarra, OP, La His-

toria de *Las Hermanas* (Historical Background), *Report* (n.d.). LHC, Box 3.

4. *Informes* (19 September 1971): 2.

5. Ibid., 2.

6. Yolanda Tarango, CCVI, interview conducted by author, 12 June 1990. For a discussion of the same limitations placed on Chicano seminarians and priests, see Moisés Sandoval, *On The Move: A History of the Hispanic Church in the United States* (Maryknoll, N.Y.: Orbis Books, 1990), 64–66.

7. Gregoria Ortega, interview conducted by author, 7 May 1997. Ortega left religious life in the early 1980s.

8. María Carolina Flores, CDP, interview conducted by author, 26 April 1997.

9. Sylvia Sedillo, SL, interview conducted by author, 8 April 1997.

10. Teresita Basso, interview conducted by author, 7 March 1997. Basso left religious life in the 1980s after twenty-eight years of service. She continues to provide administrative consulting services to the Presentation sisters.

11. See Carmen Tafolla, "The Church in Texas"; Luciano C. Hendren, "The Church in New Mexico"; and Moisés Sandoval and Salvador E. Alvarez, "The Church in California," in *Fronteras: A History of the Latin American Church in the USA Since 1513,* ed. Moisés Sandoval (San Antonio: Mexican American Cultural Center, 1983).

12. Hendren, "The Church in New Mexico," in *Fronteras,* 195–207. For an excellent discussion of Lamy and the penitente brotherhood, see Albert Pulido, *The Sacred World of the Penitentes* (Washington, D.C.: Smithsonian Institution, 2000).

13. Michael E. Engh, SJ, "From *Frontera* Faith to Roman Rubrics: Altering Hispanic Religious Customs in Los Angeles, 1855–1880," *U.S. Catholic Historian* 12, no. 4 (1994): 91. See also Michael Neri, "Hispanic Catholicism in Transitional California: The Life of José González Rubio, O.F.M., 1804–1875" (Ph.D. diss., Graduate Theological Union, 1974), 138.

14. Engh, "From *Frontera* Faith," 91–94.

15. Albert Camarillo, *Chicanos in a Changing Society* (Cambridge, Mass.: Harvard University Press, 1979), 63.

16. George Sánchez, *Becoming Mexican American: Ethnicity, Culture and Identity in Chicano Los Angeles, 1900–1945* (New York: Oxford University Press, 1993), 166; Gilbert R. Cadena, "Chicanos and the Catholic Church: Liberation Theology as a Form of Empowerment" (Ph.D. diss., University of California at Riverside, 1987), 55–56.

17. This also occurred to Puerto Rican Catholics well into the twentieth century. See Ana María Díaz-Stevens, *Oxcart Catholicism on Fifth*

Avenue: The Impact of the Puerto Rican Migration upon the Archdiocese of New York (Notre Dame, Ind.: University of Notre Dame, 1993), 111–16.

18. Kathy Smith Franklin, " 'A Spirit of Mercy': The Founding of Saint Joseph's Hospital, 1892–1912" (master's thesis, Arizona State University, 1997), 47–48.

19. Ibid., 48; Ricardo Ramírez, "The American Church and Hispanic Migration: An Historical Analysis—Part I" *Migration Today* 6, no. 1 (1978): 16–20; Cadena, "Chicanos and the Catholic Church," 65–67.

20. Sánchez, *Becoming Mexican American*, 151–157; Leo Grebler, Joan W. Moore, and Ralph C. Guzman, *The Mexican American People* (New York: The Free Press, 1970), 486–512.

21. Clifton L. Holland, *The Religious Dimension in Hispanic Los Angeles: A Protestant Case Study* (Pasadena, Calif.: William Carey Library, 1974). Cited in Eldin Villafañe, *The Liberating Spirit* (Grand Rapids: Eerdmans, 1993), 62.

22. Victor De León, "Growth of Hispanic Pentecostals," *Paraclete* 15 (1981): 18. Cited in Villafañe, *Liberating Spirit*, 89.

23. Edwin Sylvest Jr., "Hispanic American Protestantism in the United States," in *Fronteras*, 314–15; Villafañe, *Liberating Spirit*, 66–71.

24. Sánchez, *Becoming Mexican American*, 157–59.

25. Ibid.

26. Grebler, Moore, and Guzman, *The Mexican American People*, 456–58; Cadena, "Chicanos and the Catholic Church," 65–70; Sánchez, *Becoming Mexican American*, 164.

27. Sánchez, *Becoming Mexican American*, 159.

28. Louise Año Nuevo Kerr, "The Chicano Experience in Chicago: 1920–1970" (Ph.D. diss., University of Illinois at Chicago Circle, 1976), 57.

29. Juan R. García, *Mexicans in the Midwest, 1900–1932* (Tucson: University of Arizona Press, 1996), 216–18.

30. Raquel Rubio Goldsmith, "Shipwrecked in the Desert: A Short History of the Mexican Sisters of the House of the Providence in Douglas, Arizona, 1927–1949," in *Women on the U.S.-Mexico Border*, ed. Vicki L. Ruiz and Susan Tiano (Boston: Allen & Unwin, 1987), 183.

31. Grebler, Moore, and Guzman, *The Mexican American People*, 459–60.

32. Cadena, "Chicanos and the Catholic Church," 65–67.

33. Moíses Sandoval, "The Organization of a Hispanic Church," in *Hispanic Catholic Culture in the U.S.*, ed. Jay Dolan and Allan Figueroa Deck, SJ (Notre Dame: University of Notre Dame Press, 1994), 133–34.

34. Ibid., 133–38.

35. Ibid., 139.

36. Ibid., 138–41.

37. Gilbert Cadena, "Chicano Clergy and the Emergence of Liberation Theology," *Hispanic Journal of Behavioral Sciences* 11, no. 2 (1989): 109.

38. Ibid.

39. Las Hermanas conducted a study in 1974 that revealed fifty-nine sites in the United States employing Mexican sisters as domestics. This will be discussed in Chapter 3.

40. Carmelita Espinoza, RGS, interview conducted by author, 16 October 1996.

41. María Iglesias, SC, interview conducted by author, 2 March 1997.

42. Timothy McCarthy, *The Catholic Tradition: Before and After Vatican Council II 1878–1993* (Chicago: Loyola University Press, 1994), 62–64.

43. Basso interview.

44. Karl Rahner, "Towards a Fundamental Theological Interpretation of Vatican Council II," *Theological Studies* 40 (1979): 718–20.

45. Basso interview.

46. McCarthy, *Catholic Tradition*, 68–71.

47. John O'Malley, *Tradition and Transition: Historical Perspectives on Vatican Council II* (Wilmington, Del.: Michael Glazier, 1989), 17.

48. McCarthy, *Catholic Tradition*, 67.

49. Ibid.

50. Walter M. Abbot, SJ, ed., *The Documents of Vatican Council II* (New York: Guild Press, 1966), 206.

51. Ibid., 241.

52. Ibid., 468.

53. Basso interview.

54. Tarango interview.

55. Sandra M. Schneiders, IHM, "Religious Life," in *Modern Catholicism,* ed. Adrian Hastings (New York: Oxford University Press, 1991), 158. Women religious actually began preparing for these new ideas much earlier than the 1960s. See Mary Ewens, OP, "Women in the Convent," in *American Catholic Women,* ed. Karen Kennelly, CSJ (New York: Macmillan, 1989). Ewens chronicles the historic tension for women religious seeking to be active participants in a world beyond convent walls. See also Mary Jo Weaver, *New Catholic Women: A Contemporary Challenge to Traditional Religious Authority* (San Francisco: Harper & Row, 1985).

56. Augusta Neal, *Catholic Sisters in Transition 1960s to 1980s* (Wilmington, Del.: Michael Glazier, 1984), 72.

57. Basso interview.

58. Iglesias interview.

59. Espinoza interview.

60. Tarango interview.

61. Espinoza interview.

62. Ibid.

63. Basso interview.

64. Iglesias interview.

65. Augusta Neal, "The Relation between Religious Belief and Structural Change in Religious Orders": Some Evidence," *Review of Religious Research*, Part II, XII, no. 3 (1971): 153.

66. Neal, *Catholic Sisters in Transition*, 47.

67. Iglesias interview.

68. Carlos Barron, interview conducted by author, 9 March 1997. Mario (Lucie) Barron died of leukemia in 1993. This information is based on an interview with her younger brother, who maintained a close relationship with his sister throughout her religious career.

69. Weaver, *New Catholic Women*, 83.

70. As examples, African American sisters organized as the National Black Sisters' Conference in 1968. See Shawn Copeland, "A Cadre of Women Religious Committed to Black Liberation: The National Black Sisters' Conference," *U.S. Catholic Historian* 14, no. 1 (1996). The National Association of Women Religious organized in 1970 to assist members in using their organized power to effect systemic change. See Judy Vaughan, "National Assembly of Religious Women (NARW)," in *U.S. Women's Interest Groups*, ed. Sarah Slavin (Westport, Conn.: Greenwood, 1995).

71. George Kelley, *The Battle for the American Church* (New York: Doubleday, 1979), 296.

72. Weaver, *New Catholic Women*, 84–85.

73. Kelley, *Battle*, 298–300.

74. Ibid., 296.

75. Ibid., 298.

76. Gregory Baum, "Faith and Liberation: Development since Vatican Council II," in *Vatican Council II: Open Questions and New Horizons*, ed. Gerald M. Fagin, SJ (Wilmington, Del.: Michael Glazier, 1984), 85–88.

77. Phillip Berryman, *The Religious Roots of Rebellion* (Maryknoll, N.Y.: Orbis Books, 1984), 27. Beginning in the 1970s feminist scholars argued for the integration of poor women in "developing" countries into the modernization process so that they might receive their fair share of Western capitalist development. In the late 1970s, social feminists criticized the integration approach: "development under capitalist auspices reinforces, rather than eliminates, the patriarchal relations that oppress women." For a discussion of developmentalism and its impact on gender roles, see *Women on the U.S.-Mexico Border*, ed. Vicki L. Ruiz and

Susan Tiano (Boston: Allen & Unwin, 1987; rept. Westview, 1991), 5–8.

78. Berryman, *Religious Roots*, 40–41.

79. Lawrence Littwin, *Latin America: Catholicism and Class Conflict* (Encino, Calif.: Dickenson, 1974), 2.

80. Ibid., 2–3.

81. Pauline Turner, "Religious Aspects of Women's Role in Nicaragua Revolution," in *Women, Religion and Social Change*, ed. Yvonne Yazbeck Haddad and Ellison Banks Findly (New York: State University of New York Press, 1985), 321–24.

82. Ibid., 324.

83. Susan E. Ramírez-Horton, "The Role of Women in the Nicaraguan Revolution," in *Nicaragua in Revolution*, ed. Thomas W. Walker (New York: Praeger, 1982), 148.

84. Ibid., 148–49. For additional works on women in Latin America in the 1970s, see Doris Tijerino, *Inside the Nicaraguan Revolution* (Vancouver: New Star Books, 1978); Ann Pescatello, ed., *Female and Male in Latin America* (Pittsburgh: University of Pittsburgh Press, 1973), 89–101.

85. Despite the progressive stance by the bishops, the plight of women never received direct attention from the bishops and subsequent male Latin American liberation theologians. It would take Latin American feminists to challenge liberation theology on its silence regarding the status of women in the Church and society. See Milagros Peña, "Feminist Christian Women in Latin America," *Journal of Feminist Studies in Religion* 11, no. 1 (1995): 81–94.

86. Gregory Baum, "Class Struggle and the Magisterium: A New Note," *Theological Studies* 45, no. 4 (1984): 690–92. See also the documents of Medellín, "Peace," nos. 1–13, in *The Gospel of Justice and Peace*, ed. J. Gremillion (Maryknoll, N.Y.: Orbis Books, 1976), 455–58.

87. Daniel Levine, *Popular Voices in Latin American Catholicism* (Princeton: Princeton University Press, 1992).

88. Penny Lernoux, *People of God* (New York: Penguin Books, 1989), 122–23. Cámara received many threats because of his work and between 1968 and 1977 was banned from radio and television. He eventually lost influence in the CNBB due to a conservative backlash in the hierarchy that paralleled military repression in Brazil.

89. Paulo Freire, *The Politics of Education* (South Hadley, Mass.: Bergin & Garvey, 1985), 93.

90. Lernoux, *People of God*, 116–21; Berryman, *Religious Roots*, 21–24.

91. Levine, *Popular Voices*, 33.

92. The book was translated into English in 1973. Gustavo Gutiérrez, *A Theology of Liberation* (Maryknoll, N.Y.: Orbis Books, 1973).

93. A few of the first major works include Leonardo Boff, *Jesus Christ Liberator* (Maryknoll, N.Y.: Orbis Books, 1978), first published in 1972 by Editora Vozes, Brazil; Jose Miguez Bonino, *doing theology in a revolutionary situation* (Philadelphia: Fortress, 1975); Jon Sobrino, *Christology at the Crossroads* (Maryknoll, N.Y.: Orbis Books, 1978), first published in 1976 by Centro de Reflexión Teológica, Mexico.

94. Baum, "Class Struggle and the Magisterium," 692.

95. "Evangelization in Latin America's Present and Future," in *Liberation Theology: A Documentary History*, ed. Alfred T. Hennelly (Maryknoll, N.Y.: Orbis Books, 1990), 254. See also Phillip Berryman, "What Happened at Puebla," in *Churches and Politics in Latin America*, ed. Daniel Levine (Beverly Hills, Calif.: Sage, 1980).

96. Gilbert Cadena, "The Social Location of Liberation Theology: From Latin America to the United States," in *Hispanic/Latino Theology*, ed. Ada María Isasi-Díaz and Fernando Segovia (Minneapolis: Fortress, 1996), 167–71.

97. Berryman, *Religious Roots*, 224.

98. Lernoux, *Cry of the People*, xvi–xix. Two of the women, Ita Ford and Maura Clarke, were Maryknoll sisters. Dorothy Kazel belonged to the Ursuline order and Jean Donovan was a lay missionary from Cleveland, Ohio.

99. Lernoux, *People of God*, 5–6 (quote on 6).

100. Jon Sobrino, Ignacio Ellacuría, et al., *Companions of Jesus* (Maryknoll, N.Y.: Orbis Books, 1990).

101. Weaver, *New Catholic Women*, 83. See also Debra Campbell, "Reformers and Activists," in *American Catholic Women*, ed. Karen Kennelly (New York: Macmillan, 1989), 179–80.

102. Espinoza interview.

103. Dominga Zapata, "gospel to the hispanic: unrecognized ministry?" in *Women in Ministry: A Sister's View* (Chicago: National Association for Women Religious Publications, 1972), 131–32.

104. María de Jesús Ybarra, OP, interview conducted by author, 10 April 1997.

105. Ada María Isasi-Díaz, "*Luchar por la Justicia Es Rezar:* To Struggle for Justice Is to Pray," in *Mujerista Theology* (Maryknoll, N.Y.: Orbis Books, 1996), 32.

106. See Emilio Zamora, *The World of the Mexican Worker in Texas* (College Station: Texas A&M University Press, 1993); Mario García, *Desert Immigrants: The Mexicans of El Paso, 1880–1920* (New Haven: Yale University Press, 1981); Albert Camarillo, *Chicanos in a Changing*

Society (Cambridge, Mass.: Harvard University Press, 1979); Rudolfo Acuña, *Occupied America: A History of Chicanos,* 4th ed. (New York: Longman, 2000); Mario García, *Mexican Americans* (New Haven: Yale University Press, 1989); George Sanchez, *Becoming Mexican American* (New York: Oxford University Press, 1993); David Gutiérrez, *Wall and Mirrors: Mexican Americans, Mexican Immigrants, and the Politics of Ethnicity in the Southwest, 1910–1986* (Berkeley: University of California Press, 1995); and Vicki Ruiz, *From Out of the Shadows: Mexican Women in Twentieth-Century America* (New York: Oxford University Press, 1998).

107. Ruiz, *Shadows,* 98.

108. General Social and Economic Characteristics. U.S. Summary, 1970 Census of Population, PC(1)-C1.

109. Ibid., 398.

110. Ibid., 386.

111. No author, "Another Civil Rights Headache," *U.S. News and World Report,* 6 June 1966, 47.

112. Thomas P. Carter, *Mexican Americans in School: A History of Educational Neglect* (New York: College Entrance Exam Board, 1970), 221.

113. Julie Leininger Pycior, "From Hope to Frustration: Mexican Americans and Lyndon Johnson in 1967," *The Western Historical Quarterly* 24, no. 4 (1993): 468–94.

114. Ibid., 493–94.

115. Carter, *Mexican Americans in School*s, 30. Cited in Vicki Ruiz, *Shadows,* 102–3. As an example, in 1967 Chicanos in seven southwestern colleges totaled only 3,227 students.

116. Anonymous, "The Struggle for Chicano Liberation," in *The Politics of Chicano Liberation,* ed. Olga Rodríguez (New York: Pathfinder, 1977), 50.

117. Helen Rowan, "A Minority Nobody Knows," *The Atlantic,* June 1967, 47–52.

118. Senator Joseph Montoya of New Mexico; Congressmen Edward Roybal from California; Hernan Badillo from New York; Manuel Luzan from New Mexico; Henry González and Eligio de la Garza, both of Texas. See Richard Santillan, *La Raza Unida Party* (Los Angeles: Tlaquilo Publications, 1973), 11.

119. Ernesto Chávez, "Creating Aztlán: The Chicano Movement in Los Angeles, 1966–1978" (Ph.D. diss., University of California at Los Angeles, 1994), xvii–xviii.

120. The association's name was changed to United Farm Workers (UFW) in February 1972. In September 1973, it would again be changed to the United Farm Workers of America (UFWA).

121. Carlos Muñoz Jr., *Youth, Identity and Power* (New York: Verso, 1989), 7.

122. Arturo Rosales, *CHICANO!: The History of the Mexican American Civil Rights Movement* (Houston: Arte Público, 1996), 140. The AWOC represented Filipino farm workers in Delano, California, and asked the NFWA for support in their strike against grape growers beginning 5 September 1965. See 136–37.

123. Ibid., 141–45 (quote is on 145.) A more detailed analysis of the farmworker movement is presented in Chapter 3.

124. Ibid., 145–46.

125. The 1970 victory was short-lived, as grape growers refused to renew their contracts in 1973.

126. César Chávez, "The Mexican American and the Church," *El Grito* 1, no. 4 (1968): 10. This speech took place during a twenty-five-day spiritual fast.

127. "Struggle for Chicano Liberation," in *Politics of Chicano Liberation*, 52.

128. Chávez, "The Mexican American," 11–12.

129. Rosales, *CHICANO!* 147.

130. Basso interview.

131. Irene Muñoz, SHM, interview conducted by author, 15 July 1997.

132. Muñoz interview. The involvement of Las Hermanas and PADRES in the farm labor struggle will be addressed in Chapter 3.

133. Muñoz Jr., *Youth, Identity and Power*, 58, 130.

134. Dolores Bernal, "Providing an Alternative History of the 1968 East Los Angeles Blowouts: Constructing a Theory to Better Understand Chicana School Resistance" (Ph.D. diss., University of California at Los Angeles, 1997). Bernal focuses on the leadership of Chicanas during the blow outs.

135. Ruiz, *Shadows*, 103–4.

136. Rosales, *CHICANO!* 190–94.

137. Basso interview.

138. "Chicano Woman Subject of CCC Course," *The Independent* (Marin County), 17 December 1975, 26.

139. Muñoz Jr., *Youth, Identity and Power*, 76–78. Another youth conference at the University of California at Santa Barbara occurred one month after the Denver gathering, to ensure equal access to higher education for Chicanos. The three-day conference launched the MEChA and emphasized the institutionalization of Chicano studies on college campuses. Participants produced "a master plan of action" for Chicanos in higher education. *El Plan de Santa Barbara* emphasized a strong connection between the academy and the community that has had long-lasting effects on the development of Chicano/a studies programs and departments.

140. Espinoza interview.

141. Ruiz, *Shadows,* 114–15.

142. Rosales, *CHICANO!* 201–2.

143. Ibid., 202–5, for a brief biography of Salazar and the impact of his death on the movement. A Los Angeles County Coroner's Jury decided that there was no cause for criminal action against the deputy who fired tear gas into the Silver Dollar Bar where Salazar was slain.

144. Clarita Trujillo, OLVN, interview conducted by author, 5 May 1997.

145. Ibid.

146. Juan Romero, "*PADRES*: WHO THEY ARE AND WHERE THEY ARE GOING," *PADRES* NATIONAL CONGRESS: *LA RAZA NUEVA Y NUEVA ESPERANZA,* 2–5 Feb. 1975 (N.p.: Privately printed, San Antonio, Tex., 1975), 2.

147. Timothy Matovina, "Representation and the Reconstruction of Power: The Rise of *PADRES* and *Las Hermanas,*" in *What's Left: Progressive Catholics in America,* ed. Mary Jo Weaver and R. Scott Appleby (Bloomington: Indiana University Press, 1999), 221.

148. Ibid.

149. The issue of membership would persist throughout PADRES's history and, some would argue, would lead to its demise in the mid-1980s. See ibid.

150. Juan Romero, "Charism and Power: An Essay on the History of *PADRES,*" *U.S. Catholic Historian* 9 (Winter–Spring 1990): 147–63.

151. Albert Pulido, "Are You an Emissary of Jesus Christ?: Justice, The Catholic Church, and the Chicano Movement," in *American Mosaic,* ed. Young I. Song and Eugene C. Kim (Englewood Cliffs, N.J.: Prentice Hall, 1993), 154.

152. Ibid., 156.

153. Ibid., 156–59. El Centro Padre Hidalgo will be discussed in Chapter 4.

154. Ibid., 161.

155. Ibid., 159. For a creative interpretation of these events, see Oscar Zeta Acosta, *The Revolt of the Cockroach People* (San Francisco: Straight Arrow Books, 1973), Chapter 1.

156. Teresita Basso, "The Emerging 'Chicana' Sister," *Review for Religious* 30 (1971): 1019–28. Also published in *Chicana Feminist Thought: The Basic Historical Writings,* ed. Alma M. García (New York: Routledge, 1997). Cited in García, 58.

157. See Marta Vidal, *Chicanas Speak Out* (New York: Pathfinder, 1971). Exceptions did occur as on the University of California at Santa Barbara campus during 1973–75 when two Chicanas, Norma Razo and Suzanne Manriquez, took prominent leadership roles in the student organization, La Raza Libre. I attended UCSB during these years.

158. Sonia A. López, "The Role of the Chicana within the Student Movement," in *Essays on la Mujer,* ed. Rosaura Sánchez and Rosa Martínez Cruz (Los Angeles: University of California at Los Angeles Chicano Studies Center Publications, 1977), 23–24.

159. Ibid., 24–27. The earliest groups formed on college campuses include Las Chicanas from San Diego State University and Hijas De Cuauhtémoc at Long Beach State University. Other groups formed at Fresno State College and Stanford University. The First National Chicana Conference was held in Houston, Texas, in May 1971, followed by the Chicana Regional Conference in 1972 in Whittier, California, and La Conferencia Femenil in Sacramento, California. Feminist community organizations, such as Comisión Femenil Mexicana Nacional and the National Chicana Political Caucus, also formed.

160. Ramón Gutiérrez, "Community, Patriarchy and Individualism: The Politics of Chicano History and the Dream of Equality," *American Quarterly* 45, no. 1 (1993): 47.

161. Ruiz, *Shadows,* 100.

162. Friction and disagreement among Chicana activists characterized these formative years of Chicana feminism, as many women chose to remain loyal to the cultural nationalist agenda. Chicana heterosexual feminists often met accusations of being *vendidas, falsas,* opportunists, and lesbians; and lesbians were accused of being feminists. For "loyalists," an agenda concerned with the liberation of women threatened the cultural survival of Chicanos based on traditional heterosexual unions. Chicana lesbians experienced even worse condemnation because their sexual identity was "identified as an extreme derivation of feminism." See García, "Chicana Feminist Discourse," 536–37.

163. López, "The Role of the Chicana," in *Essays on la Mujer,* 27.

164. García, *Chicana Feminist Thought,* 8.

165. Ruiz, *Shadows,* 107–8.

166. Mirta Vidal, "Women: New Voice of La Raza," in *Chicanas Speak Out* (New York: Pathfinder, 1971), 4.

167. Ibid.

168. For a telling discussion of the gender politics in CASA, see Ruiz, *Shadows,* 116–18.

169. Basso interview.

170. Virgilio Elizondo, interview conducted by author, 17 February 1997.

171. Ana María Díaz-Stevens, "Latinas and the Church," in *Hispanic Catholic Culture in the U.S.: Issues and Concerns,* ed. Jay P. Dolan and Alan Figueroa Deck (Notre Dame, Ind.: University of Notre Dame Press, 1994), 245.

172. Tarango interview.

173. See *In Our Own Voices*, ed. Rosemary Radford Ruether and Rosemary Skinner Keller (San Francisco: Harper, 1995), 21; Weaver, *New Catholic Women*, 25–36; Rubio Goldsmith, "Shipwrecked," 187.

174. For an account of Sor Juana, see Octavio Paz, *Sor Juana, or the Traps of Faith*, trans. Margaret Sayers Pedin (Cambridge, Mass.: Harvard University Press, 1988). For a revisionist interpretation, see Alicia Gaspar de Alba, "The Politics of Location of the Tenth Muse of America: An Interview with Sor Juana Inés de la Cruz," in *Living Chicana Theory*, ed. Carla Trujillo (Berkeley: Third Woman Press, 1998), 136–65. See also Alicia Gasper de Alba, *Sor Juana's Second Dream: A Novel* (Albuquerque: University of New Mexico Press, 1999).

175. Barron interview.

176. James E. Kenneally, *The History of American Catholic Women* (New York: Crossroad, 1990), 43.

177. Rosemary Radford Ruether, "Ruether Reflects on History: Nun-Lay-woman," *Probe* 12 (July–August 1984): 2. Cited in Weaver, *New Catholic Women*, 72.

178. Ibid.

179. Olivia Mercado, "*Las Hermanas*," *COMADRE*, no. 2 (1978): 34–41.

180. Vidal, "Women: New Voice of La Raza," 3.

181. "Workshop Resolutions—First National Chicana Conference," in *Chicanas Speak Out* (New York: Pathfinder, 1971), 14.

182. Ibid., 15.

183. Ibid., 13.

184. López, "The Role of the Chicana," in *Essays on la Mujer*, 24–25.

185. Basso, cited in García, *Chicana Feminist Thought*, 60.

Chapter Two: *Unidas en acción y oración*

1. Unidas en acción y oración means "united in action and prayer." La raza literally translates as "the race," a term connoting a sense of peoplehood and solidarity among persons of Latin American descent. LHC, Box 3.

2. Gloria Gallardo, SHG, to prospective members, 20 October 1970, LHC, Box 4.

3. Ortega interview, 21 April 1997.

4. Chela Sandoval, "U.S. Third World Feminism: The Theory and Method of Oppositional Consciousness in the PostModern World," *Genders*, no. 10 (1991): 3, 15.

5. Ortega interview.

6. Ibid.

7. Ibid.

8. Ibid.

9. See Rudy Acuña, *Occupied America: A History of Chicanos*, 5th ed. (New York: Pearson Longman, 2004). Arnoldo De León, *Mexican Americans in Texas, A Brief History* (Arlington Heights, Ill.: Harlan Davidson, 1993).

10. De León, *Mexican Americans in Texas*, 37, 50.

11. David Montejano, *Anglos and Mexicans in the Making of Texas, 1836–1986* (Austin: University of Texas Press, 1987), 262.

12. Ibid., 285–86. See also "Chicanos File Suit Against School Board," *Abilene Reporter-News*, 5 December 1969, sec. C, 12.

13. "School Districts Hit by U.S. Suits," *Dallas Morning News*, 8 August 1970, sec. A, 1; Rudolfo Acuña, "Judge Ignores U.S. School Demand," *Dallas Morning News*, 11 August 1970, sec. D, 1.

14. De León, *Mexican Americans in Texas*, 127.

15. Montejano, *Anglos and Mexicans*, 286.

16. Ortega interview.

17. Ibid. *Gavachos* is a slang term for whites.

18. "Chicanos Will Hold Boycott," *Abilene Reporter-News*, 30 October 1969, 1. Schools included Abilene High, Cooper High, Franklin Junior High, Lincoln Junior High, Madison and Mann Junior High.

19. Ortega interview.

20. Ibid. See also "Chicanos to Wear Brown Armbands, Ask No Trouble," *Abilene Reporter-News*, 3 November 1969.

21. "Chicanos Gather for Ninth Day," *Abilene Reporter-News*, 31 October 1969.

22. "Chicanos File Suit Against School Board," *Abilene Reporter-News*, 5 December 1969, sec. C, 12.

23. Ortega interview.

24. "Chicanos Gather for Ninth Day," *Abilene Reporter-News*, 31 October 1969.

25. Ibid.

26. "Chicanos to Wear Brown Armbands, Ask No Trouble," *Abilene Reporter-News*, 3 November 1969.

27. Ortega interview.

28. "Chicanos File Suit Against School Board," *Abilene Reporter-News*, 5 December 1969, sec. C, 12.

29. Ibid.

30. "Testimony Opens in Chicano Suit," *Abilene Reporter-News*, 9 June 1970, sec. A, 2; "Boycott Jury Rules Board Applied Absence Rule Fairly," *Abilene Reporter-News*, 13 June 1970, sec. A, 1.

31. "Absentee Lawyers Criticized by Judge," *Abilene Reporter-News*, 13 June 1970, sec. A, 1–2.

32. Ortega interview.

33. Ibid.

34. Rudy Acuña, interview conducted by author, 17 April 1997. Acuña does not have any documentation on his presence in Rotan due to his fear for many years of being prosecuted as an outside agitator. Apparently his role as a civil rights observer was misunderstood by many of the Euroamericans in Rotan.

35. Mark Smith, interview conducted by author, 17 July 1997. Smith also lacked documentation on his presence in Rotan. He was considered a "rabblerouser from Lubock" by Judge Leo Brewster during the trial in Abilene. See "Absentee Lawyers Criticized by Judge," *Abilene Reporter-News,* 13 June 1970, sec. A, 1–2.

36. Ortega interview.

37. Ibid.

38. Acuña interview.

39. Ortega interview.

40. "Genteel Activist Leads Spanish-Speaking Sisters," *National Catholic Reporter,* 13 August 1971, 1, 19. Unfortunately, Gloria Gallardo could not be located for this study.

41. In 1970, Flores would be appointed as the first Chicano bishop in the United States.

42. "Genteel Activist," 19.

43. Ibid.

44. Ortega interview.

45. Ibid. The *Dallas Morning News* included numerous articles during August 1970 on federal lawsuits against Texas school districts refusing to integrate. An example: "Quick School Suit Action Ordered of Federal Judge," which included a discussion on the "dual system of discrimination in its schools for Mexican American students." *Dallas Morning News,* 19 August 1970, sec. A, 1.

46. For a reference to the huelga schools, see "Texas Schools' Integration Has Some Bumpy Spots," *Dallas Morning News,* 6 September 1970, sec. A, 28.

47. Ortega interview. The MCDP was founded in Houston in 1930 by Sister Benita while she worked as a member of the Sisters of Divine Providence. Of Belgian ancestry, Benita was orphaned at twelve years of age and was educated in Mexico by the Sisters of Charity of the Incarnate Word. See Moisés Sandoval, "A Half-Century of Service," *Revista Maryknoll* (November 1980): 9–10.

48. Circular letter from Sister Gloria Gallardo, SHG, 21 April 1971, LCH, Box 4.

49. Tarango interview.

50. Fresquez interview.

51. Basso interview.

52. Ybarra interview.

53. Based on Ybarra interview, Fresquez interview, Tarango interview, and Ortega interview.

54. Tarango interview.

55. Espinoza interview.

56. Corrales interview.

57. Gloria Gallardo, SHG, to Leadership Conference of Women Religious, 17 November 1971, LHC, Box 4.

58. Ortega never officially presented herself to Bishop Morkovsky of the Galveston–Houston diocese because she feared reprisal from the clergy of San Angelo. Apparently Morkovsky did not object to Ortega's presence, as was evident in his support at the first Las Hermanas conference.

59. Ortega interview. The first issues of *Informes* also thanks the contemplative order of Nuns of the Perpetual Adoration of the Blessed Sacrament in El Paso as "playing a big part in the development of *Las Hermanas*" through prayer. *Informes* (19 September 1971): 3.

60. Carmelita Espinoza and María de Jesús Ybarra, "*La Historia de Las Hermanas*" (N.p.: Privately printed, 1978), 9. It is interesting to note that Susan Starr Sered in *Priestess Mother and Sacred Sister* states, "In women's religions 'sisterhood' is a symbolic expression of ongoing unity . . . sisterhood is what empowers them to translate religious participation into secular benefits" (New York: Oxford University Press, 1994), 269.

61. See Audre Lorde, *Sister Outsider* (New York: The Crossing Press, 1984), for a critique of sisterhood in the white women's movement. Also see bell hooks, *Feminism is for Everybody* (Cambridge, Mass.: South End Press, 2000).

62. See Ruiz, *Shadows*, 4.

63. Elías interview.

64. Villegas interview.

65. Browne interview.

66. Iglesias interview.

67. Gloria Gallardo, SHG, 21 April 1971, LCH, Box 4.

68. Basso interview.

69. Espinoza interview.

70. Gloria Gallardo, SHG, 21 April 1971, LHC, Box 4.

71. The experience at IPLA will be discussed more fully in Chapter 3.

72. Ybarra interview.

73. Ibid.

74. Gloria Gallardo, SHG, 21 April 1971, LHC, Box 4. The leadership structure of president and vice-president changed in 1972.

75. *Informes* (19 September 1971): 2.

76. Ibid., 2.
77. Ibid., 4. "Sisters, we have won another victory!"
78. Espinoza and Ybarra, "La Historia de *Las Hermanas*," 25. LCWR was formerly the Major Superiors of Women Religious, as discussed in Chapter 1.
79. Tarango interview.
80. Dominga Zapata, "Gospel to the Hispanic: Unrecognized Ministry?" in *Women in Ministry: A Sisters' View* (Chicago: NAWR Publications, 1972), 129.
81. Ibid., 131.
82. Ibid., 132.
83. Corrales interview.
84. Espinoza and Ybarra, "La Historia de *Las Hermanas*," 25
85. While this conference represented the second time that Las Hermanas met, more recent literature in the archives recognizes the Houston meeting as preparatory and the Santa Fe meeting as the first national conference.
86. Tarango interview.
87. Asemblea, or assembly, is often used in archival materials to refer to the annual conferences. I use the terms interchangeably.
88. Mario Barron, SJC, "*Equipos de Concientización*," proposal delivered on 24 November 1971, 3, LHC, Box 6.
89. Ibid., 3–4.
90. Anonymous, LHC, Box 6.
91. Tarango interview. The order of the Holy Ghost suggested to Gallardo that she start her own religious congregation when she explained to them the purpose of Las Hermanas. Letter from Gloria Gallardo, to Las Hermanas, 30 October 1991, LHC, Box 6.
92. Tarango interview.
93. One group of activists in Los Angeles went so far as to burn their baptismal certificates.
94. Basso interview.
95. Iglesias interview.
96. Ibid.
97. Ybarra interview.
98. Author unknown, "In Solidarity and Service, Reflections on the Problem of Clericalism in the Church," 2, LHC, Box 6.
99. Tarango interview.
100. Basso interview.
101. Other groups such as the LCWR, the NAWR, and the NBSC limited their membership to sisters in the mid-1970s. Both the NAWR and the NBSC mobilized in 1968, the former to represent "grassroots women religious" concerned with justice issues and the latter address-

ing the concerns of African American sisters. The NAWR followed the example of Las Hermanas in 1978 by opening its membership to laity, and in 1984, four laywomen joined their board of directors; however, the NAWR disbanded in 1995. The NBSC now admits laywomen only as associate members, and the LCWR continues to limit its membership to religious sisters.

102. Ortega interview.

103. Basso interview.

104. "Financial Reports," LHC, Box 8.

105. Basso interview.

106. Iglesias interview.

107. Basso interview.

108. Espinoza and Ybarra, "La Historia de *Las Hermanas*," 20.

109. Carmelita Espinoza, "Reporte Sobre la Organización *Las Hermanas* de '72/74," 1, LHC, Box 2.

110. Sisters Uniting organized in 1972 as a collaborative effort of nine women's religious congregations, including Las Hermanas, the NAWR, and the NBSC.

111. Tarango interview.

112. Ortega interview.

113. Iglesias interview.

Chapter Three: *Una Nueva Iglesia Latina*

1. "Being church" emphasizes that the institutional Church must be transformed to be a Church in solidarity with the poor. María de Jesús Ybarra, *El Quetzal Emplumece,* ed. Carmen Montalvo, OSB, and Leonardo Anguiano (San Antonio, Tex.: Mexican American Cultural Center, 1976), 293.

2. "MACC," *PADRES* (January 1972): 3. "Cultural Center Offers Specialized Spanish for Church Purposes," *National Catholic Reporter,* 30 April 1976, 3. Gloria Gallardo, SHG, then president of Las Hermanas, sat on the first steering committee. Other members included Archbishop James Davis of Santa Fe; Bishop Lawrence DeFalco of Amarillo; Bishop Thomas Tschoepe of Dallas; Frs. Peter Kellerman, Joseph Montoya, Ron Anderson, Ed Bily, and Roberto Flores; Protestant theologian Jorge-Lara Braud of Austin; Sister James Elizabeth Gonzalez of Our Lady of the Lake University; Dr. Leonard Mestas; and Richard Santos. Fr. Virgilio Elizondo served as executive director. *PADRES* (January 1972): 3.

3. Ybarra interview.

4. Ibid. Circular letter to Las Hermanas members, 14 April 1974. This program was the seed for the mini-pastoral courses now offered at MACC. Ybarra also served on the Personnel Committee in 1973.

5. "Summer at MACC," *PADRES* (July 1973): 4.

6. *Informes* (November 1974): 2.

7. Sandoval, *The Mexican American Experience in the Church*, 22.

8. "MACC Concludes Its First Evaluation," *PADRES* (October 1972): 3.

9. Romero interview.

10. Gustavo Gutiérrez, Enrique Dussell, Juan Luis Segundo, Edgar Beltran, and José Marins were among those who conducted seminars for religious and laity at MACC. "Summer at MACC," *PADRES* (July 1973): 4; Cadena, "Chicanos and the Catholic Church: Liberation Theology as a Form of Empowerment," 90.

11. Sedillo's experience at MACC will be elaborated on in Chapter 4.

12. "Summer at MACC," *PADRES* (July 1973): 4.

13. "The 'Why' of this Center," *MACC Fifth Anniversary* (N.p.: Privately published, 1977), 7.

14. San Antonio residents María Zapata and José Vásquez served as board members along with Bishop Patricio Flores; Protestant theologian Jorge Lara-Braud; Paul Sedillo, director of the Secretariat for the Spanish Speaking; Roberto Flores of PADRES; and Gloria Gallardo of Las Hermanas. "Minutes of the Evaluation Session," September 1972, *PADRES* files.

15. "MACC Board Meeting," 17 February 1973, 1, *PADRES* files.

16. Staff resignations over this issue occurred in 1973. See letter of resignation from Rubén Peña, Richard Yzaguirre, and Angélica Inda, 15 May 1973, PADRES files.

17. Tarango interview.

18. Internal Report, "Mexican American Cultural Center, Evaluation Report. Management Design, Inc.," May 1977: 22, PADRES files.

19. Elizondo interview.

20. MACC has been a model for other pastoral institutes such as the Southeast Pastoral Institute (SEPI) established in 1979, the Midwest Institute for Hispanic Ministry in 1981, and the Northwest Pastoral Institute in 1983. The Midwest and Northwest institutes no longer exist.

21. Ortega had contacted the MCDP in her initial efforts to organize Las Hermanas.

22. Ybarra interview.

23. Carmelita Espinoza and María de Jesus Ybarra, *La Historia de Las Hermanas, Report,* (n.d.), 21, LHC, Box 14.

24. The MFC arose as the Spanish-speaking version of the Christian Family Movement, an organization founded in 1949 emphasizing lay leadership, evangelization, communication, and community service as ways to strengthen Christian families. The goal of the MFC was that each family exist as a small Christian community. National MFC conventions

included the support of bishops and members of PADRES. *Movimiento Familiar Cristiano, Report,* 1978.

25. Ybarra interview.

26. María de Jesús Ybarra, Mexicans Nuns in the U.S., *Report,* (n.d.) LHC, Box 14. The report by Ybarra stated that in one of the places visited, a total of $250 was paid per month for the labor of five sisters.

27. María de Jesús Ybarra, *Reporte Sobre Trabajo Hecho de Proyecto Mexico, Report,* 25 August 1974, LHC, Box 14. See also Ana María Díaz-Stevens, "Latinas in the Church," in *Hispanic Catholic Culture in the U.S.,* ed. Jay P. Dolan and Alan Figueroa Deck (Notre Dame, Ind.: University of Notre Dame Press, 1994), 262–66; Edmundo Rodríguez, "The Hispanic Community and Church Movements: Schools of Leadership," in *Hispanic Catholic Culture,* 228–29.

28. Executive Board Meeting Minutes 1973, LHC, Box 2.

29. Financial Report, LHC, Box 8.

30. Ybarra interview.

31. Díaz-Stevens, "Latinas and the Church," in *Hispanic Catholic Culture,* 265.

32. Browne interview.

33. Individual amounts ranged between $100 and $500 for workshops and courses addressing diverse issues such as Chicanas in management, homosexuality and the church, immigration, liturgy, theology, film, and law. Recipients could apply the funds toward courses at secular or religious institutions. In addition, the organization awarded limited financial assistance to laywomen for their attendance at Las Hermanas national conferences. "Scholarship/Grant Expenditures 1981–82; 1982–83," LHC, Box 16.

34. "*Las Hermanas* to Bishops," 27 May 1974, LHC, Box 3.

35. Ybarra interview.

36. Ibid.

37. "*Las Hermanas* to Bishops," 27 May 1974, LHC, Box 14. *Hispano* is a term used by some Latinos to refer to Spanish-speaking persons. It is historically used in New Mexico and Colorado.

38. Ibid.

39. Ybarra interview.

40. Tarango interview. PADRES's decision to limit its membership to clergy emphasized its concern for institutional power.

41. Corrales interview.

42. "Interview with Bishop Elect Chávez," *PADRES* (May 1974): 3; "*PADRES* and the Selection of the Bishop," *PADRES* (May 1974): 8.

43. Juan Romero, "Charism and Power: An Essay on the History of *PADRES,*" *U.S. Catholic Historian* 9 (Winter–Spring 1990): 157.

44. Between 1970 and 1990 a total of twenty-one Latinos were ordained as bishops in the United States. Not all, however, have held a progressive vision for the Church as did the earlier Chicano bishops. See Romero, "Charism and Power," 158.

45. Ybarra interview. Sedillo's office refers to the Division for the Spanish-Speaking of the U.S. Catholic Conference in Washington, D.C.

46. Letter to Rev. Jean Jadot, 15 August 1978, *PADRES* files.

47. Traditionally bishops have been selected from the diocesan level where priests do not have ties to religious communities but act as individual clergy responsible directly to their bishop. More Latino candidates belonged to religious orders.

48. Juan Romero, "New Bishop for San Bernardino," unpublished paper, 18–19. The four bishops invited were John Quinn of San Francisco, then president of the NCCB; Cardinal Manning of Los Angeles; John Cummings of Oakland, then president of the California Catholic Conference; and Auxiliary Bishop Roger Mahony of Fresno.

49. Ibid.

50. Ibid., 21–22.

51. Ibid.

52. "San Bernardino," *Entre Nosotros* (Winter 1978): 2.

53. Espinoza interview.

54. *Proceedings of the II Encuentro Nacional Hispano de Pastoral,* Secretariat for Hispanic Affairs National Conference of Catholic Bishops/United States Catholic Conference, n.d, 64.

55. Sandoval, "The Organization of a Hispanic Church," in *Hispanic Catholic Culture,* 142.

56. Ibid., 141–43.

57. The role of Las Hermanas in the III Encuentro will be discussed in Chapter 4.

58. Many others participated, including Olga Villa and Lupe Anguiano.

59. Iglesias interview.

60. Castañeda interview. See *"II Encuentro Nacional Hispano: 'Somos una Gran y Rica Potencia,'"* *PADRES* (Summer 1977): 6–7.

61. Castañeda interview.

62. Ibid.

63. "II *Encuentro* Nacional Hispano de Pastoral, Conclusions," *El Visitante Dominical,* 27 November 1977, 7. Author's translation.

64. Castañeda interview.

65. Sandoval, "Organization of a Hispanic Church," in *Hispanic Catholic Culture.*

66. *Proceedings of the II Encuentro Nacional,* 66.

67. *The Hispanic Presence: Challenge and Commitment* (Washington, D.C.: USCC Office of Publishing and Promotion Services, 1983).

68. The III Encuentro held in 1985 had an attendance of 1,148 persons, including approximately fifty bishops, and concluded with the broad outlines for a national pastoral plan for Hispanic ministry. The plan was finally approved in 1987 by the U.S. Catholic bishops, but with no allocation of funds for its implementation. It would be up to individual dioceses to implement their own plan of action for Latino ministry. See Sandoval, "Organization of a Hispanic Church," in *Hispanic Catholic Culture.*

69. Although the battle against racism and sexism in the church continues, the encuentros helped to construct the foundation on which to build resistance.

70. Richard Griswold del Castillo and Richard García, *César Chávez: A Triumph of Spirit* (Norman: University of Oklahoma Press, 1995), 76.

71. *Rerum novarum* inaugurated a Catholic position on labor, as it supported a worker's right to humane conditions, a just wage, freedom to organize, and the right to own private property. In 1931 these ideals were developed further by Pope Pius XI in *The Reconstruction of the Social Order* (*Quadragesimo anno*). Writing in the midst of a worldwide economic depression, Pius XI addressed the abuses of capitalism and communism and stressed the duty of the Church and governments to address social injustices. This letter broadened the Church's concern for exploited workers by addressing oppressive economic systems. In 1961, on the seventieth anniversary of *Rerum novarum,* Pope John XXIII issued another papal encyclical, *Christianity and Social Progress* (*Mater et magister*). Addressing the growing gap between the rich and the poor, the pope confirmed workers' rights and the social responsibility of employers. Subsequent pastoral letters, *Peace on Earth* (*Pacem en terris,* 1963), *The Church in the Modern World* (*Gaudium et spes,* 1965), and *The Development of Peoples* (*Popolorum progressio,* 1967), continued the strong tradition of social justice teaching within the Roman Catholic Church. See Peter J. Henriot, Edward P. DeBerri, and Michael J. Schultheis, *Catholic Social Teaching: Our Best Kept Secret* (Maryknoll, N.Y.: Orbis Books, 1985).

72. See Victor Salandini, *The Tortilla Priest* (San Diego: The San Diego Review, 1992); Patrick Hayes McNamara, "Bishops, Priests, and Prophecy: A Study in the Sociology of Religious Protest" (Ph.D. diss., University of California at Los Angeles, 1968).

73. The Catholic Church had officially initiated ministry to migrant workers in 1950 under the Spanish Mission Band in response to

the increased number of Mexican Catholics working under the *bracero* system. Under the Spanish Mission Band, four priests, Frs. Thomas McCullough, Donald McDonnell, John García, and Ralph Duggan, organized direct ministry to migrant workers in the San Francisco archdiocese, which included numerous rural areas. Their work focused initially on spiritual needs but soon turned to socioeconomic issues. In 1958, McCullough began the Agricultural Workers Association (AWA), based on the model of a mutual aid society. Dolores Huerta, then an organizer for the Community Service Organization (CSO), collaborated with the priests in writing the AWA's constitution. One year later, the AWA joined with the AWOC, a union that would eventually join with the National Farm Workers Association under the direction of César Chávez and Dolores Huerta. As the priests spoke publicly against the bracero program for increasing unemployment, depressing wages, and hindering the unionization of farmworkers, they met the wrath of agricultural growers. Between 1958 and 1959, numerous growers in the Stockton and San Diego area threatened local bishops to stop the Mission Band's efforts at social justice. In 1964, the Band was brought to an end; however, McDonnell and McCullough's efforts to organize farmworkers had led them to work closely with Huerta and Chávez. See Jeffrey M. Burns, "Migrants and Braceros," in *Mexican Americans the Catholic Church, 1900–1965*, ed. Jay P. Dolan and Gilberto M. Hinojosa (Notre Dame, Ind.: University of Notre Dame Press, 1994); Margaret Elenor Rose, "Women in the United Farm Workers: A Study of Chicana and Mexicana Participation in a Labor Union" (Ph.D. diss., University of California at Los Angeles, 1988). See also Susan Ferriss and Ricardo Sandoval, *The Fight in the Fields: Cesar Chavez and the Farmworkers Movement* (Orlando: Paradigm Productions, 1997), 37–60; Fred Ross, *Conquering Goliath: Cesar Chavez at the Beginning* (Keene, Calif.: El Tallerr Grafico Press, 1989). Dolores Huerta interview, conducted by the author, May 2002.

74. Pulido, "Are You an Emissary of Jesus Christ?" in *American Mosaic*.

75. Msgr. George G. Higgins with William Bole, *Organized Labor and the Church: Reflections of a Labor Priest* (New York: Paulist Press, 1993). *Labor priest* became popularized during the New Deal era and referred to clergy heavily involved with union organizing. See Higgins and Bole, 20.

76. Initially aimed at the Guimarra Corporation, the largest table grape grower in the country, the boycott soon spread to the entire grape industry. Other table grape companies illegally lent Guimarra their labels for clandestine shipping into grocery stores, forcing the union to broaden the boycott. See Rosales, *Chicano!* 145.

77. UFWOC organizing efforts also occurred in Texas, but lasted only a few years. The Arizona Farm Workers Organizing Committee mobilized in Arizona and the Farm Labor Organizing Committee targeted the Midwest. See Rosales, *Chicano!* 150; W. K. Barger and Ernesto M. Reza, *The Farm Labor Movement in the Midwest* (Austin: University of Texas Press, 1994).

78. Msgr. George Higgins of the Social Action Department of the U.S. Catholic Conference served as staff advisor and Father Roger Mahony of Fresno acted as field secretary in California. Roger Mahony was appointed archbishop of Los Angeles in 1985. According to Higgins, the working committee essentially consisted of Donnelly, Higgins, and Mahony, as Manning and Donohoe opted out in the early stages. Higgins and Bole, *Organized Labor*, 90.

79. Ibid., 91.

80. Ibid.

81. The growers settled for a pay rate of $1.80 per hour, forty cents more than what the workers originally had demanded. An additional ten cents an hour would be paid to a health and welfare fund for the workers and their families.

82. Higgins and Bole, *Organized Labor*, 91–93; Griswold del Castillo and García, *Triumph of Spirit*, 92–94; Ferriss and Sandoval, *Fight in the Fields*, 157.

83. Ortega interview.

84. The union's name was changed to the UFW in February 1972. In September 1973 it would again be changed to the UFWA. See Ferriss and Sandoval, *Fight in the Fields*, 159–76; Griswold del Castillo and García, *Triumph of Spirit*, 116–17.

85. Ferriss and Sandoval, *Fight in the Fields*, 181–82.

86. Ibid., 181–89, for descriptive accounts of the violence; Griswold del Castillo and García, *Triumph of Spirit*, 122–23. Two deaths occurred along with numerous serious injuries of UFW supporters and farmworkers.

87. Ferriss and Sandoval, *Fight in the Fields*, 184.

88. Ibid., 186. See also Juan Romero, "3,000 Arrested Backing Chavez," *PADRES* (September 1973): 5–7.

89. For a narrative account of the arrest, see Romero, "3,000 Arrested," 5–7.

90. Ybarra interview.

91. John Dart, "Some Go to Picket: *Las Hermanas* Divide Forces for Meeting," *Los Angeles Times*, 11 August 1973, sec. A, 26.

92. Ortega interview.

93. María de Jesús Ybarra, *El Quetzal Emplumece*, 292–93. Author's translation.

94. "Chavez Tells Parishioners UFW Will Win," *PADRES* (September 1973): 7.

95. Nagi Daifullah, a twenty-four-year-old Arab picket captain, died of a fractured skull. The coroner's jury ruled that Daifullah fractured his skull when he fell to the pavement after being hit with a club by a sheriff deputy. Another victim, sixty-year-old Juan de la Cruz, died from a bullet wound near his heart as he sat with his wife in their automobile. A speeding pickup truck had fired five shots aimed at the elder. The accused slayer of de la Cruz was acquitted several years later. See Ferris and Sandoval, *Fight in the Fields,* 187–89. Both funerals of these UFW martyrs had a strong presence of Catholic clergy, including many members of PADRES. See *PADRES* (September 1973): 2.

96. These hermanas included Sylvia Sedillo, Paulina Apodaca, Teresita Basso, and Mario (Lucie) Barron.

97. "20 Protesters Arrested," *Colorado Springs Gazette Telegraph,* 25 March 1973, sec. B, 1. Clarita Trujillo served as captain of the picket line.

98. Corrales interview. The lettuce boycott proved to be more difficult, as consumers were less likely to give up a dietary staple. In contrast, the boycott of Gallo wines gained greater success as the public easily recognized the brand name, its lower-priced products, and the role it played in alcoholism. After two years the boycott culminated in a UFW march from San Francisco to Gallo headquarters in Modesto as a way to persuade not only Gallo but also Governor Jerry Brown to pass a farm labor law. See Ferris and Sandoval, *Fight in the Fields,* 189–94.

99. Ibid., 195–210.

100. *Probe* (January–February 1981): 1. The NFWM emerged in 1971 after much negotiation from the collaborative efforts of the Protestant-based California Migrant Ministry, Church Women United, the National Council of Churches of Christ in the USA (NCCUSA), Protestant denominations, several Catholic religious orders, and PADRES "as a way to organize Church folks to support farm workers who are organizing themselves." National Farm Worker Ministry, "Brief History of the Church's Ministry with Farm Workers," *Report,* May 1995.

101. Browne interview. Funds from the Wisconsin Migrant Mission supported her work at JPC to strengthen the boycott in the Midwest.

102. "Short Hoe Ban Victory for UFW," *McAllen [Texas] Monitor,* 18 June 1981, sec. D, 1; *NFWM: 75 Years of Farm Worker Ministry 1920–1995, Report,* 1995, 35; Ferriss and Sandoval, *Fight in the Fields,* 206–7.

103. *NFWM: 75 Years of Farm Worker Ministry 1920–1995,* 35.

104. "Short Hoe Ban Victory for UFW," 1.

105. The march drew 30,000 people and reflects the resurgence of

the UFW since Chávez's death in 1993, under the leadership of Arturo Rodríguez, Chávez's son-in-law. "March in Support of Farm Workers Draws Thousands," *San Francisco Chronicle*, 14 April 1997, sec. A, 13; "Thousands Take Part in UFW March," *San Jose Mercury News*, 14 April 1997, sec. A, 1; "The UFW's Resurgence," *San Francisco Chronicle*, 1 September 1997, sec. A, 22.

106. Iglesias interview.

107. Yolanda Tarango and Timothy Matovina, "*Las Hermanas*," in *Hispanics in the Church: Up From the Cellar*, ed. Phillip E. Lampe (San Francisco: Catholic Scholars Press, 1994). See, for example, *Informes* (February 1975); (February 1978); (June 1978); (March 1990).

108. Tarango and Matovina, "*Las Hermanas*," in *Hispanics in the Church*. FLOC was founded in 1967 by Baldemar Velásquez to organize farmworkers in the Midwest.

109. Marylyn Shaefer, CSJ, interview conducted by author, June 1997. Shaefer was a member of NAWR and in the same religious community as Mario (Lucie) Barron, CSJ.

110. Browne interview.

111. "*Asamblea Nacional de Hermanas*," *PADRES* (Fall 1976): 5.

112. News clipping of picket line with caption, no citation, LHC, Box 18.

113. Browne interview.

114. "Theology in the Americas," *Informes* (February 1978): 8.

115. *Informes* (April 1977): 2; (June 1982): 7. Iglesias is of Puerto Rican and Cuban ancestry.

116. Sergio Torres and John Eagleson, eds., *Theology in the Americas* (New York: Orbis Books, 1976), 263.

117. Ibid., 357–60.

118. Ibid., 207–12 (quote on 210); see also "The Chicano Struggle," *PADRES*, October 1975, 9–10. Members of this group included Mario (Lucie) Barron from *Las Hermanas*, Fr. Lonnie Reyes, Fr. Edmundo Rodríguez, Fr. Juan Romero, Fr. Luciano Hendren, and Fr. Roberto Peña of PADRES.

119. Torres and Eagleson, *Theology in the Americas*, 210.

120. In 1986, Mexican theologian Elsa Tamez produced an article exploring the myth of the Toltecan god of life, Quetzalcoatl, as a resource for women, and the relationship between Quetzalcoatl and the Christian God of the Bible. See "Introduction: The Power of the Sacred," in *Through Her Eyes: Women's Theology from Latin America*, ed. Elsa Tamez (Maryknoll, N.Y.: Orbis Books, 1989). The 1998 annual meeting of the Academy of Catholic Hispanic Theologians of the United States (ACHTUS), first formed in 1989, addressed the relationship between

the pre-Hispanic indigenous spirituality of "cosmic order" and the European Christian "spirituality of redemption." The insights of the "Chicano Reflection Group" clearly preceded these more recent deliberations on the "authentic import of the indigenous cosmologies" on Christian thought in the Americas. Quotes taken from Dr. Jean-Perre Ruiz, letter to ACHTUS members, 17 March 1998.

121. See, for example, Miguel A. De La Torre and Edwin Aponte, *Introducing Latino/a Theologies* (Maryknoll, N.Y.: Orbis Books, 2001); Arturo J. Bañuelas, ed., *Mestizo Christianity* (Maryknoll, N.Y.: Orbis Books, 1995).

122. Torres and Eagleson, *Theology in the Americas*, 210.

123. See Virgilio Elizondo, "Popular Religion as the Core of Cultural Identity Based on the Mexican American Experience in the United States," in *An Enduring Flame: Studies on Latino Popular Religiosity*, ed. Anthony M. Stevens-Arroyo and Ana María Díaz-Stevens (New York: Bildner Center for Western Hemisphere Studies, City University of New York, 1994), 113–32; Roberto S. Goizueta, *Caminemos Con Jesus* (Maryknoll, N.Y.: Orbis Books, 1995); Orlando Espín, *The Faith of the People* (Maryknoll, N.Y.: Orbis Books, 1998).

124. Gregory Baum, "The Christian Left at Detroit," in *Theology in the Americas*, 399–429 (quote on 425–26).

125. Aurora Camacho de Schmidt, interview conducted by author, 23 July 1997.

126. Baum, "The Christian Left at Detroit," in *Theology in the Americas*, 401.

127. Castañeda interview.

128. Baum, "The Christian Left at Detroit," in *Theology in the Americas*, 426.

129. Castañeda interview.

130. Ada María Isasi-Díaz and Yolanda Tarango, *Hispanic Women: Prophetic Voice in the Church* (San Francisco: Harper & Row, 1988).

131. Tarango and Isasi-Diaz interviews. This will be explored further in Chapter 5.

132. See Rosemary Radford Ruether and Rosemary Skinner Keller, eds., *In Our Own Voices: Four Centuries of American Women's Religious Writing* (New York: HarperCollins, 1995), 447–51. Many other U.S. Latinos outside of Las Hermanas have also produced significant theological works. See, for example, María Pilar Aquino, Daisy L. Machado, and Jeanette Rodriguez, *A Reader in Latina Feminist Theology: Religion and Justice* (Austin: University of Texas Press, 2002).

133. "Informes y Análisis De La Reunión De NAC," *Informes* (March 1987): 5. Translation by author.

Chapter Four: The Challenge of Being Chicana/Latina, Catholic, and Feminist

1. "Santa María del Camino," song used by Las Hermanas at 1985 annual conference, LHC, Box 6.

2. "Summary of National Priorities," Las Hermanas Third National Conference, Lake Forest, Ill., 13–17 August 1972, LHC, Box 6.

3. Carmelita Espinoza to National Coordinating Team, 31 August 1976, LHC, Box 4.

4. Among these organizations were Comisión Femenil Mexicana, Chicana Action Service Center, and numerous university student organizations. For an analysis of Chicana feminists in the movement, see Chapter 5 of Ruiz, *Shadows,* and Elizabeth Martinez, *De Colores Means All of Us: Latina Views for a Multi-Colored Century* (Cambridge, Mass.: South End Press, 1998). For a selection of Chicana feminist historical writings produced during the 1960s and 1970s, see Alma M. García, *Chicana Feminist Thought: The Basic Historical Writings* (New York: Routledge, 1997).

5. Ruiz, *Shadows,* 112.

6. Corrales interview.

7. Las Hermanas National Coordinating Team to PADRES National and Regional Directors, 7 September 1973, PADRES files.

8. Ibid.

9. "*PADRES* and Priestly Formation," *PADRES* (November 1974): 11.

10. In 1990, the Bishops' Committee for Hispanic Affairs abolished the NAC due to its increasing criticism of the bishops' failure to allocate funds to implement the national pastoral plan for Hispanic ministry that was approved following the III Encuentro. See Edmundo Rodríguez, "The Hispanic Community and Church Movements," in *Hispanic Catholic Culture,* 160.

11. Juan Romero, *PADRES National Congress* "La Raza Nueva y Nueva Esperanza," *February 2–5, 1975,* San Antonio, Texas (N.p.: Privately printed, 1975), 1.

12. Clarita Trujillo, "Aporte de *Las Hermanas* in *PADRES National Congress* "La Raza Nueva y Nueva Esperanza," 70.

13. Ibid.

14. Ibid., 88.

15. Ibid., 71. Author's translation.

16. "*PADRES* National Congress—Press Release," in *PADRES National Congress* "La Raza Nueva y Nueva Esperanza," 13.

17. Ibid.

18. Text of address included in Anthony Stevens-Arroyo, *Prophets Denied Honor,* 286–88 (quote on 288).

19. "Call to Action Conference Detroit," *PADRES* (Fall 1976): 8–9; "Hispanic Statement on Call to Action," *PADRES* (Fall 1976): 10.

20. "Hispanic Statement on Call to Action," 10.

21. National conferences attract 2,000 to 5,000 members and in 1997 membership totaled 18,000. See *Call to Action News Special Edition* 18, no. 3; "Catholic Reform Group Conference Set," *Los Angeles Times,* 2 August 1997. See also "Bishops Vote Strong 'Action' Implementation," *National Catholic Reporter,* 13 May 1977, 1.

22. Martinez interview. See also "Bishops Vote Strong 'Action' Implementation," *National Catholic Reporter,* 13 May 1977, 1.

23. Minutes of Planning Meeting, "Joint Hermanas-*PADRES* Conference," 27 October 1977, LHC, Box 6. Fr. Juan Romero of PADRES suggested a joint meeting in 1973.

24. "*Encuentro PADRES*/Hermanas de Modelos para la 'Nueva Iglesia Hispana,'" *El Visitante Dominical,* 24 September 1978, 6–7; Juan Romero, interview conducted by author, 9 October 1997.

25. Romero interview.

26. "Hispanic Priests, Nuns Act Politically, Personally," *National Catholic Reporter,* 1 September 1978, 1. Other partnership teams included Ana María Díaz-Ramirez and Antonio Stevens-Arroyo; Teresita Basso and Anastacio Rivera; and Rosa Martha Zárate and Frank Ponce and provided a variety of experiences.

27. "Hispanic Priests, Nuns Act Politically, Personally," *National Catholic Reporter,* 1 September 1978, 1.

28. Ibid., 7.

29. Ibid.

30. Basso interview. For a complete review of the conference, see *Entre Nosotros* (Fall 1978). *Entre Nosotros* was the joint PADRES–Las Hermanas newsletter resulting from the conference.

31. "Open Letter to *Hermanas,*" *Entre Nosotros* (Fall 1978): 5.

32. Balthasar Janacek, interview conducted by author, March 1997.

33. Minutes of PADRES–Hermanas Joint Board Meeting, August 18, 1978, LHC, Box 6.

34. Trino Sánchez, SJ, and Margarita Castañeda, CND, were the co-editors.

35. *National Catholic Reporter,* 18 March 1977. Iglesias authored this statement as chair of Sisters Uniting 1975–1976, a network of sister groups including Association of Contemplative Sisters, Las Hermanas, National Coalition of American Nuns, National Sisters Vocation Conference, Religious Formation Conference, Sisters for Christian Community, National Assembly of Religious Women, National Black Sisters Confer-

ence, and the National Sisters Communication Conference. See Weaver, *New Catholic Women,* 234.

36. *Informes* (April 1977): 4.

37. *La Guadalupe Que Camina,* prod. Beva Sánchez, dir. Ruby Perez, Mujeres Indigenas Productions, 1990, videocassette.

38. Minutes of PADRES–HERMANAS Joint Board Meeting, August 18, 1978, LHC, Box 6.

39. "Report of National Coordinators," n.d., LHC, Box 2. A deeper analysis of the relationship between Las Hermanas and the WOC follows in this chapter.

40. Clarita Trujillo, interview conducted by author, 5 May 1997.

41. Romero interview. Romero credits Bishop Patricio Flores, Bishop Gilbert Chávez, and Fr. Roberto Peña as strong advocates for continuing educational opportunities for Las Hermanas.

42. Basso interview; Martínez interview.

43. Trujillo interview.

44. Tim Matovina analyzes the limitations PADRES faced by choosing to remain a clerical organization. See "Representation and the Reconstruction of Power: The Rise of *PADRES* and *Las Hermanas,*" in *The Catholic Left,* ed. Mary Jo Weaver (Indianapolis: Indiana University Press, 1999).

45. Sedillo interview.

46. For additional viewpoints on Gutiérrez's openness to feminist concerns, see "On Gustavo's side," *National Catholic Reporter,* 10 January 1997, 19; "No Rift with Gutiérrez," *National Catholic Reporter,* 10 January 1997, 32.

47. Sedillo interview.

48. Tarango interview.

49. Letter from Ricardo Ramírez, executive vice-president, to María Iglesias, 22 January 1979, LHC, Box 13.

50. Letter from Ricardo Ramírez to Margarita Castañeda, 12 November 1979, LHC, Box 13.

51. Letter from Ricardo Ramírez to Margarita Castañeda, 18 January 1980, LHC, Box 13.

52. Letter from Margarita Castañeda to three nominees, 4 February 1980, LHC, Box 13.

53. Trujillo interview.

54. Las Hermanas Board Meeting Minutes, 17 August 1977, 3, LHC, Box 2.

55. Castañeda interview.

56. Tarango interview.

57. Ibid.

58. Ibid.

59. See Yolanda Tarango, "The Hispanic Woman and Her Role in the Church," *New Theology Review* 3, no. 4 (1990): 56–61; Yolanda Tarango, "La Vida es la Lucha," *Texas Journal of Ideas, History and Culture* 2 (Spring–Summer 1990): 11.

60. "Nun Wages Internal Battle to Reform 'Sexist' Church," *Austin American Statesman,* 9 September 1987, sec. A, 8.

61. Ada María Isasi-Díaz and Yolanda Tarango, *Hispanic Women: Prophetic Voice in the Church* (San Francisco: Harper & Row, 1988), x.

62. *Informes* (January 1986): 4.

63. Ibid.

64. Ibid., Author's translation. Also cited in Matovina and Tarango, "*Las Hermanas,*" 9; Ada María Isasi-Díaz and Yolanda Tarango, *Hispanic Women: Prophetic Voice in the Church,* 104; *Informes* (May 1986): 2.

65. Carmen Villegas, interview conducted by author, 17 May 1997.

66. Radford Ruether, *In Our Own Voices,* 57. See also "Catholics Speak Out, Reject the Pastoral on Women's Concerns," *National Catholic Reporter,* 20 November 1992, 13; "Why the Pastoral Was Defeated," *National Catholic Reporter,* 4 December 1992, 2–5.

67. National Conference of Catholic Bishops, *The Hispanic Presence: Challenge and Commitment* (Washington, D.C.: USCC Office of Publishing and Promotion Services, 1983).

68. See Margarita Castañeda, "Annual Report to the Hispanic Advisory Committee of the USCC/NCCB," 4, LHC, Box 4.

69. "At *Encuentro,* Vision, Debate Mold Future," *National Catholic Reporter,* 30 August 1985, 1.

70. Forty-six persons comprised the national leadership along with twelve bishops.

71. Ernie Cortés Jr. began COPS in 1973 in San Antonio with the support of local parishes. Based on Alinsky-style organizing, residents mobilize and negotiate with city officials to improve the material conditions of their neighborhoods. COPS has influenced the use of community development block grants and federal urban renewal funds. COPS now has twenty-five chapters in San Antonio and has influenced the formation of similar organizations in the Southwest, including United Neighborhood Organization (UNO), South Central Organizing Committee (SCOC), and East Valleys Organization (EVO). For a discussion of COPS, see Ruiz, *Shadows,* 138–41. See also Mary Beth Rogers, *Cold Anger: A Story of Faith and Politics* (Denton: University of North Texas Press, 1990).

72. "Nun Embodies *Encuentro* Process for Her People," *National Catholic Reporter,* 14 December 1984, 21.

73. Elisa Rodríguez interview, 4 August 1997.

74. Romero interview.

75. Dolorita Martínez, "Basic Christian Communities: A New Model of Church Within the U.S. Hispanic Community," *New Theology Review* 3, no. 4 (1990): 36.

76. Ana María Piñeda, "Pastoral de Conjunto," *New Theology Review* 3, no. 4 (1990): 30.

77. Moíses Sandoval, "The Organization of a Hispanic Church," in *Hispanic Catholic Culture*, 145–46.

78. *Prophetic Voices: The Document on the Process of the III Encuentro Nacional Hispano de Pastoral* (Washington, D.C.: Secretariat for Hispanic Affairs—United States Catholic Conference, n.d.), 24–25.

79. Circular mailing, "*Las Hermanas*, Día de Reflexión: La Mujer y El III *Encuentro*," n.d. 1, LCH, Box 6. Author's translation.

80. Isasi-Díaz, communication to author, March 1998.

81. *Informes* (January 1986): 2.

82. "Dia de Reflexión: La Mujer y El III *Encuentro* Nacional Hispano de Pastoral, 1985," 1, LHC, Box 6. Author's translation.

83. Denise A. Segura, "Chicanas and Triple Oppression in the Labor Force," in *Chicana Voices: Intersections of Class, Race and Gender*, ed. Teresa Córdova et al. (Austin: Center for Mexican American Studies, 1986), 54–55. Based on data from U.S. Bureau of the Census, "Money Income of Households, Families, and Persons in the United States: 1981," *Current Population Reports*, Series P-60, No. 137. Tables 1 and 2.

84. U.S. Department of Commerce, *Poverty in the United States: 1988 and 1989* (Washington, D.C.: U.S. Government Printing Office, 1991), Table 1.

85. Bureau of Justice Statistics, *Violence against Women: Estimates from the Redesigned Survey* (Washington, D.C.: U.S. Government Printing Office, 1995), 1. This report was based on a survey questionnaire redesigned beginning in 1985. By 1992 it was in wide use to produce more accurate reporting of incidents of rape and sexual assault committed by family members. Statistics from previous years are less reliable.

86. U.S. Department of Justice, *Criminal Victimization in the United States, 1983* (Washington, D.C.: U.S. Government Printing Office, 1985), Table 8.

87. "*Las Hermanas*: VOZ PROFETICA," *Informes* (January 1986): 2.

88. 'Dia de Reflexión," 2, LHC, Box 6. A permanent diaconate assists in priestly duties but is open only to married men.

89. "Tercer *Encuentro*," *Informes* (January 1986): 7.

90. María Luisa Gastón, communication to author, May 1998. Gastón co-chaired the on-site proceedings.

91. "Terar Encuentro," *Informes* (January 1986):7. Emphasis mine.

92. "Hispanics Back Women Priests: 'Process' Intervenes," *National Catholic Reporter,* 30 August 1985, 5; "La Mujer Hispana Fue Protagonista," *La Voz,* 30 August 1985, 8.

93. María Luisa Gastón, interview conducted by author, 27 July 1997.

94. Isasi-Díaz, communication to author, April 1998.

95. Isasi-Díaz interview.

96. Villegas interview; Isasi-Díaz interview. Both women were present at the III Encuentro. "La Mujer Hispana Fue Protagonista," states that 200 women gathered; however, those present believe the number to be 500.

97. Villegas interview.

98. "The Conclusions of the III *Encuentro,*" *Prophetic Voices: The Document on the Process of the III Encuentro Nacional Hispano de Pastora* (Washington, D.C., Secretariat for Hispanic Affairs-USCC/NCCB, 1986), 6.

99. Romero interview.

100. "Hispanics Back Women Priests;" *National Catholic Reporter,* 30 August 1985, 5.

101. Gastón interview.

102. "Informes y Análisis De La Reunión De NAC," *Informes* (March 1987): 5. Author's translation.

103. *Informes* (January 1986): 1.

104. See, for example, "Bonding Together as Women," *Informes* (March 1986): 1; "La Mujer Trabajadora . . . ," *Informes* (September 1986): 3; "Nicaragua En Acción," *Informes* (March 1987): 3.

105. "*Las Hermanas DE NUEVA YORK,*" *Informes* (May 1986): 6.

106. "*Las Hermanas DE NUEVA YORK,*" *Informes* (May 1986): 6.

107. Ibid.

108. *Informes* (June 1989): 4. Also cited in Matovina and Tarango, "*Las Hermanas,*" 20.

109. Zárate interview.

110. *Integral education* refers to a well-rounded learning process focusing on economic, cultural, political, and religious issues. It became a term widely used by U.S. Latino religious leaders.

111. "Debemos Dar El Ejemplo Personal De Educarnos," *El Visitante Dominical,* 16 October 1974, 12.

112. "Nun to Head Service Center," *The San Diego Union,*" 1 June 1974; "Sister Murrieta Named Padre Hidalgo Director," *Southern Cross,* 25 April 1974, 3.

113. "Nun to Head Service Center."

114. "Padre Hidalgo Center: A Decade of Success," *Private Industrial Council Report* 1, no. 12 (1982): 3.

115. Sara Murrieta, interview conducted by author, 26 July 1997.

116. "1981: Chicano Headlines of the Year," *La Prensa*, 31 December 1981, 1.

117. The phone call was followed by a letter from Bishop Chávez dated 14 March 1983, officially notifying Sara Murrieta of the change in her appointment and responsibilities. Personal files of Sara Murrieta; "Mendez Co-director at Padre Hidalgo," *Southern Cross*, 31 March 1983, 3.

118. Bishop Chávez to Sara Murrieta, 14 March 1983, personal papers of Sara Murrieta.

119. Enrique Méndez, interview conducted by author, 13 April 1997. See also "Mendez Co-director at Padre Hidalgo," *Southern Cross*, 31 March 1983, 3.

120. *La Prensa*, 2 September 1983, 1.

121. Ibid.

122. "Tezozomoc Speaks," *La Prensa*, 2 September 1983, 4.

123. Murrieta interview.

124. Lilia López, interview conducted by author, 19 April 1997.

125. "Centro Padre Hidalgo," talk given by Sara Murrieta on 23 November 1996 at the anniversary celebration of Padre Hidalgo Center, personal papers of Sara Murrieta.

126. Cited in Rosamaría Mora, "FROM DECH TO CAPULLI: A Hispanic Catholic service organization's struggle and change," unpublished paper, 13–14.

127. In 1978, the San Diego diocese was divided into San Diego and San Bernardino dioceses.

128. Statistics cited in Albert Pulido, "Race Relations within the American Catholic Church: An Historical and Sociological Analysis of Mexican American Catholics" (Ph.D. diss., University of Notre Dame, 1989), 100.

129. "Rosa Martha Zárate, Comunidades, Guitarra, Canciónes . . . ," *El Visitante Dominical*, 6 June 1976, 12.

130. Zárate interview. Her work sometimes took her 300 miles in one day; Moises Sandoval, "From Mexico with love," *Revista Maryknoll*, February 1984, 28–29.

131. "Rosa Martha Zárate, Comunidades, Guitarra, Canciónes . . . ," *El Visitante*, 12.

132. Zárate interview.

133. Sandoval, "From Mexico with love," *Revista Maryknoll*, 298–99.

134. Ibid.; "Hispanics Now 'Enter Desert, Hard Part of the Journey,'" *National Catholic Reporter*, 5 September 1985, 7; "Two Hispanic Centers Dedicated," *San Bernardino and Riverside Newsletter*, 28 October 1981, 6–7.

135. "Lay Ministers Molding New Model of Church," *National Catholic Reporter*, 14 December 1984, 20.

136. "Hispanics Now 'Enter Desert," *National Catholic Reporter*, 5 September 1985, 7.

137. Patricio Guillen, interview conducted by author, 12 March 1994.

138. *Rosa Martha Zárate Plaintiff v. Roman Catholic Diocese of San Bernardino*, 8 March 1989, 7, LHC, Box 21.

139. "Diocese Unveils Plan to Strengthen Hispanic Ministry," *Inland Catholic*, 12 June 1986, 12.

140. *Rosa Martha Zárate Plaintiff v. Roman Catholic Diocese of San Bernardino*, 8, LHC, Box 21.

141. Zárate interview.

142. "Diocese Unveils Plan," 12.

143. Zárate interview.

144. Cited in Rosamaría Mora, "FROM DECH TO CAPULLI," 15.

145. Guillen interview.

146. See *Cantos Para Animar La Esperanza* (N.p.: Privately published, 1996).

147. "LA LUCHA ES LA VIDA," *Informes* (May 1986): 3.

148. *La Prensa*, 10 June 1983, 4.

149. "HAPPY NEW YEAR!" *Informes* (December 1986): 1.

150. "LA LUCHA ES LA VIDA," 3.

151. Murrieta interview.

152. "HAPPY NEW YEAR!" 1.

153. "Brief Herstory of Women-Church Convergence," n.d. For a concise overview of the Women-Church movement, see Rosemary Radford Ruether, "Women-Church: An American Catholic Feminist Movement," in *The Catholic Left*, 8. See also Rosemary Radford Ruether, "Reflection of Woman-Church," *PROBE* (February–March 1984): 3.

154. The WOC and later the WCC and the Women-Church Convergence led the Women-Church movement on a national basis.

155. The WOC mobilized not simply for women's ordination, but also for the transformation of the Church from patriarchal clericalism to a collaborative model of ministy. See Anne Marie Gardiner, ed., *Women and Catholic Priesthood: An Expanded Vision: Proceedings of the Detroit Conference* (New York: Paulist Press, 1976).

156. See *Informes* (December 1975): 2; (February 1976): 4–5; *Entre Nosotros* (Winter 1978): 9.

157. Iglesias interview.

158. "Brief Herstory of Women-Church Convergence."

159. Rosemary Radford Ruether, "Women-Church: An American Catholic Feminist Movement," in *The Catholic Left*, 8.

160. "Woman Church Speaks in Chicago Nov. 11–13," *PROBE* XII, 1 (December 1983–January 1984): 6.

161. "MUJER-IGLESIA HABLA DE GENERACION EN GENERACION," *Informes*, n.d., 19.

162. "Brief Herstory of Women-Church Convergence"; Rosemary Radford Ruether states that she proposed the plural term in order to address the diversity among women. Radford Ruether, "Women-Church," in *The Catholic Left*, 31.

163. Letter from Ada María Isasi-Díaz to Las Hermanas national coordinators, 28 March 1987, LHC, Box 13.

164. Ibid. These concerns were reiterated in a letter addressed to Women Church Conference Planners from Las Hermanas national coordinators, 6 April 1987, LHC, Box 13.

165. Isasi-Díaz to Las Hermanas national coordinators, 28 March 1987, LHC, Box 13.

166. *Informes* (March 1993): 4–5.

167. *Informes* (May 1993): 2; Browne interview.

168. Radford Ruether, "Women-Church," 25.

169. Browne interview.

170. *Informes* (May 1993): 2.

171. Radford Ruether, "Women-Church," 23–24. Also cited in Anne E. Patrick, "A Ministry of Justice: The 25 Year Pilgrimage of the National Assembly of Religious Women (NAWR/NARW)," in *The Catholic Left*. In 1991 the NAWR notified the WCC that they would sever their membership if the WCC did not diversify their membership.

172. A letter to Judy Vaughn and Maureen Reiff of the NARW from representatives of the WCC Conference Planning Groups attempts to explain the WCC's concern for diversity, yet also outlines several perceived obstacles. 1 June 1990, LHC, Box 13.

173. Browne interview.

174. Rosemary Radford Ruether, "Women-Church," 24.

175. Ibid. The Black Sisters Conference ceased to be part of the WCC in the early 1980s.

176. Cortera, "Feminism," 226–28. For a collection of experiences, see "And When You Leave, Take Your Pictures With You: Racism in the Women's Movement," in *This Bridge Called My Back: Writings by Radical Women of Color* (New York: Kitchen Table: Women of Color Press, 1981), 60–101; Alma M. García, "The Development of Chicana Feminist Discourse, 1970–1980," 538–41.

177. García, "Chicana Feminist Discourse."

178. Matovina and Tarango, "*Las Hermanas*," 10.

179. Anita de Luna was never a member of Las Hermanas; however, her appointment exemplified the progress that Latinas were making in the leadership of religious communities.

180. Matovina and Tarango, "LAS HERMANAS," 20.

Chapter Five: Transformative Struggle

1. Rosa Martha Zárate, "Lucha, Poder, Esperanza," song composed for Las Hermanas conference in 1989. Courtesy of the author.

2. Carmen Villegas, "Informes y Análisis De la Reunión De NAC," *Informes* (March 1987): 5. Author's translation.

3. Timothy Matovina and Yolanda Tarango, "*Las Hermanas* History Revisited," *Informes* 8, no. 1 (1994):7.

4. I have been influenced by numerous feminist writers to arrive at this definition, including Anne E. Carr, *Transforming Grace* (San Francisco: Harper & Row, 1988); Audre Lorde, "The Power of the Erotic," in *Weaving the Vision*, ed. Judith Plaskow and Carol P. Christ (San Francisco: Harper & Row, 1989); and Yolanda Tarango, "La Vida es la Lucha," *Texas Journal of Ideas, History and Culture* 2 (1990): 11.

5. Tarango, "La Vida es la Lucha;" see also "La Vida es la Lucha," *Informes* (March 1990): 1.

6. "La Vida es la Lucha," *Informes* (March 1990): 9–10.

7. Isasi-Díaz and Tarango, *Hispanic Women*, 103.

8. See Ruiz, *Shadows*, 108–9; García, "The Development of Chicana Feminism," 535–36.

9. Ruiz, *Shadows*; García, "The Development of Chicana Feminism."

10. Ada María Isasi-Díaz, "*Mujeristas*: A Name of Our Own," in *The Future of Liberation Theology: Essays in Honor of Gustavo Gutiérrez*, ed. Marct Ellis and Otto Maduro (Maryknoll, N.Y.: Orbis Books, 1989), 410. See also Ada María Isasi-Díaz, "Toward an Understanding of Feminismo Hispano in the U.S.A.," in *Women's Consciousness, Women's Conscience*, ed. Barbara Hilkert Andolsen, Christine E. Gudorf, and Mary D. Pellauer (Minneapolis: Winston Press, 1985), 51–61.

11. Isasi-Díaz, "*Mujeristas*: A Name of Our Own," in *Future of Liberation*, 410.

12. Ibid.

13. Ada María Isasi-Díaz, "*Mujerista* Theology: A Challenge to Traditional Theology," in *Mujerista Theology* (Maryknoll, N.Y.: Orbis Books, 1996), 61. Isasi-Díaz notes that "Latino men as well as men and women from other racial/ethnic groups can also opt to be *mujeristas*."

14. Cited in Isasi-Díaz, "*Mujeristas*: A Name of Our Own," in *Future of Liberation*, 411; see also full text of song in 1989 Las Hermanas

Conference Program and Rosa Martha Zárate, *Cantos para animar la esperanza* (San Bernardino, Calif.: Rosa Martha Zárate, 1996), 1. Used with permission of the author.

15. A complete list of contributors is provided in Isasi-Díaz and Tarango, vii. Included are many of the religious communities of the members of Las Hermanas.

16. Isasi-Díaz interview.

17. Sylvia Vasquez, interview conducted by author, 23 August 1996. Vasquez went on to become an ordained minister in the Episcopal Church.

18. *Praxis* is defined as critical reflective action. See Paulo Freire, *The Politics of Education* (South Hadley, Mass.: Bergin & Garvey, 1985).

19. Isasi-Díaz and Tarango, *Hispanic Women,* xii.

20. Ibid., Chapter 5.

21. Ibid., 101.

22. Ibid., 102.

23. Ibid., 1.

24. Ibid., 104.

25. Mary Fainsod Katzenstein, "Discursive Politics and Feminist Activism in the Catholic Church," in *Feminist Organizations: Harvest of the New Women's Movement,* ed. Myra Marx Ferree and Patricia Yancey Martin (Philadelphia: Temple University Press, 1995), 35.

26. Program pamphlet, "Mujeres Hispanas en la Iglesia," 1980, 1, LHC, Box 6.

27. Castañeda interview.

28. See Fabiola Santiago, "Our Legacy of Silence," *Latina,* February 2003, 102–6, for an excellent discussion of the cultural and religious influences on Latina sexuality.

29. "15th Asamblea Nacional, El Don De Ser: La Mujer Hispana Ayer, Hoy Y Mañana," 1987, 3, LHC, Box 6.

30. In 1983 the organization decided to hold biennial conferences due to a lack of financial resources.

31. Veronica Méndez, interview conducted by author, 12 July 1997.

32. Teresa Barajas, interview conducted by author, August 1997.

33. Minutes from Las Hermanas meeting with Catholics for Free Choice, 27 September 1986, LHC, Box 14.

34. Ibid.

35. *Informes* (June 1989): 4. As cited in Matovina and Tarango,"*Las Hermanas,*" 20.

36. In 1989 the organization also filed incorporation papers within the state of Texas under a new name, Las Hermanas-U.S.A. to distinguish the national group from the regional chapters.

37. This was the same community that offered Las Hermanas's national coordinators emergency housing in 1971. Prior to this, the national office had moved where the new national coordinator lived or worked. Besides the cumbersome logistics of moving an office every two years, Las Hermanas had to deal with state laws that required new incorporation papers to be filed with each move, creating a burdensome expense.

38. Vásquez interview. In 1990 Vásquez left her staff position and the Roman Catholic Church to begin her studies for ordination in the Episcopal Church.

39. Consuelo Covarrubias, PBVM, "Chicago Perspective," *Informes* (December 1989): 3.

40. *Informes* (December 1989): 1. The bylaws called for a seven-member national board. The additional board members were Martha Obregon of Illinois; Lucy Ortiz of Florida; Dolorita Martínez of Nebraska; and Rosa Martha Zárate and María Inez Martínez, both from California. A lack of nominees for the National Coordinating Team, however, necessitated Yolanda Tarango serving as the sole coordinator for an additional year, considered to be a "transitional year," while the new national board and staff stabilized.

41. "Special Issue! La Mujer Hispana: Poder, Lucha Y Esperanza, *Las Hermanas* 1989 Conference," *Informes* (December 1989).

42. Synopsis of presentation by María Antonietta Berriozábal, *Informes* (December 1989): 5.

43. Teresa Barajas, "Reflexiones desde San Antonio," *Informes* (December 1989): 2. Author's translation.

44. Rosa Martha Zárate, "Encuentro Nacional de *Las Hermanas*," *Informes* (December 1989): 3. Author's translation.

45. María Inez Martínez, IHM, "Empowerment, Enablement, Hope," *Informes* (December 1989): 1.

46. The U.S. Catholic Conference of Bishops disbanded the NAC in 1990 due to its criticism of the bishops' failure to allocate funds to implement the National Pastoral Plan for Hispanic Ministry resulting from the III Encuentro. See Moíses Sandoval, "The Organization of a Hispanic Church," in *Hispanic Catholic Culture in the U.S.*, 159–60.

47. Regional retreats take place annually in Denver and La Habra, California. These sites are beyond the scope of this immediate study.

48. Isasi-Díaz interview.

49. Florez interview. Dolores continued her involvement with Las Hermanas and served on the National Coordinating Team from 1993 to 1996. Besides being involved on the national level she remains very active in the regional chapter of Las Hermanas in Denver and works in pastoral and grief counseling for the archdiocese of Denver.

50. Ada María Isasi-Díaz, "On the Birthing Stool: *Mujerista* Liturgy," in *Mujerista Theology* (Maryknoll, N.Y.: Orbis Books, 1996), 171.

51. Based on interview with María Inez Martínez, 7 June 1997.

52. Ada María Isasi-Díaz, "Rituals and Mujeristas' Struggle for Liberation," in *Mujerista Theology*, 201.

53. Isasi-Díaz, "On the Birthing Stool," in *Mujerista Theology*, 171.

54. Each mujerista ritual and communal altar is distinct and reflects the particular women planning and participating in the ritual. Our Lady of Guadalupe is the devotional icon of many Chicanas and Mexicanas. Nuestra Señora de la Caridad del Cobre is the most popular female icon among Cubans. Both are traditionally interpreted as ethnic representations of Mary, the mother of Jesus, while some devotees argue they stand on their own merit as the feminine face of God. For creative and diverse interpretations of Our Lady of Guadalupe, see Ana Castillo, ed., *Goddess of the Americas* (New York: Riverhead Books, 1996). For an indepth study on Mexican American women and Our Lady of Guadalupe, see Jeannette Rodriguez, *Our Lady of Guadalupe: Faith and Empowerment among Mexican-American Women* (Austin: University of Texas Press, 1994). For an in-depth study of Nuestra Señora de la Caridad del Cobre, see Tom Tweed, *Our Lady of the Exile* (New York: Oxford University Press, 1998).

55. Isasi-Díaz, "On the Birthing Stool," in *Mujerista Theology*, 171.

56. Holding a Eucharist celebration at the end of Las Hermanas conferences with a male cleric presiding is due to the preferences of the rotating conference planners, as some members feel more committed to a traditional Mass. Las Hermanas has been able to make room for both types of liturgies and both perspectives.

57. Isasi-Díaz provided an in-depth analysis of this ritual in "On the Birthing Stool," in *Mujerista Theology*, 170–91, which informed my synopsis for this section.

58. Ibid., 176.

59. Ibid., 177.

60. Ibid., 178.

61. Katzenstein, "Discursive Politics and Feminist Activism in the Catholic Church," in *Feminist Organizations*, 48.

62. Isasi-Díaz, "On the Birthing Stool," in *Mujerista Theology*, 179–80.

63. Ibid., 182–84.

64. Isasi-Díaz interview.

65. Rosa Ramírez Guerrero was inducted in the Texas Women's Hall of Fame in 1994 for her cultural and humanitarian work. See *Informes* (March 1994): 1. She has received numerous awards and honors over the years for her artistic productions and her International Ballet Folklorico.

For an oral interview with Ramírez Guerrero, see Vicki Ruiz, "Oral History and La Mujer: The Rosa Guerrero Story," in *Women on the U.S. Mexico Border*, ed. Vicki Ruiz and Susan Tiano (Winchester, Mass.: Allen and Unwin, 1987), 219–31; reprinted by Westview Press, 1991.

66. Virgilio Elizondo, "Popular Religion as the Core of Cultural Identity in the Mexican American Experience," in *An Enduring Flame: Studies on Latino Popular Religiosity*, ed. Anthony M. Stevens-Arroyo and Ana María Díaz-Stevens (New York: Bildner Center, 1994), 116.

67. Villegas interview.

68. Catherine Bell, *Ritual Theory, Ritual Practice* (New York: Oxford University Press, 1992), 196.

69. Isasi-Díaz, "Rituals and Mujeristas' Struggle for Liberation," in *Mujerista Theology*, 193.

70. Enedina Casarez Vásquez, interview, conducted by author, August 1997.

71. Isasi-Díaz, "Rituals and Mujeristas' Struggle for Liberation," 193–94. See also "Constitution of the Sacred Liturgy," in Walter M. Abbott, SJ, ed., *The Documents of the Vatican II* (New York: American Press, 1966), 137–54.

72. Ruiz, *Shadows*, 27. See also Orlando Espin, *The Faith of the People* (Maryknoll, N.Y.: Orbis Books, 1998), for a collection of articles on popular religiosity.

73. *Mujeres Grandes Anthology Premier Issue* 1, ed., Angela de Hoyos (San Antonio: M&A editions, 1993); *Mujeres Grandes 2*, Angela de Hoyos (San Antonio: M&A editions, 1995).

74. Juanita Luna Lawhn, *Mujeres Grandes Anthology 2*, 5.

75. Privately printed by Enedina Casarez Vásquez. Courtesy of the author.

76. Rosie Castro, "The Coronation," *Informes* (June 1990): 7.

77. *La Guadalupe Que Camina*, prod. Beverly Sánchez-Padilla, dir. Ruby Perez, Mujeres Indigenas Productions, San Antonio, Tex., 1990 (videocassette).

78. Previous national coordinator Sylvia Sedillo had invested monies into a certificate of deposit enhancing the financial stability of the organization.

79. Tarango, *Informes* (June 1990): 3.

80. "Surviving as an Organization," *Informes* (January 1992): 7–8.

81. "Hermanas Words and Deeds Shaping New Church," *National Catholic Reporter*, 15 November 1991, 6–7.

82. Martínez interview.

83. Yolanda Tarango served as editor of *Informes* beginning in 1985.

84. Rocio Talfur-Salgado, "Transcisiones De La Conferencia," *Informes* (November 1993): 3.

85. Isasi-Díaz, "Rituals and Mujeristas' Struggle for Liberation," in *Mujerista Theology,* 196–97.

86. "Special Report," *Informes* (October 1994).

87. The personal expense, however, does keep some board members from attending all board meetings, which weakens leadership endeavors.

88. Rosa Martha Zárate, Sara Murrieta, and Alicia Salcido, group interview conducted by author, 26 July 1997.

89. Castañeda interview.

90. Isasi-Díaz interview.

91. Presenters included Teresita Basso, Margarita Castañeda, Maria Iglesias, Lucy Ortiz, Sylvia Sedillo, Yolanda Tarango, and Dolores Florez.

92. González also delivered a presentation at the 1999 conference in Denver on the failures of the global economy and local solutions.

93. *"Las Hermanas* Evolving," *Informes* 4, no. 1 (March 2002): 1.

94. Ibid.

Conclusion

1. MANA, founded in 1974, continues to advocate for the full and equal participation of Latinas in the social, educational, economic, and political arenas in the United States. MALCS is dedicated to the support of Chicanas/Latinas in institutions of higher education and to bridging the gap between the academy and the community.

2. Tarango interview.

3. "Hispanic trends create pastoral puzzles," *National Catholic Reporter,* January 1998, 7.

4. Ibid. Gastón served as director of Hispanic and multicultural services for the Paulist National Catholic Evangelization Association in Washington, D.C.

5. See Larry B. Stammer, "Archdiocese's Programs, Staff Hit Hard by Cuts," *Los Angeles Times,* 20 September 2002, sec. B-1.

6. Conversation with theologians and priests in 1998 at Loyola Marymount University, Los Angeles.

7. Feminist theologian Elizabeth Schussler Fiorenza coined the term kyriarchy "to refer to interlocking structures of oppression that result in the "lordship" of one person or group over another." See "It's inevitable: Women Will Be Ordained," *National Catholic Reporter,* 21 February 1997, 25.

Bibliography

Books, Articles, and Essays

Abbott, Walter M., ed. *The Documents of Vatican II*. New York: Guild Press, 1966.

Acuña, Rodolfo. *Occupied America: A History of Chicanos*. 5th ed. New York: Pearson Longman, 2004.

"Another Civil-Rights Headache—Plight of Mexican-Americans." *U.S. News & World Report*, 6 June 1966, 46–48.

Barger, W. K., and Ernesto M. Reza. *The Farm Labor Movement in the Midwest*. Austin: University of Texas Press, 1994.

Basso, Teresita. "The Emerging 'Chicana' Sister." *Review For Religious* 30 (1971): 1019–28.

Baum, Gregory. "Class Struggle and Magisterium: A New Note." *Theological Studies* 45 (December 1984): 690–701.

———. "Faith and Liberation: Development Since Vatican II." In *Vatican II: Open Questions and New Horizons*, 75–104. Ed. Steven Duffy et al. Wilmington, Del.: Michael Glazier, 1984.

Bell, Catherine. *Ritual Theory, Ritual Practice*. New York: Oxford University Press, 1992.

Bernal, Dolores. "Providing an Alternative History of the 1968 East Los Angeles Blowouts: Constructing a Theory to Better Understand Chicana School Resistance." Ph.D. diss., University of California at Los Angeles, 1997.

Berryman, Phillip. *The Religious Roots of Rebellion: Christians in Central American Revolutions*. Maryknoll, N.Y.: Orbis Books, 1984.

———. *Liberation Theology: The Essential Facts about the Revolutionary Movement in Latin America and Beyond*. New York: Pantheon, 1987.

Bureau of Justice Statistics. *Violence Against Women: Estimates from the Redesigned Survey.* Washington, D.C.: U.S. Government Printing Office, 1995.

Burns, Jeffrey M. "The Mexican Catholic Community in California." In *Mexican Americans and the Catholic Church, 1900–1965,* 127–233. Ed. Jay P. Dolan and Gilberto M. Hinojosa. Notre Dame, Ind.: University of Notre Dame Press, 1994.

Cadena, Gilbert R. "Chicanos and the Catholic Church: Liberation Theology as a Form of Empowerment." Ph.D. diss., University of California at Riverside, 1987.

————. "Chicano Clergy and the Emergence of Liberation Theology." *Hispanic Journal of Behavioral Sciences* 11, no. 2 (May 1989): 107–21.

————. "Latino Ethnic Identity: A Socio-Religious Portrait of Latinos and Latinas in the Catholic Church." In *Old Masks, New Faces: Religious and Latino Identities,* 33–59. Ed. Anthony M. Stevens-Arroyo and Gilbert R. Cadena. New York: Bildner Center, CUNY, 1995.

————. "The Social Location of Liberation Theology: From Latin America to the United States." In *Hispanic/Latino Theology: Challenge and Promise,* 167–182. Ed. Ada María Isasi-Díaz and Fernando F. Segovia. Minneapolis: Fortress Press, 1996.

————. "Latino and the Catholic Church: Cohesion and Conflict." In *Religion in a Changing World: Comparative Studies in Sociology,* 111–20. Ed. Madeleine Cousineau. Westport, Conn.: Greenwood, 1998.

Cadena, Gilbert R., and Lara Medina. "Liberation Theology and Social Change: Chicanas and Chicanos in the Catholic Church." In *Chicanas and Chicanos in Contemporary Society,* 99–111. Ed. Roberto M. de Anda. Boston, Mass.: Allyn and Bacon, 1996, reprint forthcoming.

Camarillo, Albert. *Chicanos in a Changing Society.* Cambridge, Mass.: Harvard University Press, 1979.

————. *Chicanos in California: A History of Mexican Americans in California.* Sparks, Nev.: Materials For Today's Learning, 1990.

Campbell, Debra. "Reformers and Activists." In *American Catholic Women,* 152–81. Ed. Karen Kennelly. New York: Macmillan, 1989.

Carter, Thomas P. *Mexican Americans in School: A History of Educational Neglect.* New York: College Entrance Examination Board, 1970.

Castañeda, Antonia I. "Women of Color and the Rewriting of Western History: The Discourse, Politics, and Decolonization of History." *Pacific Historical Review* (1992): 501–33.

————. "Sexual Violence in the Politics and Policies of Conquest." In *Building with our Hands: New Directions in Chicana Studies,* 15–33. Ed. Adela de la Torre and Beatríz M. Pesquera. Berkeley: University of California Press, 1993.

Chavez, César E. "The Mexican-American and the Church." *El Grito* 1, no. 4 (Summer 1968): 9–12.

Chávez, Ernesto. "Creating Aztlán: The Chicano Movement in Los Angeles, 1966–1978." Ph.D. diss., University of California, at Los Angeles, 1994.

Cohen, Elizabeth. *Making a New Deal: Industrial Workers in Chicago, 1919–1939.* Cambridge: Cambridge University Press, 1990.

Cotera, Marta. "Feminism: The Chicana and Anglo Versions." In *Twice a Minority: Mexican American Women,* 217–34. Ed. Margarita B. Melville. St. Louis, Mo.: C. V. Mosby, 1980.

Covarrubias, Consuelo. "Dear Mom." In *Así Es: Stories of Hispanic Spirituality,* 21–26. Ed. Arturo Pérez, Consuelo Covarrubias, and Edward Foley. Collegeville, Minn.: The Liturgical Press, 1994.

Coy, Patrick G., ed. *A Revolution of the Heart: Essays on the Catholic Worker.* Philadelphia: Temple University Press, 1988.

De Hoyos, Angelica, ed. *Mujeres Grandes Anthology 2.* San Antonio, Tex.: M&E editions, 1995.

De León, Arnoldo. *Mexican Americans in Texas: A Brief History.* Arlington Heights, Ill.: Harlan Davidson, 1993.

Díaz-Stevens, Ana María. *Oxcart Catholicism on Fifth Avenue: The Impact of the Puerto Rican Migration upon the Archdiocese of New York.* Notre Dame, Ind.: University of Notre Dame Press, 1993.

———. "Latinas in the Church." In *Hispanic Catholic Culture in the U.S.: Issues and Concerns,* 240–77. Ed. Jay P. Dolan and Allan Figueroa Deck. Notre Dame, Ind.: University of Notre Dame Press, 1994.

Eagleson, John, and Philip Scharper, eds. *Puebla and Beyond.* Maryknoll, N.Y.: Orbis Books, 1979.

Elizondo, Virgilio. "Popular Religion as the Core of Cultural Identity in the Mexican American Experience." In *An Enduring Flame: Studies on Latino Popular Religiosity,* 113–32. Ed. Anthony Stevens-Arroyo and Ana María Díaz-Stevens. New York: Bildner Center, 1994.

Engh, Michael E. "From *Frontera* Faith to Roman Rubrics: Altering Hispanic Religious Customs in Los Angeles, 1855–1880." *U.S. Catholic Historian* 12, no. 2 (September 1994): 85–105.

Ewens, Mary. "Women in the Convent." In *American Catholic Women,* 17–47. Ed. Karen Kennelly. New York: Macmillan, 1989.

Ferriss, Susan, and Ricardo Sandoval. *The Fight in the Fields: César Chávez and the Farmworkers Movement.* New York: Harcourt Brace, 1997.

Franklin, Kathy Smith. " 'A Spirit of Mercy': The Founding of Saint Joseph's Hospital, 1892–1912." Master's thesis, Arizona State University, 1997.

Freire, Paulo. *The Politics of Education: Culture, Power and Liberation.* South Hadley, Mass.: Bergin & Garvey, 1985.

García, Alma M. "The Development of Chicana Feminist Discourse, 1970–1980." In *Unequal Sisters: A Multi-Cultural Reader in U.S. Women's History*, 2nd ed., 531–44. Ed. Vicki L. Ruiz and Ellen Carol DuBois. New York: Routledge, 1994.

———, ed. Chicana Feminist Thought: The Basic Historical Writings. New York: Routledge, 1997.

García, Juan R. *Mexicans in the Midwest, 1900–1932.* Tucson: University of Arizona Press, 1996.

García, Mario. *Mexican Americans: Leadership, Ideology, and Identity, 1930–1960.* New Haven: Yale University Press, 1989.

Gaspar de Alba, Alicia. "The Politics of Location of the Tenth Muse of America: An Interview with Sor Juana Inéz de la Cruz." In *Living Chicana Theory*, 137–65. Ed. Carla Trujillo. Berkeley, Calif.: Third Women Press, 1998.

Goldsmith, Raquel Rubio. "Shipwrecked in the Desert: A Short History of the Mexican Sisters of the House of the Providence in Douglas, Arizona, 1927–1949." In *Women on the U.S.-Mexico Border*, 177–95. Ed. Vicki L. Ruiz and Susan Tiano. Boston: Allen & Unwin, 1987.

González, Gilbert. "Racism, Education, and the Mexican Community in Los Angeles, 1920–30." *Societas* 4 (Autumn 1974): 287–301.

Goodpasture, H. McKennie, ed. *Cross and Sword: An Eyewitness History of Christianity in Latin America*, Maryknoll, N.Y.: Orbis Books, 1989.

Grebler, Leo, Joan Moore, and Ralph Guzmán. *The Mexican American People: The Nation's Second Largest Minority.* New York: The Free Press, 1970.

Greeley, Andrew. "Defection Among Hispanics." *America*, 30 July 1988, 61–62.

Griswold del Castillo, Richard, and Richard A. García. *Cesar Chavez: A Triumph of Spirit.* Norman: University of Oklahoma Press, 1995.

Gutiérrez, David G. *Walls and Mirrors.* Berkeley: University of California Press, 1995.

Gutiérrez, Gustavo. *A Theology of Liberation.* Maryknoll, N.Y.: Orbis Books, 1973.

Gutiérrez, Ramón A. "Community, Patriarchy and Individualism: The Politics of Chicano History and the Dream of Equality." *American Quarterly* 45, no. 1 (March 1993): 44–72.

Hayes-Bautista, David E., Aída Hurtado, R. Burciaga Valdez, and Anthony C. R. Hernández. *No Longer a Minority: Latinos and Social Policy in California.* Los Angeles: UCLA Chicano Studies Research Center, 1992.

Hendren, Luciano C. "The Church in New Mexico." In *Fronteras: A History of the Latin American Church in the USA Since 1513*, 195–207. Ed. Moisés Sandoval. San Antonio, Tex.: Mexican American Cultural Center, 1983.

Hennelly, Alfred T., ed. *Liberation Theology: A Documentary History.* Maryknoll, N.Y.: Orbis Books, 1990.

Henriot, Peter J., Edward P. DeBerri, and Michael J. Schultheis. *Catholic Social Teaching: Our Best Kept Secret.* Maryknoll, N.Y.: Orbis Books, 1988.

Higgins, George G. *Organized Labor and the Church: Reflections of a "Labor Priest."* New York: Paulist Press, 1993.

Hurtado, Aída. "The Politics of Sexuality in the Gender Subordination of Chicanas." In *Living Chicana Theory,* 383–428. Ed. Carla Trujillo. Berkeley, Calif.: Third Women Press, 1998.

Isasi-Díaz, Ada María. "Toward an Understanding of Feminismo Hispano in the U.S.A." In *Women's Consciousness, Women's Conscience: A Reader in Feminist Ethics,* 51–61. Ed. Barbara Andolsen, Christian Gudorf, and Mary Pellauer. Minneapolis, Minn.: Winston Press, 1985.

———. *En La Lucha, In the Struggle: A Hispanic Women's Liberation Theology.* Minneapolis, Minn.: Fortress Press, 1993.

———. *Mujerista Theology: A Theology for the Twenty-First Century.* Maryknoll, N.Y.: Orbis Books, 1996.

Isasi-Díaz, Ada María, and Yolanda Tarango. *Hispanic Women, Prophetic Voice in the Church: Toward a Hispanic Women's Liberation Theology.* San Francisco: Harper and Row, 1988.

Katzenstein, Mary Fainsod. "Discursive Politics and Feminist Activism in the Catholic Church." In *Feminist Organizations: Harvest of the New Women's Movement,* 35–52. Ed. Myra Marx Ferree, and Patricia Yancey Martin. Philadelphia: Temple University Press, 1995.

Kelly, George A. *The Battle for the American Church.* Garden City, N.Y.: Doubleday, 1979.

Kenneally, James J. *The History of American Catholic Women.* New York: Crossroads, 1990.

Kerr, Louise Año Nuevo. "The Chicano Experience in Chicago: 1920–1970." Ph.D. diss., University of Illinois, Chicago Circle, 1976.

Leo XIII. "Apostolic Constitution Conditae a Christo, December 8, 1900." In *The States of Perfection, The Benedictine Monks of Solesmes.* Boston, Mass.: Daughters of St. Paul, 1967.

Lernoux, Penny. *Cry of the People.* New York: Doubleday, 1980.

———. *People of God: The Struggle for World Catholicism.* New York: Penguin Books, 1989.

Levine, Daniel H. *Popular Voices in Latin American Catholicism.* Princeton, N.J.: Princeton University Press, 1992.

Littwin, Lawrence. *Latin America: Catholicism and Class Conflict.* Encino, Calif.: Dickenson, 1974.

López, Sonia A. "The Role of the Chicana within the Student Movement." In *Essays on La Mujer,* 16–29. Ed. Rosaura Sánchez and Rosa

Martínez Cruz. Los Angeles: UCLA Chicano Studies Center Publications, 1977.

Madeleva, M. "The Education of Our Young Religious Teachers." In *The Education of Sister Lucy: A Symposium on Teacher Education and Teacher Training*, 5–10. Holy Cross, Ind.: Saint Mary's College, 1949.

Martínez, Dolorita. "Basic Christian Communities: A New Model of Church Within the U.S. Hispanic Community." *New Theology Review* 3, no. 4 (November 1990): 35–42.

Martínez, Elizabeth. "Seeds of a New Movimiento." *Z Magazine*, September 1993, 52–56.

Matovina, Timothy M. "Representation and the Reconstruction of Power: The Rise of *PADRES* and *LAS HERMANAS.*" In *What's Left? Liberal American Catholics*, 220–37. Ed. Mary Jo Weaver and R. Scott Appleby. Bloomington: Indiana University Press, 1999.

McCarthy, Timothy G. *The Catholic Tradition: Before and After Vatican II, 1878–1993*. Chicago: Loyola University Press, 1994.

McGovern, Arthur F. *Liberation Theology and its Critics: Toward an Assessment*. Maryknoll, N.Y.: Orbis Books, 1989.

McNamara, Patrick. "Bishops, Priests and Prophecy." Ph.D. diss., University of California at Los Angeles, 1968.

Medina, Lara. "Los Espírtus Siguen Hablando: Chicana Spiritualities." In *Living Chicana Theory*, 189–213. Ed. Carla Trujillo. Berkeley, Calif.: Third World Press, 1998.

———. "Broadening the Discourse at the Theological Table: An Overview of Latino Theology 1968–1993." *Latino Studies Journal* 5, no. 3 (September 1994): 10–36.

Meyer, Michael C., and William L. Sherman. *The Course of Mexican History*. New York: Oxford University Press, 1995.

Meyers, Bertrande. *The Education of Sisters: A Plan for Integrating the Religious, Social, Cultural, and Professional Training of Sisters*. New York: Sheed and Ward, 1941.

———. *Sisters for the Twenty-First Century*. New York: Sheed and Ward, 1965.

Moraga, Cherríe, and Gloria Anzaldua, eds. *This Bridge Called My Back*. Latham, N.Y.: Kitchen Table: Woman of Color Press, 1981.

Muñoz, Carlos Jr. *Youth, Identity, Power: The Chicano Movement*. London: Verso Books, 1989.

Neal, Maria Augusta. "The Relation Between Religious Belief and Structural Change in Religious Orders: Some Evidence." *Review of Religious Research* 12 (Spring 1971): 153–64.

———. *Catholic Sisters in Transition: From the 1960s to the 1980s*. Wilmington, Del.: Michael Glazier, 1984.

Neri, Michael. "Hispanic Catholicism in Transitional California: The Life of Jose Gonzáles Rubio O.F.M., 1804–1875." Ph.D. diss., Graduate Theological Union, Berkeley, 1974.

Oates, Mary. "Religion and Gender in American Higher Education: A Case Study of the College of Notre Dame of Maryland, 1869–1996." Unpublished paper presented at the Louisville Institute Winter Seminar, January 1998.

Official Catholic Directory. Wilmette, Ill.: P. J. Kennedy and Sons, 1990.

O'Malley, John. *Tradition and Transition: Historical Perspectives on Vatican II.* Wilmington, Del.: Michael Glazier, 1989.

Pardo, Mary. "Doing if for the Kids: Mexican American Community Activists, Border Feminists?" In *Feminist Organizations: Harvest of the New Women's Movement,* 356–71. Ed. Myra Marx Ferree and Patricia Yancey Martin. Philadelphia: Temple University Press, 1995.

Patrick, Anne E. "A Ministry of Justice: The 25-Year Pilgrimage of the National Assembly of Religious Women (NAWR/NARW)." In *What's Left: Progressive Catholics in America.* Ed. Mary Jo Weaver and R. Scott Appleby. Bloomington: Indiana University Press, 1999.

Piñeda, Ana Maria. "Pastoral de Conjunto." *New Theology Review* 3, no. 4 (November 1990): 28–34.

Pulido, Albert L. "Are You an Emissary of Jesus Christ?" In *American Mosaic,* 147–63. Ed. Young I. Song and Eugene C. Kim. Englewood, Cliffs, N.J.: Prentice Hall, 1993.

Pycior, Julie Leininger. "From Hope to Frustration: Mexican Americans and Lyndon Johnson in 1967." *Western Historical Quarterly* 24, no. 4 (November 1993): 468–94.

Rader, Rosemary. "Catholic Feminism: Its Impact on U.S. Catholic Women." In *American Catholic Women,* 182–197. Ed. Karen Kennelly. New York: Macmillan, 1989.

Rahner, Karl. "Towards a Fundamental Theological Interpretation of Vatican II." *Theological Studies* 40 (December 1979): 716–27.

Ramírez, Ricardo. "The American Church and Hispanic Migration: An Historical Analysis (Part 1)." *Migration Today* 6, no. 1 (1978): 16–20.

Randall, Margaret. *Doris Tijerino: Inside the Nicaraguan Revolution.* Vancouver: New Star Books, 1978.

Roberts, Nancy L. *Dorothy Day and the Catholic Worker.* Albany: State University of New York Press, 1984.

Rodríguez, Edmundo. "The Hispanic Community and Church Movements: Schools of Leadership." In *Hispanic Catholic Culture in the U.S.: Issues and Concerns,* 206–39. Ed. Jay P. Dolan and Allan Figueroa Deck. Notre Dame, Ind.: University of Notre Dame Press, 1994.

Rodríguez, Olga, ed. *The Politics of Chicano Liberation,* New York: Pathfinder, 1977.

Romero, Juan. "New Bishop for San Bernardino." Unpublished paper, 6 November 1978.

————. "Charism and Power: An Essay on the History of PADRES." *U.S. Catholic Historian* 9, nos. 1–2 (Winter–Spring 1990): 147–64.

Rosales, F. Arturo. *Chicano!: The History of the Mexican American Civil Rights Movement.* Houston, Tex.: Arte Publico Press, 1996.

Rose, Margaret. "Gender and Civic Activism in Mexican American Barrios in California." In *Not June Cleaver: Women and Gender in Postwar America, 1945–1960,* 177–200. Ed. Joanne Meyerowitz. Philadelphia: Temple University Press, 1994.

Rose, Margaret Eleanor. "Women in the United Farm Workers: A Study of Chicana and Mexicana Participation in a Labor Union, 1950 to 1980." Ph.D. diss., University of California at Los Angeles, 1988.

Rowan, Helen. "A Minority Nobody Knows." *The Atlantic Monthly,* 1976, 47–52.

Ruether, Radford Rosemary. "Women-Church: An American Catholic Feminist Movement." In *What's Left: Progressive Catholics in America.* Ed. Mary Jo Weaver and Scott R. Appleby. Bloomington: Indiana University Press, 1999.

Ruether, Rosemary Radford, and Rosemary Skinner Keller, eds. *In Our Own Voices: Four Centuries of American Women's Religious Writing.* New York: HarperCollins, 1995.

Ruiz, Vicki L. " 'Star Struck:' Acculturation, Adolescence, and the Mexican American Woman, 1920–1950". In *Building with Our Hands: New Directions in Chicana Studies,* 109–29. Ed. Adela de la Torre and Beatríz M. Pesquera. Berkeley: University of California Press, 1993.

————. "Dead Ends or Gold Mines? Using Missionary Records in Mexican American Women's History." In *Unequal Sisters: A Multi-cultural Reader in U.S. Women's History,* 298–315. Ed. Vicki L. Ruiz and Ellen Carol DuBois. New York: Routledge, 1994.

————. *From Out of the Shadows: Mexican Women in Twentieth-Century America.* New York: Oxford University Press, 1998.

Ruiz, Vicki L., and Susan Tiano, eds. *Women on the U.S.-Mexico Border.* Boston: Allen & Unwin, 1987.

Salandini, Victor. *The Confessions of the Tortilla Priest.* San Diego, Calif.: The San Diego Review, 1992.

Sánchez, George J. *Becoming Mexican American: Ethnicity, Culture and Identity in Chicano Los Angeles, 1900–1945.* New York: Oxford University Press, 1993.

Sandoval, Chela. "U.S. Third World Feminism: The Theory and Method of Oppositional Consciousness in the Postmodern World." *Genders* 4, no. 10 (1991): 2–24.

Sandoval, Moisés. "The Church and 'El Movimiento'." In *Fronteras: A History of the Latin American Church in the USA Since 1513*, 377–412. Ed. Moisés Sandoval. San Antonio, Tex.: Mexican American Cultural Center, 1983.

———, ed. *The Mexican American Experience in the Church*. New York: Sadlier, 1983.

———. *On the Move: A History of the Hispanic Church in the United States*. Maryknoll, N.Y.: Orbis Books, 1990.

———. "The Organization of the Hispanic Church." In *Hispanic Catholic Culture in the U.S.: Issues and Concerns*, 131–165. Ed. Jay P. Dolan and Allan Figueroa Deck. Notre Dame, Ind.: University of Notre Dame Press, 1994.

Sandoval, Moisés, and Salvador E. Alvarez. "The Church in California." In *Fronteras: A History of the Latin American Church in the USA Since 1513*, 209–221. Ed. Moisés Sandoval. San Antonio, Tex.: Mexican American Cultural Center, 1983.

Santillan, Richard. *La Raza Unida*. Los Angeles: Tlaquilio, 1973.

Schneiders, Sandra M. "Religious Life." In *Modern Catholicism*, 157–62. Ed. Adrian Hastings. New York: Oxford University Press, 1991.

Schoenherr, Richard A., and Lawrence A. Young. *Full Pews and Empty Altars: Demographics of the Priest Shortage in United States Catholic Dioceses*. Madison: University of Wisconsin Press, 1993.

Segura, Denise A. "Chicanas and Triple Oppression in the Labor Force." In *Chicana Voices: Intersection of Class, Race and Gender*, 47–65. Ed. Teresa Córdova et al. Austin, Tex.: Center for Mexican American Studies, 1986.

Smith, Christian. *The Emergence of Liberation Theology: Radical Religion and Social Movement Theory*. Chicago: University of Chicago Press, 1991.

———. *Resisting Reagan: The U.S. Central America Peace Movement*. Chicago: University of Chicago Press, 1996.

Sobrino, Jon, et al. *Companions of Jesus: The Jesuit Martyrs of El Salvador*. Maryknoll, N.Y.: Orbis Books, 1990.

Soto, Antonio Robert. "The Chicano and the Church in Northern California, 1848–1978: A Study of an Ethnic Minority Within the Roman Catholic Church." Ph.D. diss., University of California at Berkeley, 1978.

Stevens-Arroyo, Anthony M., ed. *Prophets Denied Honor: An Anthology on the Hispanic Church in the United States*. Maryknoll, N.Y.: Orbis Books, 1980.

Sylvest, Jr Edwin. "Hispanic American Protestantism in the United States." In *Fronteras: A History of the Latin American Church in the*

USA Since 1513, 279–338. Ed. Moíses Sandoval. San Antonio, Tex.: Mexican American Cultural Center, 1983.

Tafolla, Carmen. "The Church in Texas." In *Fronteras: A History of the Latin American Church in the USA Since 1513*, 183–94. Ed. Moíses Sandoval. San Antonio, Tex.: Mexican American Cultural Center, 1983.

Tarango, Yolanda. "The Hispanic Women and Her Role in the Church." *New Theology Review* 3, no. 4 (November 1990): 56–61.

————. "A Hispanic Women's 'Spirituality'." In *Así Es: Stories of Hispanic Spirituality*, 10–15. Ed. Arturo Pérez, Consuelo Covarrubias, and Edward Foley. Collegeville, Minn.: The Liturgical Press, 1994.

Tarango, Yolanda, and Timothy M. Matovina. "LAS HERMANAS." In *Hispanics in the Church: Up From the Cellar*, 95–120. Ed. Phillip E. Lampe. San Francisco: Catholic Scholars Press, 1994.

Torres, Sergio, and John Eagleson, eds. *Theology in the Americas*. Maryknoll, N.Y.: Orbis Books, 1976.

U.S. Bureau of the Census. *General Social and Economic Characteristics— United States Summary*. Washington, D.C.: U.S. Government Printing Office, 1970.

————. *Persons of Spanish Ancestry*. Washington, D.C.: U.S. Government Printing Office, February 1973.

————. *Characteristics of the Spanish Surname Population By Census Tract, for SMSA's in Texas: 1970*. Washington, D.C.: U.S. Government Printing Office, May 1974.

U.S. Department of Commerce. *Poverty in the United States: 1988 and 1989*. Washington, D.C.: U.S. Government Printing Office, 1991.

U.S. Department of Justice. *Criminal Victimization in the United States, 1983*. Washington, D.C.: U.S. Government Printing Office, 1985.

Vidal, Mirta. *Chicanas Speak Out, Women: New Voice of La Raza*. New York: Pathfinder, 1971.

Villafañe, Eldin. *The Liberating Spirit: Toward an Hispanic American Pentecostal Social Ethic*. Grand Rapids: Eerdmans, 1993.

Walker, Thomas W., ed. *Nicaragua in Revolution*, New York: Preager, 1982.

Weaver, Mary Jo. *New Catholic Women: A Contemporary Challenge to Traditional Religious Authority*. San Francisco, Calif.: Harper and Row, 1985.

Ybarra, María de Jesús, OP. "Sister María de Jesús Ybarra." In *El Quetzal Emplumece*, 292–93. Ed. Carmela Montalvo, Leonardo Anguiano, and Cecilio Garcia Camarillo. San Antonio, Tex.: Mexican American Cultural Center, 1976.

Yoo, David. "For Those Who Have Eyes to See: Religious Sightings in Asian America." *Amerasia Journal* 22, no. 1 (1996): xiii–xxii.

Zapata, Dominga. "Gospel to the Hispanic: Unrecognized Ministry?" In *Women in Ministry: A Sister's View*, 131–32. Chicago: NAWR Publications, 1972.

Zavella, Patricia. "Reflections on Diversity Among Chicanas." In *Challenging Fronteras: Structuring Latina and Latino Lives in the U.S.*, 187–94. Ed. Mary Romero, Pierrette Hondagneu-Sotelo, and Vilma Ortiz. New York: Routledge, 1997.

Interviews

Acuña, Rudy. 18 April 1997, Sacramento, California.

Barajas, Teresa. 21 August 1996, San Antonio, Texas.

Barron, Carlos. 9 March 1997, Pasadena, California.

Basso, Theresa. 7 March 1997, Moreno Valley, California.

Browne, Tess. 20 May 1997, Telephone Interview, Boston, Massachusetts.

Camacho de Schmidt, Aurora. 23 July 1997, Telephone Interview, Swarthmore, Pennsylvania.

Castañeda, Margarita. 15 March 1997, Burlingame, California.

Chávez, Linda. 26 July 1997, New York, New York.

Corrales, Ramona Jean. 15 April 1997, Telephone interview, Somerton, Arizona.

Covarrubias, Consuelo. 11 July 1997, Chicago, Illinois.

Elías, Rosamaría. 20 May 1997, Telephone Interview, Hartford, Connecticut.

Elizondo, Virgilio. 17 February 1997, Pasadena, California.

Espinoza, Carmelita. 16 October 1996, Telephone Interview, Seattle, Washington.

Flores, Cecilia. 14 July 1997, Denver, Colorado.

Flores, María Carolina. 26 April 1997, Pasadena, California.

Florez, Dolores. 24 August 1996, Denver, Colorado, and 14 July 1997, Denver, Colorado.

Fresquez, Catalina. 13 May 1997, Los Angeles, California.

Gastón, María Luisa. 27 July 1997, New York, New York.

Guillen, Patricio. 12 March 1994, San Bernardino, California.

Iglesias, María. 2 March 1997, San Luis Obispo, California and 15 March 1997, Salinas, California.

Isasi-Díaz, Ada María. 21 August 1996, San Antonio, Texas.

Janacek, Balthasar. 3 March 1997, Telephone Interview. San Antonio, Texas.

Lovato, Flor. 14 July 1997, Denver, Colorado.

Martínez, María Inez. 7 June 1997, Santa Barbara, California.

Méndez, Veronica. 12 July 1997, Chicago, Illinois.

Muñoz, Irene. 15 July 1997, Denver, Colorado.
Murrieta, Sara. 26 July 1997, New York, New York.
Ortega, Gregoria. 21 April 1997, Los Angeles, California, and 7 May 1997, Los Angeles, California.
Ortiz, Lucy. 27 July 1997, New York, New York.
Peña, Lydia. 15 July 1997, Denver, Colorado.
Piñeda, Ana María. 12 July 1997, Chicago, Illinois.
Rodríguez, Elisa. 4 August 1997, Sierra Madre, California.
Romero, Juan. 9 October 1997, Los Angeles, California.
Salcido, Alicia. 26 July 1997, New York, New York.
Sandoval, Moises. 29 July 1997, Maryknoll, New York.
Sedillo, Sylvia. 23 April 1997, Telephone Interview, Santa Fe, New Mexico.
Segura, Marylou. 14 July 1997, Denver, Colorado.
Smith, Mark. 17 July 1997, Telephone Interview, Lubbock, Texas.
Tarango, Yolanda. July 1990, San Antonio, Texas and 22 August 1996, San Antonio, Texas.
Trujillo, Clarita. 5 May 1997, Telephone Interview, Española, New Mexico.
Vásquez, Sylvia. 23 August 1996, San Antonio, Texas.
Vásquez, Cásarez Enedina. 22 August 1996, San Antonio, Texas.
Vaughn, Judy. 9 July 1997, Los Angeles, California.
Villegas, Carmen. 17 May 1997, Telephone Interview, New York, New York.
Ybarra, María de Jesús. 10 April 1997, Telephone Interview, Yakima, Washington.
Zárate, Rosa Martha Mácias. 6 March 1997, Los Angeles, California, and 26 July 1997, New York, New York.

Manuscript Collection, Songs, and Visual Media

LAS HERMANAS Collection, Mexican American Studies Department, Our Lady of the Lake University, San Antonio, Tex.

Zárate, Rosa Martha Mácias. "Cántico de Mujer." In *Cantos para animar la esperanza.* San Bernardino: CA: by the author, 1996.

La Guadalupe Que Camina: A Performance Piece. *Mujeres Indigenas.* Ruby Perez. San Antonio, TX: 1990.

Index